D1076827

New Migrants in the UK:

education, training and employment

New Migrants in the UK:
education, training and employment

Jenny Phillimore and Lisa Goodson

Trentham Books

Stoke on Trent, UK and Sterling, USA

Trentham Books Limited

Westview House   22883 Quicksilver Drive
734 London Road   Sterling
Oakhill   VA 20166-2012
Stoke on Trent   USA
Staffordshire
England ST4 5NP

© 2008 Jenny Phillimore and Lisa Goodson

All rights reserved. No part of this publication may be reproduced or
transmitted in any form or by any means, electronic or mechanical
including photocopying, recording or any information storage or retrieval
system, without prior permission in writing from the publishers.

First published 2008

British Library Cataloguing-in-Publication Data
A catalogue record for this book is available from the
British Library

ISBN: 978 1 85856 350 3

Cover painting by Robert Aswani, an influential Kenyan artist who is
currently working both in Nairobi and Arusha, Tanzania. His biography
and additional paintings can be seen at www.insideafricanart.com
<http://www.insideafricanart.com/>

Designed and typeset by Trentham Print Design Ltd., Chester and printed
in Great Britain by Hobbs the Printers Ltd, Hampshire.

Contents

Acknowledgements • vi

Chapter One
Migration and asylum policy • 1

Chapter Two
**Education, training and employment for
integration and inclusion • 25**

Chapter Three
**Exploring new migrants' experiences of education,
training and employment: methodological
considerations and research approach • 57**

Chapter Four
The exclusion of new migrants from learning • 91

Chapter Five
Providing learning for new migrants • 115

Chapter Six
Supporting refugees into employment and learning • 135

Chapter Seven
Employing new migrants • 155

Chapter Eight
From exclusion to integration via employability • 179

References • 195

Index • 211

Acknowledgements

Thanks are due to all our friends, family and colleagues, who have given us encouragement and support through the process. We hope that one day Joe and Abby will understand why so much time was spent on the computer writing a book that had no interesting pictures. In particular it is important for us to acknowledge the contributions of, Yanina Dutton and Jane Watts from NIACE. It was originally intended that they would be the authors of chapters five and six and while they were unfortunately unable to do this and they put in a great deal of time to gather data and draft ideas. The contribution of Ann Bolstridge, our loyal and supportive friend and colleague was also critical to the completion of this book. The work she put in helping the editing and proof reading process and her constant encouragement is greatly appreciated. Special thanks are also due to Yvonne Harley who has provided an ongoing contribution through her continued support over the past few years, sometimes under great pressure, in order for us to deliver on our research projects. In addition the work of colleagues Carolyn Fox and Jane Simpson should be acknowledged.

The past eight years of our working lives have been spent researching the lives and experiences of new migrants – initially, with the advent of the dispersal programme, in the West Midlands and subsequently across the remainder of the UK and Europe. We are profoundly grateful to all the organisations that have aided our research both in terms of sponsorship and other kinds of support, from introducing us to respondents or providing space for interviews. We would like to give thanks to members of the research teams at NIACE led by Fiona Aldridge, and the Centre for Urban Studies, who have supported us and worked with us throughout all the projects that have contributed data to this book. Special thanks are due to the Progress GB EQUAL programme for sponsoring three years of activity aimed at making a difference for skilled refugees and providing us with time and ideas to write this book.

We would like to thank all the refugees and asylum seekers who have participated in our studies. The time and effort they gave to take part when their lives were in turmoil, is acknowledged and greatly appreciated. Without them this book could not have been written. The stories and experiences of some of our respondents have inspired us to actively work towards fairer treatment of newcomers. We hope that this book will go some way in making the argument for making the most of the potential new migrants bring to the UK.

1

Migration and asylum policy

People have moved around the world for thousands of years. The flow of refugees to countries in Europe is not a new phenomenon. The past forty years have seen the arrival of significant numbers of asylum seekers and refugees in the European Union countries (European Commission, 2001). Comparatively recently most refugees arrived in the UK under the auspices of specific refugee programmes established as a result of international action pertaining to particular global political issues, for example the expulsion of Asians from Uganda, boat-people fleeing Vietnam, or the conflict in Bosnia (Sales, 2002; Kuepper *et al*, 1975).

The significant difference in the 1990s was that the numbers of asylum applicants arriving spontaneously in Europe as individuals rather than as part of a planned programme increased to such an extent that successive governments have felt the need to create specific policy initiatives to deal with this influx.

The situation in the UK mirrors that in much of Europe. In the past ten years the number of people seeking asylum increased dramatically, reaching an all time high of 103,080 applications in 2002 (www.ecre.org). In response to the pressure placed on services in London and Southern England, the National Asylum Support Service (NASS) was established in 1999 to coordinate and fund the dispersal of asylum seekers around the UK.

This policy has come under a great deal of criticism from refugee and civil rights groups, particularly over concerns that moving people away from the well-developed networks of friends, family, legal and support services in London will hamper their ability to settle and make a place for themselves in the UK (Zetter and Pearl, 2000). This book examines the background to policy-making, and the effects recent policies have had.

As the numbers seeking asylum in the UK increased so has the level of interest in integration. This interest, and the extent to which refugees were accessing the support and services they needed to make a home for themselves in the UK, were highlighted in the publication of the first Home Office strategy for the integration of refugees, *Full and Equal Citizens* (2000). The emphasis in this document was placed upon developing ideas for the integration of 're-cognised refugees', and the 'promotion of citizenship'. A National Refugee Integration Forum was established to explore the different dimensions of integration and to examine how they might be implemented in policy terms.

More recently two key documents were published. Ager and Strang's (2004) paper set out an Indicators of Integration framework. *Integration Matters*, the Home Office's (2005) national strategy for refugee integration, proposes a set of actions aimed at taking the strategy forward and presents some indicators, based on Ager and Strang's framework, for measuring success. Central to the notion of integration used in their work is the issue of self-sufficiency and the need to build the 'provision of opportunities for language training, acquisi-tion of work experience, retraining and re-accreditation where necessary and commitment and openness from employers' (2004: 6).

Whilst previous research has explored different aspects of education, training and employment (ETE) and how migrants access them, there has been no systematic study of refugees' experiences of ETE and little consideration of the perspectives of providers and agencies charged with facilitating access. Furthermore, the vast majority of research has examined one or more dimen-sions of ETE often within London alone, and not in the dispersal regions.

The dispersal system has now been running for seven years. Refugees have settled in all the major cities as well as London. It is important to explore the experiences of those individuals who in this book we refer to by the collective term newcomers or new migrants. They are the product of the new system.

New communities are forming in urban and rural areas where there was, and still is, little infrastructure to support their development and little experience of integrating newcomers, certainly on the scale now being seen in the regions. Questions need to be asked about the kinds of support these new-comers are receiving, their aspirations for the future, the types of provision they are seeking and the extent to which it is being provided. How are new-comers to the regions faring? Are they able to access ETE? What mechanisms have been put in place to help them to integrate via these means? This book aims to plug a gap in existing knowledge by taking an in-depth look at the ex-periences of newcomers, and providers, in the regions.

The book focuses upon the West Midlands region, in particular the cities of Birmingham, Coventry and Wolverhampton, where the needs and experiences of refugees and asylum seekers, and the organisations who have some responsibility for their integration, are explored through a range of methodologies including household surveys, questionnaires, focus groups and in depth interviews. The book is less concerned with offering a critique of the dispersal system than with examining how dispersal developed, the needs of those who have been dispersed and the reactions of organisations to those needs. Throughout the book, consideration is given to the ways in which policies have been, and might yet be, developed at local, regional and national levels to help better facilitate the integration of newcomers into the region via ETE.

It is hoped that whilst the research considered highlights challenges facing newcomers and organisations working with them, we can propose a range of policy focused solutions to help those who have been dispersed to maximise their contribution to society and the economy in the regions.

This first chapter sets out the context to the development of the dispersal system. It considers in brief the history of migration to the UK and looks in some detail at the factors that underpin the introduction of dispersal. It includes a discussion of some of the key legislation introducing dispersal and then outlines the main implications of legislation introduced since 2000, an era described by some as the most intensive period for the introduction of immigration legislation that the UK has ever seen (Refugee Council, 2000). The chapter concludes by setting out the structure for the rest of the book.

History of immigration in the UK

The British Isles is the product of colonisation. British school children are taught about the arrival of the Romans in 55BC and the sophistication of their culture and technologies in comparison to the native population which itself was made up of Celtic and Pictish tribes who formed some of the first communities in fledgling Britain. The Romans were followed by Jutes, Angles and Saxons from Europe and Vikings from Scandinavia. The final phase in the early colonisation of the island was the arrival of the French following the Norman Conquest in 1066. Each of these peoples helped to shape the English language, culture and ceremonies that we celebrate today as British. They influenced many aspects of our society, from the names of towns and villages to the way in which Parliament is run.

These early colonisations share a common characteristic: apart from the occasional black legionnaire, migrants who came to the UK were white Europeans. It was not until the conquest of the so-called New World in the 1500s that the English began to take part in the trade of African slaves, which became such a lucrative part of the English economy for the next three hundred or so years (Rawley, 1981). Freed slaves and other black settlers were numerous enough by 1601 that Queen Elizabeth I declared in a royal proclamation that all 'negroes and blackamoors' should be speedily deported in the interests of the 'good and welfare of her own natural subjects' (File and Power, 1981).

In 1672 Charles II created the Royal African Company, which established England as the world's greatest slave trader. Cities such as Bristol and Liverpool were built around the slave trade and their fortunes were founded upon the trade itself and the products of factories that manufactured imports from the colonies (Thomas, 1997). As the slave trade became more entrenched in the economy so did the appearance of black slaves in the households of wealthy industrialists. By 1770, 14,000 black people lived in England and abolitionists began the movement to win their freedom. Policy change was slow but gradually the attitude of the populus changed and by 1833 slavery was banned across the Empire. This largely meant an end to the arrival of Africans in England. Some foreign seamen, some of them black and Chinese, began to settle in port areas because of the decline in the sea trade and their lack of a passage home.

The long history of immigration to the UK has been accompanied by increasingly organised attempts to use policy to exclude particular groups. The first attempt to use legislation to exclude immigrants from the UK was Grenville's Aliens Act, which was passed in 1793, and gave parliamentary sanction for the expulsion of 'aliens' for the first time (Cohen, 1994). The Act made a clear legal distinction between an 'alien' and 'privileged foreigner' or 'denizen', making clear that its provisions applied only to those defined as 'aliens'. Later, in 1848, the Removal of Aliens Act gave the Home Secretary the right to expel foreigners if it was deemed that they threatened the 'preservation of the peace and tranquillity of the realm'. This act was viewed as a direct response to the influx of Russian and Eastern European Jews in the 1800s; immigration which had a negative effect on public opinion and the media of the time who depicted Jews as wicked capitalists.

The first twentieth century act concerning migration, the Aliens Act of 1905, defined 'undesirables' as 'previous deportees, fugitive offenders, the mad and the destitute'. Cohen argues that while black people and other ethnic minorities were all victims of restrictionist attitudes, the main targets of animosity just before the First World War were the Jews and that at that time the term 'alien' meant Jew. The tide changed after the outbreak of the First World War when the focus was placed upon those with German roots. Men and women over military age with a German background were obliged to show why they shouldn't be expelled. In the period 1914-1919, 28,744 aliens were repatriated, of whom 23,571 were Germans. An order-in-council in 1920 reserved the Home Secretary's right to deport someone if he considered it 'conducive to public good' (Cohen, 1994).

Whilst both World Wars saw rises in xenophobia and the exclusion of migrants, they also saw high levels of immigration from the colonies. Many hundreds of thousands of men from India and the colonies fought for Britain. Some 130,000 Indian soldiers served on the Western Front (Visram, 1989). Thousands of Asian seamen played a role in both world wars, and many stayed on in Britain permanently, working for instance in collieries and factories. Despite their role in providing labour and soldiery during and after the wars, there were concerns about the long term settlement of black or Asian people in Britain, particularly after the race riots which took place in a number of cities in 1919. However, notwithstanding the unpopular nature of migration in relation to certain ethnic groups, the Government had economic imperatives for its continuance. When labour shortages occurred at the end of the Second World War the government sought solutions. They first turned to white Europeans and invited over 100,000 Poles and Italians to live in Britain. They experienced little opposition from the general population. The numbers arriving were insufficient to meet the labour needs of recovering Britain so the Government looked farther afield to the West Indies where servicemen had returned to unemployment and few long-term prospects.

Large-scale immigration from what was to become the New Commonwealth began in the late 1940s and continued throughout the 1950s (Favell, 1998). Immigrants came first in great numbers from the West Indies and later the Asian sub-continent. The 1948 Nationality Act ushered in an open door policy to members of the Commonwealth who, as sovereign subjects, had the same rights of entry and abode as British citizens. Initially there was almost universal support amongst the political parties towards the Commonwealth. This was short-lived and in 1958 the first race riots broke out in Notting Hill and Nottingham, organised by white extremists targeting the black population. Race relations became a central political concern.

In response to the riots, the 1962 Commonwealth Immigrants Act was put into place. It could be argued that this Act set the stage for a scenario repeated to the present day, when acts of xenophobia or extremism are met with a response from the Government intended to placate rather than to take legislative action against racism. The Act placed restrictions on immigration, stopping open immigration from the New Commonwealth, and thus clearly demarking and limiting future non-white immigration (Favell, 1998). Despite the new Act, racial discrimination by whites against blacks persisted and the black community began to show signs of discontent and even willingness to incite disorder in an attempt to resist discrimination.

When Labour came into power in 1964, it tried to resolve these problems with progressive legislation. In the end, in what by now has become a familiar bow to popular opinion led by right-wing media, Labour left behind its promise to repeal or reform the immigration controls and reinforced them with amendments of its own. In 1968, Enoch Powell made his famous 'rivers of blood' speech. The speech depicted immigrants as 'invading hordes who, with their peculiar practices and origins and predilection for crime', would never fit in to society and the British way of life.

Throughout the period 1960-68, the relationship between Britain and the Commonwealth was eroded. Immigration laws culminated in the concept of 'patriality' as the basis for citizenship (Lloyd, 2000): the right accorded by birth of a parent or grandparent. The legislation extended the reasons for deportation and the categories of people who could be deported. Commonwealth citizens had their rights reduced to those of Aliens. Cohen (1994) argues that colour was the determining factor in the right to remain in the UK. Right of abode was granted to patrials, most of whom were white, and denied to non-patrials most of whom were not. In this way the immigration issue was racialised and that racialisation confirmed by Powell's speech.

Cohen credits Enoch Powell's speech with the linking of the issues of race relations and immigration to the point where it is now impossible to separate the two in British political discourse: Even those who were liberals on domestic race relations matters were nonetheless induced into accepting Powell's political agenda by arguing that harmonious race relations in Britain depended on rapidly cutting down the numbers of non-whites admitted to the country (Cohen, 1994).

Although Powell was sacked and marginalised, and the Second Race Relations Act in 1968 outlawed direct discrimination in employment and other public places, the speech incited and almost legitimised race hatred.

Favell (1998) sees Powell's argument as being behind the rise of the National Front, the forerunner to the British National Party.

However, there were positive moves to deal with increases in racial discrimination and hatred. A further Race Relations Act was introduced in 1976 and continued in the progressive vein of the 1968 Act. It included new provisions which extended the legislation to cover indirect discrimination, where cases could also be brought against organisations that unintentionally behaved in a discriminatory way. The Commission for Racial Equality was created to ensure that anti-discrimination cases were pursued and assistance provided to those wishing to bring a case.

By the end of the 1970s racial tension again increased. Riots erupted in Toxteth, Brixton and Southall during 1981. In a response to the unrest, Lord Scarman was charged with examining the cause of the riots and to suggest possible solutions. He found deprivation to be at the heart of the problem, but also found institutional racism to have had a role in provoking challenges to public order. New community-focused approaches to policing were proposed and introduced as a result of the report. Whilst the aftermath of the riots may have seen some progress for those who had settled in the UK, the New Nationality Act of 1981, which came into force in 1983, included tougher measures to reduce the number of immigrants. The Act extended new controls to British overseas dependencies, closed loopholes for certain types of New Commonwealth family reunification, and ended the practice of automatic citizenship for children born on British soil of non-British parents (Cohen, 1994). Clause 4 of the 1988 Nationality Act went even further, outlining who had the right to live in the UK. In a move since echoed in recent legislation it limited the scope and availability of appeals against deportation for those seeking refugee status. For overstayers, appeals would not be granted.

Cohen (1994) argues that the Conservative party with its thirteen years in power did much to demonise immigrants. Thatcher built upon Powell's rhetoric by making speeches about her concerns around the possibility of Britain becoming 'swamped' with migrants. In fact, the number of people emigrating from Britain at that time was pretty much the same as those coming in and the motivation pretty similar: people were looking for a better life.

More countries were selected for new visa controls, including for the first time Commonwealth countries. The use of the powers of removal and deportation were increased throughout the period the Conservatives were in power, both in relation to individuals entering or overstaying in the UK and in the British outpost of Hong Kong. The case of the Vietnamese boat people is cited as an indication of the change in attitudes to refugees in this period. Prior to 1988 most of the Vietnamese arriving in Hong Kong were admitted as a country of first asylum, with the expectation that most would move to other countries of settlement. As the number of arrivals grew, the West became reluctant to offer them residence. Detention centres were created as holding camps whilst individual cases were assessed to determine their eligibility for refugee status. By 1989 a forcible deportation procedure was invoked and the mass deportations were watched on television sets across the UK.

Up to the 1980s much of the migration to the UK had been related to employment or family re-unification. Increased migration had been coupled with an increase in racial hatred and discrimination. Legislation was introduced to reduce levels of economic migration and to prevent chain migration. Whilst there had been a serious deterioration in race relations, progressive legislation aimed to reduce discrimination and introduce new offences aimed at addressing some of the problems associated with the collapse of community cohesion. The nature of migration was about to change. With routes to economic migration severely reduced and major changes underway in global power structures, seeking political asylum was to become the main focus of migration and legislation governing immigration and asylum.

The flow of refugees

Britain makes much of its history of welcoming immigrants and refugees into the country. Emphasis was placed on this in Home Office publications such as *Integration Matters* (2005). However, historically we have tended to favour those with whom we have some political allegiance and who arrive in small numbers which are less of a challenge to accommodate and integrate. An early example might include conservatives and aristocrats fleeing the French Revolution. However, even when the numbers of refugees became more significant, the Aliens Act of 1905 sought to limit unwanted immigrants but allowed admittance to those who could prove they were seeking access to escape persecution on religious or political grounds.

Following the end of World War Two, sanctuary in Britain was offered to around 200,000 Poles and other East Europeans escaping Nazi occupation who now sought to remain to avoid returning to Soviet rule. They and thousands of others who had been displaced into camps around Europe were allowed to remain (Cohen, 1994). These European voluntary workers were the last large group of refugees to be allowed to enter and automatically remain in Britain because they were anti-Soviet, and therefore politically aligned to Britain and because they offered a solution to the labour shortage.

Thereafter the main flow of refugees into the UK was via a quota system. Three thousand Chilean refugees were permitted to enter and join integration programmes after the political crisis and repression following the military coup and assassination of President Allende (Cohen, 1994). In 1979 a quota of 18,000 Vietnamese was agreed with the UN following pressure to take a more active role in dealing with the arrivals in Hong Kong. East African Asians came to Britain when East Africa was approaching independence and in particular when Idi Amin insisted that non-Africans should decide if they wanted to remain British nationals or become Ugandans.

In the late 1980s and early 1990s the number of refugees continued to increase as poverty and political instability increased across the world. The collapse of communism in the Soviet Union and Eastern Europe was a precursor to inter-ethnic violence in 1991/92 in the former Yugoslavia, and led to the largest number of displaced people in Europe since the Second World War (Cohen, 1994). Britain reluctantly accepted some displaced persons from ex-Yugoslavia but the main support came from countries in mainland Europe: this crisis in Eastern Europe was the last in the wave of quota resettlements before the development of the Gateway Protection Programme in 2003.

Overbeek (1995) suggests a range of reasons for the development of the 'refugee crisis' of the 1990s. The widening demographic and development gap between the north and the south encouraged ever greater numbers of migrants to improve their prospects by migrating or fleeing to the rich north. Other factors were the restructuring of the world political and economic order, political events such as the collapse of socialism and the effects of civil war and famines or natural disasters in many developing states. The size and extent of refugee crises expanded as they coincided with the reduction of aid to the developing world in response to nationalist and protectionist pressures in the industrialised countries (Cohen, 1994). Tariffs and trade agreements, such as the General Agreement on Tariffs and Trade, have all in some way had an impact on the ability of the developing world to survive economically. As the volume of refugee migration expanded through the 1990s many potential host states began to argue that refugees were in effect 'disguised economic migrants' who did not meet the criteria set out under the 1951 UN Geneva Convention.

Whilst Britain has only recently become one of the most important refugee-receiving countries in Europe, attitudes to refugees have deteriorated and public opinion and policy have become increasingly hostile (Marfleet, 2006). Cohen (1994) argues 'the construction of a new stigmatised group, the 'disguised economic migrant', was necessary to the deconstruction of the morally untouchable category of the 'deserving political refugee'.' Thus, in a bid to get around the responsibilities of the 1951 Convention, refugees now have to demonstrate that they are genuine asylum seekers escaping persecution by meeting stringent criteria and jumping through ever more hoops as policy and practice evolve to meet the explicit political goal of reducing refugee numbers.

The main approach first used for reducing arrivals was the introduction of visa requirements on so-called 'pressure to migrate' or 'refugee-producing' countries such as Sri Lanka, Bangladesh and Pakistan. Visa restrictions became so severe that it is now difficult for family visitors from the Indian sub-continent to visit the UK because documentation is difficult to obtain in those countries (Cohen, 1994). Another approach has involved legislation which put the onus on air, land and sea carriers to ensure that passengers have the correct documentation and to check that their vehicles are not carrying immigrants without documentation. Failure to comply with the legislation can result in on the spot fines which are so high that they threaten unwitting carriers, such as lorry drivers, with bankruptcy. Thus much of the policing of borders was turned over to carriers, while Immigration Officers policed these carriers and processed illegal immigrants identified by them.

The changing face of asylum-seeking in Europe

The UK actions coincided with the alignment of immigration controls within the EU that began in the mid-1980s. This happened when there was an increased flow of refugees from Central and Eastern Europe and from Africa, the Indian sub-continent and South-East Asia. The predominant principle was again exclusion and the standardisation process included a raft of policies limiting the admission and settlement of refugees (Thranhardt and Miles, 1995). During the 1980s a debate emerged about the meaning of the concept of the 'free movement of persons'. Some Member States felt this should apply to EU citizens only, which would involve keeping internal border checks in order to distinguish between EU and non-EU nationals. Others argued in favour of free movement for everyone, which would mean an end to internal border checks altogether. Since the Member States found it impossible to reach agreement, France, Germany, Belgium, Luxembourg and the Netherlands decided in 1985 to create a territory without internal borders. This became known as the Schengen area. Britain, Denmark and

Greece expressed extreme opposition to free movement and Britain has remained outside the agreement (Geddes, 2000). Inter-governmental cooperation expanded to include thirteen countries in 1997, following the signing of the Treaty of Amsterdam, which was incorporated into EU law in May 1999. The Treaty adopted all the decisions taken since 1985 by Schengen group members and the associated working structures.

Cohen (1994) outlines how the EU ended up taking a collectively restrictive position on asylum. The historically more liberal states showed concern at the restraints imposed by the traditionally restrictive countries, which in reality were beginning to resemble their own increasingly tough attitudes. The states that had traditionally adopted harsh attitudes to migrants declared that they would not abandon national border restrictions until all the other states adopted their more draconian approaches to immigration. Ultimately, in a bid to see the agreement through, the liberal states yielded and each state prepared for a significant clampdown on immigration from non-EU countries, thus constructing what has been described as Fortress Europe.

When Schengen came into effect, the agreement abolished the internal borders of the signatory states and created a single external border where immigration checks were carried out in accordance with a single set of rules. Common rules regarding visas, asylum rights and checks at external borders were adopted to allow the free movement of persons within the signatory states without disturbing law and order. To help reconcile freedom and security, the freedom of movement was accompanied by so-called 'compensatory' measures. This involved improving coordination between the police, customs and the judiciary and taking measures to combat important problems such as terrorism, organised crime and to deal with asylum issues. Specific measures affected asylum-seekers: the definition of the role of all carriers in combating illegal immigration; the drawing up of rules for asylum seekers under the Dublin Convention; and the harmonisation of rules regarding entry. The Schengen Information System was set up to enable EU states to exchange data on people's identities. The system was designed with a two-track approach: fast and open for EU residents and slow and restrictive for those arriving from outside the EU.

The main objective of the Dublin Convention was to determine which Member State was responsible for examining an application for asylum, which had not been resolved by the Geneva Convention on the Status of Refugees (1951). The application of the Dublin Convention was intended to ensure that every asylum seeker's application would be examined by a

Member State, unless a 'safe' non-Member country could be considered as responsible. The rationale behind the convention was two-fold. Its main aim was to avoid applications to more than one state at the same time. A secondary aim was to avoid a situation where refugees were shuttled from one Member State to another, with none accepting responsibility for assessing their claim. In theory all asylum seekers arriving in Europe had the right to have their claim processed: they were also expected to do this in the country of arrival rather than selecting a country they perceived as having a more lenient approach to asylum, or 'asylum shopping'.

The Convention also agreed common definitions for terms such as alien, (which meant any person other than a national of a Member State) and applicant for asylum (which meant an alien seeking protection of a Member State under the Geneva Convention). All signatories, including Britain, reaffirmed their obligations under the Geneva Convention to make a commitment to protecting those in need of sanctuary whilst ensuring thorough examinations of claims to ensure authenticity. They also agreed a resolution on manifestly unfounded applications for asylum (Overbeek, 1995) and that asylum could be refused where there was no fear of persecution in the applicant's own country or if the claim was based on deception or an abuse of procedures. The sentiment behind this resolution is apparent throughout recent UK legislation, and is echoed in the media by claims about 'bogus asylum seekers'.

The Dublin Convention was signed in 1990. Together with the Schengen Agreement, it was designed to come to terms with the actions of countries attempting to discourage possible immigrants and asylum seekers by introducing daunting immigration and asylum procedures, and provided a framework for the Europeanisation of asylum and immigration policy (Marfleet, 2006).

The Amsterdam Treaty (1997) proposed the creation of 'an area of freedom, justice and security' covering free movement, immigration and asylum, and the potential for expanded anti-discrimination provisions to cover racial or ethnic discrimination (Geddes, 2000). Britain had always resisted treaties proposing the abolition of internal frontier controls which it felt might compromise its highly restrictive immigration policy framework. The Amsterdam Treaty did propose common policies on immigration but allowed Member States to maintain or introduce national provisions in their immigration policies providing that they were compatible with the treaty. The treaty covered areas such as criteria for assessing claims and set out minimum standards for reception, temporary protection and the granting or withdrawing of status. Britain is subject to this treaty.

The British situation

Applications for asylum in the UK began to rise dramatically at the end of the 1980s. By the mid-1990s numbers reached 37,000 applications in 1996 rising to a peak of 103,080 recorded in 2002 (Home Office, 2003). Peach and Henson point to the extreme difficulty of trying to assess the number of refugees resident in the UK:

> The numbers of those with refugee status or some other forms of protection who subsequently leave the UK are not recorded and the settlement figures for dependents only include those who are granted settlement at the same time as the principal applicant. (2005: 13)

Adding the cumulative totals of settlement figures given in the monthly Home Office asylum statistics reports is one way of estimating the size of the refugee population in the UK. This data indicates that some 322,875 individuals (including dependants) have received asylum status between 1996 and 2005 (see Table 1.1).

	1996	1997	1998	1999	2000	2001
Excluding dependants	4,195	4,830	6,680	22,505	25,355	17,965
	2002	**2003**	**2004**	**2005**	**1996-2005**	
	18,235	12,190	19,460	25,710	157,155	
	1996	**1997**	**1990**	**1999**	**2000**	**2001**
Including dependants	9,445	11,780	12,630	38,660	45,950	28,520
	2002	**2003**	**2004**	**2005**	**1996-2005**	
	29,940	22,105	54,310	69,535	322,875	
(After Home Office, 2006)						

Table 1.1: The total number of asylum seekers given leave to remain in the UK

The UNHCR (2005) estimates that by 2004 there were 290,000 refugees in the UK, a figure which accounted for 0.5 per cent of the UK population and 3 per cent of the world's ten million refugees (Employability Forum, 2006). One hundred and forty four thousand refugees have been granted leave to remain in the UK since 2001 (Home Office, 2006). With thousands of asylum seekers arriving in the UK annually, around 25 per cent of whom are likely to receive some kind of leave to remain, and a large backlog of cases, this number is clearly set to increase considerably. The backlog was calculated to be around 60,000 at December 2003 (Bourn, 2004) and the Home Office announced it would review 460,000 such 'legacy' cases in 2007. There is no data on the number of individuals in the regions who receive status but by calculating the figure on a pro-rata basis using the number of asylum seekers allocated to each region since dispersal it is possible to make some kind of estimate.

Figure 1.2 indicates that the North West, Yorkshire and Humberside, and the West Midlands have received the largest number of asylum seekers. Extrapolation of these figures suggests that these regions support 23,664, 28,544 and 22,980 post-dispersal refugees respectively. The combination of a significant increase in arrivals and negative media reporting is seen as having strongly influenced the Government's thinking around immigration policy, and was swiftly followed by several pieces of legislation aimed at 'securing our borders' (Home Office, 2002) against those individuals who were allegedly taking advantage of the system. This legislation, the first aimed specifically at asylum seekers, was followed rapidly by what is described by the Refugee Council as a 'phenomenal' spate of legal developments.

Research commissioned by the Home Office (see Robinson and Segrott, 2002) indicated that it was not the attractions of supposedly available housing and benefits that drew asylum seekers to the UK, but notions of the country as peaceful, safe, democratic and economically prosperous. Many were attracted to the UK because their country of origin had colonial links with it or they had relatives living there. However, the UK was generally seen as being sympathetic to asylum seekers and was therefore an attractive destination.

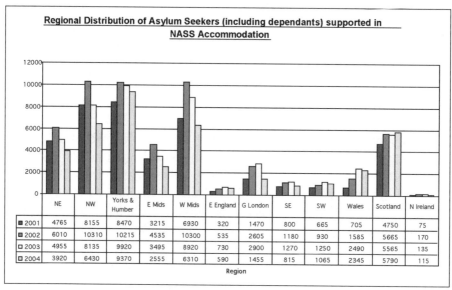

Figure 1.2: The regional distribution of asylum seekers in the regions

Others had little knowledge of their final destination and had merely been offered the UK as an option by the people smugglers who brought them into the country (Robinson and Segrott, 2002).

There is some correlation between political situations within the country of origin and seeking asylum in the UK. For example, in the years 2000 to 2002 Iraq and Afghanistan were at the top of the list but by 2004, following the US invasion of both countries, neither featured in the top five. Similarly, whilst 6,480 Europeans were granted asylum in 1999 only 165 were successful in 2004 following the resolution of the conflicts in Bosnia, Serbia and Croatia. Furthermore, 4,130 Sri Lankans were given asylum in 2001 and only 160 in 2004 following the ceasefire in Sri Lanka.

Disregarding the findings of the Robinson and Segrott's (2002) study, and the evidence that asylum flows were directly related to the political situation in unstable countries, the Government pressed on with its reforms and by 2004 achieved a reduction of more than 50 per cent in asylum applications to 40,625. It is unclear whether numbers have reduced in response to the increased restrictions, to a change in political situations leading fewer people to need sanctuary, or to immigrants electing to evade the asylum system altogether and disappear into the grey economy as illegal immigrants. What is clear is that immigration and asylum in particular are hot political issues and that the media have played a key role in highlighting so-called asylum abuses and piled on populist pressure for more and more restrictions.

Media, politics and asylum

Negative media attitudes to migration have become increasingly apparent over the past decade, when refugee numbers have increased and migration has become an important facet of European policy. A review of the literature by Hubbard (2005) revealed suggestions that anxieties about the 'flood' of asylum seekers seemingly threatening to 'swamp' Britain had triggered a series of draconian measures designed to protect the boundaries of the nation. The media depiction of asylum seekers as a social, welfare and security problem encouraged this boundary protection further. Huysmans (1995) shows how images in the media show big cities as places full of criminals and violence, and feed the growth of xenophobia and racism in Europe. The predominant message is that acts of violence against migrants and refugees are commonplace and are part of the discourse of 'They are not welcome' or 'They do not belong here'. These images of crime, insecurity and migrants were linked, leading to a situation where migrants and refugees were seen as the source of the insecurity.

Huysmans (1995) argues that political leaders in Western Europe are also putting migration on the security agenda. For example, both Schengen and Dublin linked migration with the struggle against drugs, terrorism and national security. Huysmans (1995) also found links between migration and insecurity in western European academic literature. Debate in strategic and security studies migration was gaining increasing attention. The linking of migration and security is not an innocent activity: it creates a crisis and provides a rationale for action against migrants in the interest of national security. It has increased markedly since the 9/11 and 7/11 bombings in New York and London, particularly as some of the suspects had gained refugee status in the UK. Increased concern about who should be allowed to enter the UK and move around undocumented now has the ultimate justification: a link between terrorism and asylum.

The extent to which asylum seekers and refugees have entered the national consciousness as a negative facet of modern life is illustrated by Lemos' (2005) work with young people. This study explored both their attitudes towards racial and ethnic groups and the things they said influenced their attitudes and behaviour. Refugees and asylum seekers were prominent amongst groups the young people identified as being 'disliked'. They were perceived as receiving preferential treatment in terms of benefits and housing and were sometimes connected to perceived security threats. These ideas appeared to be drawn from friends and family, local events and circumstances, personal experiences and media reporting.

In a report from the Council of Europe's racism commission, racism directed at refugees and asylum seekers in Britain was considered to be particularly acute. The report found that the xenophobic attitude evident in the British media, political debate and government policy exacerbated intolerance amongst the general population (ECRI, 2005).

Politics and asylum are inextricably linked in the UK. The 2005 General Election campaign was an excellent example of how migrants are used by political parties to score points for being the toughest against illegal immigration and 'bogus' asylum seekers. Labour kicked off its campaign with the publication of the Government's Five Year Asylum and Immigration Strategy (February, 2005), setting out some far-reaching measures which the Refugee Council (2005) describe as having 'serious implications for the future of asylum in the UK'. These included suggestions, of which some have now been implemented, such as reviewing an individual's refugee status after five years and returning those whose countries conditions have improved; fast-tracking the removals of failed asylum seekers, increasing detention and introducing tagging; fingerprinting non EU nationals entering and leaving the UK; and returning unaccompanied asylum-seeking children (UASC).

In response, the Conservative Party proposed the unprecedented step of pulling out of the Geneva Convention altogether and placing an arbitrary cap on asylum numbers to make sure that Britain 'only took its fair share' of asylum seekers, and that those permitted to enter the UK were 'genuine'. For the second election in a row the Conservatives found that making tough immigration policy the centrepiece of their campaign did not compensate for a lack of policies generally.

Whilst derided at the time for even thinking the unthinkable and suggesting that the UK should be the first country to pull out of the Geneva Convention, the Labour Party subsequently found itself making similar proposals. In May 2005 it was revealed that illegal immigrants who had been jailed for crimes committed in the UK had not been deported on their release. Headlines revealed that nine Afghani hijackers had been permitted to remain in the UK because it was deemed unsafe for them to return to their country of origin. In response the Prime Minister decided to deport all criminals of migrant background, regardless of whether or not they would be safe in their destination country. Any liberal attitudes that had once informed the support of asylum seekers were now replaced with a knee jerk approach to policy making which increasingly demonised and penalised asylum seekers whilst simultaneously trying to make an argument for the integration of refugees and the importance of multiculturalism and community cohesion.

Growing restrictionalism

Favell (1998) makes a case for there being two separate aspects of a British legislative framework: nationality law and the border control it institutes; and subsequent provision to promote social harmony and create conditions for ethnic minority integration within these borders. Border controls, he argues, are justified if they maintain a balanced control on immigrant numbers, prevent the majority population from becoming intolerant about existing immigrants and instil in the immigrant population a demographic stability that enables them to settle. Human rights and humanitarian norms, he observes, generally have no part in the existing legislation on asylum. Instead there has been a distinct lack of charity extended towards post-1989 refugees, most of whom, because of our island geography, can be kept out of Britain more easily than out of the rest of Europe.

Until 1993 there was no legislation that established the rights and status of refugees as set out under the 1951 United Nations Convention on the Status of Refugees. The Asylum and Immigration Appeals Act, introduced in 1993, incorporated the UK's obligations under the UN Convention. It gave asylum seekers a right to appeal but also announced that all asylum seekers must be fingerprinted and could be detained. Although previous legislation had sought to reduce the numbers of immigrants from overseas, this was the first initiative to adopt a restrictionist attitude towards asylum seekers. It restricted their access to housing by stating that only those who could demonstrate that they had no accommodation could be expected to be housed by a housing authority.

This Act was followed by the Asylum and Immigration Act 1996, which removed the entitlement of in-country asylum seekers to benefits and housing. It created a new criminal offence of employing someone 'subject to immigration control' who does not have leave to enter, to remain, or who is subject to conditions on such leave. This Act dictated that employers who were not able to produce documentary evidence that they had checked the papers of their employees could be liable for a fine. The implications of this measure are discussed in the next chapter. It also removed asylum seekers' right to child benefit. Related measures in the 1996 Housing Act restricted asylum seekers' access to housing by denying them access to local authority housing waiting lists.

These Acts were the first in a stream of legislation which introduced measures aimed at acting as a deterrent to asylum seekers coming to the UK: they were in response to media and public concern about asylum seekers' use of resources and in particular housing, which was in short supply in the South East of England where most asylum seekers were housed at that time.

Of all the immigration legislation, the 1999 Immigration and Asylum Act has had the biggest impact on the support of asylum seekers in the UK. It removed all remaining benefit entitlement for asylum seekers and created NASS to support and disperse destitute asylum seekers. In the first instance the Act made it hard for asylum seekers to reach the UK by ensuring that all means of transport were covered by carriers' liability legislation so that any carrier transporting a passenger without valid documentation had to pay a fine of £2,000 per person. The concept of 'safe third countries' enshrined in the Dublin Convention was written into legislation, meaning that asylum seekers who had passed through a country deemed safe could be removed to that country without appeal. Anyone entering the country using deception could be charged with a criminal offence.

NASS began operating in April 2000. It provided a basic package of support for all asylum seekers who declared themselves destitute. This support was equivalent to 70 per cent of Income Support. Those who could be housed by a relative or friend were entitled to receive a 'support only' package. Those with no access to housing were offered accommodation on a no choice basis. This meant they could be dispersed to accommodation in any one of the regions outside London. Refusal to accept the location could lead to withdrawal of support. Dispersal was the main innovation of the 1999 Act. It was primarily intended to reduce the pressure on services in the South East which had borne the main brunt of asylum support. Consequently, the selection of dispersal areas depended largely upon the availability and cost of accommodation. The drive to locate areas by housing availability rather than applicants' needs was, and still is, criticised by organisations such as the Refugee Council and in examinations of the impact of dispersal policy (Robinson *et al*, 2003).

Concerns have been expressed about the lack of support services to help asylum seekers deal with their immigration claims and indeed their everyday life. Early research in Wolverhampton, one of the West Midlands dispersal cities, showed that in 2000 there was no knowledge about the needs or entitlements of asylum seekers in the city (Phillimore and Goodson, 2001). The local authority could not provide translation services. This situation was mirrored elsewhere in the region and the UK (Robinson *et al*, 2003). Whilst the 1999 Act made some provision for payments to be made to local authorities and voluntary organisations in connection with the provision of support to asylum seekers, no amount was specified nor the mechanisms for gaining access to further sums of money. Often local authorities found themselves providing support to individuals who had been dispersed to their area without prior consultation.

The secondary aim of the 1999 Immigration and Asylum Act was to make asylum in the UK less attractive to asylum seekers, which was further developed in the legislation which followed. The Nationality, Asylum and Immigration Act 2002 placed emphasis on the control and removal of unsuccessful applicants. Detention centres were renamed removal centres, rights to appeal were reduced, the likelihood of removal to a safe third country was increased and the possibility of removal prior to appeal was reintroduced. Support was withdrawn for in-country asylum seekers, thus rendering destitute, and with no recourse to public funds, all those who had not applied for asylum within a 'reasonable time' after arrival.

However, Section 55, as it was known, was successfully challenged under Human Rights legislation. The 2002 Act proposed the setting up of Induction and Accommodation centres where asylum claims could be processed quickly whilst applicants lived in dormitory style accommodation. This policy was also abandoned because of widespread public opposition to the siting of the centres. Finally, this Act removed the right of applicants to work or undertake vocational training. It widened the range of measures aimed at reducing illegal working, including allowing immigration officers to enter a place of work without a warrant. This measure had major implications for the employability of refugees and is discussed in Chapter Seven.

On a more positive note, the 2002 Act recognised the need for measures to help refugees to integrate. It doubled funding to the Home Office Challenge Fund, designed to support projects which addressed specific social needs amongst refugee communities. This measure was criticised as being insignificant. There were also concerns about the lack of financial support for the work of the National Refugee Integration Forum (NRIF) that was introduced following the publication of *Full and Equal Citizens* (Home Office, 2000), the Government's first integration strategy.

In the Asylum and Immigration Bill, introduced in 2003, greater emphasis still was placed on removal and assessing the credibility of applicants' claims. The 2004 Asylum and Immigration Act withdrew basic support for failed asylum seeking families in a bid to encourage voluntary return. It also legislated for a 'local connection' by requiring only the authority in which an individual was already housed as an asylum seeker to support their claim for social housing once they received leave to remain. This made it difficult for refugees to move around the UK in search of employment or to re-unite with other family members who might be settled elsewhere in the country. The Immigration, Asylum and Nationality Bill 2005 furthered previous regulations around employment by introducing on the spot fines for employers of £2,000 per illegal worker. It also raised the possibility that individuals who had been granted temporary leave to remain under Exceptional Leave to Remain or Humanitarian Protection would not automatically be permitted to remain in the UK once this period expired.

Whilst the raft of legislation introduced throughout the 1990s and 2000s mainly acted to reduce the rights of asylum seekers and to make the UK less attractive as a location for seeking asylum, the Government view was that they had introduced strategies to help improve the opportunities for refugees to integrate. *Integration Matters* (Home Office, 2005) and *Working to Rebuild*

Lives (DWP, 2005) were, in an unusually joined up approach to working with refugees, released simultaneously in March 2005. *Integration Matters* builds upon the earlier integration policies set out in *Full and Equal Citizens* (Home Office, 2000). It lists the range of problems that need to be addressed and proposes both policy and practical solutions. It also highlights the need for better data about refugees.

Much emphasis was placed upon helping refugees to achieve their full potential, and the need to provide opportunities for language training, early contact with Jobcentre Plus, work experience, retraining and accreditation, and commitment and openness from employers. Importance was placed upon mobilising the voluntary sector, the Challenge Fund and the NRIF in helping refugees to achieve these goals. In addition, a Strategic Upgrade of National Refugee Integration Services, known as the SUNRISE initiative, was piloted in four areas across the UK, this is scheduled to be rolled out across the UK in 2008. The SUNRISE programme would enable each refugee engaged in the initiative to work with a caseworker to create a Personal Integration Plan.

Working to Rebuild Lives (DWP, 2005) discussed the need to develop partnerships to help in the creation of services for refugees and set out plans to encourage refugees to undertake Basic Skills and ESL (English as a second language) training and to enhance the support refugees are given by advisers in Jobcentres. It also outlines the hope that the NRIF might work to locate some solutions for professionally qualified refugees. Neither of these strategies has a designated resource to aid their implementation.

In 2006 what can only be viewed as a retrograde step in the development of integration policy occurred: the NRIF, the only organisation charged with reviewing progress on the national integration strategies, was abolished. At the same time the obligation for each NASS region to produce a regional integration strategy was withdrawn and it was announced that all integration funds would be channelled into a new National Refugee Integration Service. This service would build on the experience of the SUNRISE pilot, which had not been fully evaluated, and would add further dimensions, such as offering mentors to all new refugees and specialist support for refugee professionals. Refugee Community Organisations (RCOs) and Non Governmental Organisations (NGOs) expressed concern at the withdrawal of Home Office funding from their sector. In addition the logic of providing a service intended only for new refugees was questioned, given the evidence that refugees required support far beyond the first six months after receiving their status. In a subsequent move that indicated a shift towards further restrictionalism, the Immigration and Nationality Directorate (IND) became the Border and Immigration Agency and then the UK Borders Agency. Furthermore, the Social Policy Unit, which had held responsibility for integration policy, was dissolved.

Refugees and migration in the West Midlands

The West Midlands region has become one of the primary dispersal areas for asylum seekers in the UK and forms the case study region explored in Chapters Four to Seven. The region is situated in the heart of England and covers an area of nearly 13,000 square kilometres from Stoke-on-Trent in the north, Evesham in the south, Shrewsbury in the west and Rugby in the east. It houses 9 per cent of the UK's population, of about 5.27 million people, with the majority living in large conurbation areas. There is also a significant rural population. The region now has a varied economic base with 20.4 per cent of employment in manufacturing and nearly 70 per cent in the service sector.

Birmingham is the capital city of the region and Britain's second city. It has gained a reputation as one of Britain's foremost multicultural cities. In terms of ethnicity Birmingham is expected to become Europe's first non-white majority city by 2011 (Birmingham Chamber of Commerce, 2005). At present the city is home to a wide range of communities, including descendants of the Jewish people who fled discrimination in Eastern Europe during the eighteenth and nineteenth centuries, those escaping conflicts and persecution in Chile, Indo-China and East Africa in the 1970s and 1980s (Dick, 2004) and the Irish, African-Caribbean and South Asian economic migrants of the 1960s and 1970s. The cities of Coventry and Wolverhampton and the urban centres of Dudley, Walsall, and Sandwell have long-established African-Caribbean and Asian populations. More recently people from Afghanistan, Bosnia, Iran, East Africa, Kosovo and Kurdistan, fleeing from war, genocide and tyranny, have been sent to live in these areas as part of the NASS dispersal programme.

Whilst Birmingham has provided a home or new opportunities to those who seek sanctuary, and other urban areas in the West Midlands also view their multicultural identity as one of their defining characteristics, new communities in the region have faced difficulties when striving to make a place for themselves. The majority of newcomers move, or are dispersed to, multicultural parts of the inner city (Phillimore, 2005) which have been associated with high levels of deprivation. Across the region, asylum seekers and refugees have been housed in the most deprived areas, where housing is cheap and plentiful. While these areas were predominantly and historically multicultural, they had little experience of providing support for refugees in terms of health, education, training or employment.

The change in populations that occurred in the West Midlands following the introduction of the dispersal programme was rapid and there was little or no consultation with local residents or service providers. ETE providers had little awareness about the rights or entitlements to their services of asylum seekers or refugees and no one knew how many asylum seekers or refugees were living in the region. In order to try to understand the needs, requirements and entitlements of the new arrivals, studies were commissioned that explored these issues in some depth, with a view to informing the development of policy across the region. The data from these studies in the West Midlands with its multicultural communities and its embrace of, and early involvement in, the dispersal system, provides an excellent case study region within which to explore the experiences of refugees and asylum seekers who have been dispersed to the English regions. This data forms the basis of the empirical evidence utilised in this book. Chapter Three provides details of these studies and outlines the methodological approach adopted.

The past decade has seen massive developments in the fields of asylum and migration. Numbers have increased enormously, and asylum in particular has become the hottest political issue in the UK, if not Europe, and has dominated debate in two elections. New legislation in both the EU and the UK has been developed at breakneck speed and implemented, with varying degrees of success. At the same time there has been some realisation that refugees are a permanent feature of life in the UK and that action needs to be taken to integrate them into society. The 2001 Bradford and Oldham riots highlighted the need to ensure that new migrants become part of civil life in the UK (Cantle, 2001). Clearly getting policy right is critical, particularly in relation to the sensitive issue of asylum and integration. The impact and development of such policies are the main concern of this book.

Emphasis is placed on the issue of ETE because these, in policy terms, have been identified as having primary roles in securing social and economic integration of new arrivals, and secondly, because research suggests that asylum seekers and refugees view these factors as of primary importance in making a life in the UK (see Bloch, 2002). While research has been undertaken in these areas, particularly in the field of employment studies, the majority of studies pre-date dispersal and there is a tendency to focus research on London, which until 2000 was the primary destination for asylum seekers entering the UK. Whilst London continues to be the premier destination for asylum seekers, and refugees once they receive their status, there are now significant asylum seeker and refugee populations in many urban areas across England. It is important to understand how newcomers are faring in the regions; the kinds of challenges and opportunities they face when trying to access ETE; the skills and experiences they can offer the urban areas in which they reside; the ways in which the host communities can make the most of the opportunities offered by newcomers; and the types of policy response that can be put in place to support such integration through ETE.

Structure of the book

Having set out the context to the current situation of asylum seekers and refugees in the UK, the next chapter examines the concept of integration and recent policy developments, then moves on to explore the importance of post-compulsory education and training, and employment to integration. Chapter Two looks specifically at policy and practice around ETE provision, including entitlement, access and cost. The third chapter considers the challenges facing those researching asylum seekers in dispersal regions and leads into the field research itself.

Chapter Four analyses issues around education and training from the point of view of newcomers themselves and Chapter Five looks at provision from the perspective of providers. An overview of statutory and non-statutory sectors is given in Chapter Six, looking at ways of working with the target group and implementing government policy. Chapter Seven deals with employment, examining experiences of employment, including barriers and constraints, from the point of view of asylum seekers and refugees and then examines the attitudes of employers. Each chapter suggests ways forward.

In the final chapter, the main findings in relation to ETE are brought together to draw out the key issues facing newcomers. These findings are considered in the context of existing asylum and integration policy and the negative attitudes to newcomers perpetuated by policy and the use of asylum policy as a pawn in political debate. This last chapter explores what measures are needed to help increase the employability of newcomers. In order to support the case for change, integration policy in Northern Europe is considered. Lastly a model for increasing employability in the UK is set out and the case is made for a targeted and resourced approach to engaging new migrants.

2

Education, training and employment for integration and inclusion

Understanding integration

Between 1992 and 2002, nearly 255,000 people were granted refugee status or Exceptional Leave to Remain (ELR) in the UK (Home Office, 2005). Chapter One documented how this recent influx of newcomers has become a highly politicised and contentious issue (Robinson *et al*, 2003; Zetter *et al*, 2006). This has fuelled a debate around the issue of integration, what it is, and how it can be achieved. Within the academic literature the difficulties migrants experience in integration has received growing attention (Berry, 1997; Castles and Davidson, 2000).

The concept of integration itself is much contested and the various aspects of what constitutes an 'integrated community' are the focus of much debate (Castles *et al*, 2002; Crisp, 2004). The literature focuses on various types of integration, social, economic or cultural (cf. Baubock, 1994; Portes, 1997, 1998; Zetter *et al*, 2002), and the various aspects or indicators of integration (cf. Ager and Strang, 2004; Weiner, 1996; White, 1998). In policy and practice this interest is borne out in the Home Office's strategy documents on refugee integration: *Full and Equal Citizens* (2000), *Secure Borders, Safe Haven* (2002) and *Integration Matters* (2005), which outlines a set of actions and indicators aimed at taking integration strategies forward and measuring success based on a framework proposed by Ager and Strang (2004). In 2004 the Department of Work and Pensions' strategy on refugee employment *Working to Rebuild Lives* (DWP, 2005) was published. The National Refugee Integration Forum (NRIF) and the SUNRISE programme were set up. Interest in integration has lately been shown by the proposal of a National Refugee Integration Service which is said to represent a more strategic and targeted approach to helping newcomers to settle in the UK.

In both the academic and policy debates stress is put upon the importance of the provision of and access to education, training and employment (ETE): these stand out as having a central role in facilitating integration.

What indicators of integration should be used in exploring the significance of ETE and the experience these indicators are intended to measure, and how is integration conceptualised in the literature? Favell believes the term integration has been used to characterise 'progressive-minded, tolerant and inclusive approaches to dealing with ethnic minorities' (1998: 3). He traces the term back to Parson's (1937) synthesis of Weber and Durkheim, and society's need for socially inclusive unity based on 'value integration'. The Chicago School applied the concept of integration to the study of ethnicity in an attempt to give it a policy application (Favell, 1998). This school of thought sees integration as a process through which people pass *en route* to assimilation, although there is some recognition of the importance of the mediating role of the host society, whose actions can impact negatively on the process if migrants experience intolerance and xenophobia.

For Berry (1994) integration is just one possible dimension of the acculturation process, where acculturation is a culture change that emanates from unbroken contact between two distinct cultural groups. He takes a social psychology perspective on integration, seeing it as one of four possible acculturation strategies (Berry, 1991, 1994, 1997). For him, integration is where individuals have an interest both in maintaining their original culture and in taking part in daily interactions with other groups (Berry, 1991). He believes that integration is a strategy that is 'chosen' by migrants. They could, alternatively, elect to 'assimilate', deciding not to maintain their original cultural links; 'separate', where they do not mix with the indigenous [*sic*] population; or, if excluded, become 'marginalised' and have little contact with the indigenous population and little desire to maintain their own cultural links. All these strategies require substantial adaptation to the dominant culture, but integration is considered to be psychologically the most desirable way of acculturating (Berry, 1997).

Integration in the fullest sense of the concept can only occur freely if mutual accommodation is possible by the host society (Banton, 2001; Berry, 1997; Korac, 2003). Whilst this process requires migrants to adopt the basic values of the wider society, it also requires national institutions to adapt to meet the needs of all groups living together in multicultural society.

In a discussion of the refugee integration literature, Fyvie *et al* (2003) highlight education and training, the labour market, health and housing as being critical to integration because progress in these areas is the minimum requirement for the integration process to start. However, in a more recent review of the integration literature, Atfield *et al* (2007) draw upon the work of Temple and Moran (2005) and White (1998) to bring out the nuances beyond the functional side of integration to identify further socio-demographic and political factors that are acknowledged to affect the integration process and experience. These include gender, class, religion, legal status, characteristics of the refugee's ethnic community in the UK, including exit conditions, asylum and immigration policies and public attitudes to refugees. Thus a whole range of factors, often linked or overlapping, can influence integration experiences and make the process variable within and between ethnic groups.

Several authors argue that a holistic approach to studying integration is important as integration consists of multi-layered processes and a combination of complex and interrelated issues (Castles *et al*, 2002; Fyvie *et al*, 2003). This complexity means that the integration process does not necessarily generate a linear experience whereby access to certain rights accumulate over time, offering the opportunity for further integration. Individuals tend to make use of their rights in different ways and at different speeds, depending on factors such as their education and employment background and their willingness to utilise their rights (Gans, 1992). For example, having permission to work does not mean that a person will seek or secure work immediately.

The notion of integration as a non-linear process accounts for the fact that interruptions may occur, which may impede other aspects of integration, making any assumptions about how integration should ideally proceed problematic (Atfield *et al*, 2007). Furthermore, if the integration process is interrupted, individuals may arguably become both socially and economically marginalised (Bloch, 2000; Garvie, 2001; Geddes, 2003).

Whilst academics acknowledge that integration is bi-directional and non-linear, Crisp (2004), Korac (2003) and Schibel *et al* (2002) argue that it is also a highly subjective process. They suggest that refugees' perceptions of their integration should be central to our understanding. In policy, and to some extent in academia, emphasis is generally placed upon tangible, quantifiable aspects of the process or a top down approach focused on structural and organisational elements of the system (Korac, 2003), as opposed to providing refugees with a platform to express their views and experiences. This can mean that the nuances and complexities of their experiences are overlooked. This book aims to go some way towards redressing this imbalance. Refugees' own experiences and stories are at the heart of several chapters and we consider the role of ETE in the integration process from the perspective of refugees looking to rebuild their lives.

Developing indicators of integration

Policy makers require a more traditionally empirical approach to measuring integration so that progress can be evaluated and generalisations made about the effectiveness of policy interventions. To aid policy development and evaluation a number of authors have developed indicators for monitoring and evaluating how integration has occurred in various contexts. In the UK, Ager and Strang (2004) led the way by identifying a set of indicators which address some of the issues around subjectivity. Their indicators can be used flexibly to provide a basic framework to compare integration initiatives whilst allowing organisations to add their own indicators.

There are two main approaches to selecting indicators. Mestheneos and Ioannidi (2002) and Coussey (2000) believe that integration can be measured by using objective indicators that compare refugees' position to that of the majority and include factors such as jobs, education, housing, political representation and participation, whereas Ager and Strang (2004) and Zetter *et al* (2003) propose a series of indicators which show levels of integration within a number of domains.

Ager and Strang suggest ten policy indicators in four domains. They intend them to function both practically and at policy level to encourage a general understanding of the dimensions of integration and how it can be achieved and measured. Practically, the indicators are intended to assist the planning and delivery of services.

They suggest the following:

- 'means and markers', including employment, housing, education and health. These terms were selected because they are not only markers of integration but also facilitators of integration

- 'social connections', including social bridges, social bonds and social links. These are taken from Putnam's (2002) work on social capital and include the three dimensions of social capital: bonds within a refugee's own community, bridges with members of other communities and links with institutions of power and influence

- 'facilitators', including language and cultural knowledge and safety and stability. These represent the key skills and situational contexts required to enable refugees to engage confidently within communities

- 'foundation', which relates to the rights expected of the state, other people and the refugee themselves. This domain also includes the rights, expectations and obligations that go with citizenship (Ager and Strang, 2002).

Zetter *et al* (2003) similarly propose a typology of four domains in which integration takes place: the legal, statutory, functional and social domains.

While both approaches are intended to be as comprehensive as possible, the users of these frameworks and typologies will have a range of different requirements and different users may focus upon different combinations of domains or indicators at different times. These frameworks may be of use in assisting policy reviews (locally, regionally and nationally); helping with local consultations (to identify areas of achievement or concern); service monitoring and evaluation (helping services to reflect on their goals and purposes) and benchmarking (to define and measure local needs and achievements). Little consideration has been given to how data might be collected to help measure progress in achieving integration within the different dimensions and certainly not about how progress can be monitored across indicators. It is possible that a body of knowledge generated in one area may offer little insight or understanding of the others.

Recent indicators used by Government

Building upon the integration indicators literature, and specifically on the work of Ager and Strang (2004), the Government accepted the need for flexibility and for distinct but interrelated domains. In the most recent integration strategy, *Integration Matters* (Home Office, 2005), a set of higher-level indicators is proposed, with the aim of measuring success at local, regional and national levels. A total of seven indicators were identified and presented under three themes or domains. The first, 'achieving full potential', relates to employment rates of refugees and levels of English attainment over time. The second, 'contributing to the community' is concerned with the number of refugees involved in voluntary work, the number of refugees in touch with community organisations and the proportion of refugees reporting racial, cultural or religious harassment. The final indicator, 'accessing services', refers to rates of access to housing services and the proportion of parents indicating satisfaction with their children's education.

The Home Office (2005) indicators are a key part of their strategy and their purpose is to develop an understanding and a coherent approach to refugee integration work. They are also intended to help refugee-focused projects to plan and evaluate their services and to measure the progression of their clients. Employment and the learning of English are given priority, whereas issues around social capital and other, arguably less functional, aspects of integration are given short shrift.

Other issues around definitions and indicators of integration

This discussion of the ways in which integration is conceptualised demonstrates that although there are differences in interpretation of the term, there are some common themes that may have application at a policy level.

In academic terms integration is viewed as a process that begins with arrival and ends when refugees are in an equal position to the majority. Most argue that attempts to integrate newcomers should commence when they claim asylum. Concern has been expressed over the length of time it takes for some asylum seekers to have their claims resolved. This means they are left in limbo for months or even years, unable to settle down and make a life for themselves. The Government, on the other hand, is clear that it opposes any attempt to integrate asylum seekers, stating that 'proper' integration can only commence once an individual has leave to remain. Funding for asylum seeker activities is therefore restricted solely to actions that promote 'meaningful activity', and is limited. In practice some funds make their way to asylum seekers through the activities of the Big Lottery Fund or philanthropic work of trusts such as Barrow Cadbury and the Paul Hamlyn Foundation.

There is also some agreement in the academic arena that integration involves a two-way interchange of culture and understanding: the host community and institutions must adapt, not just the refugees (Mestheneos and Ioannidi, 2002; Schibel *et al*, 2002). Policy does not necessarily follow this line of thinking: it places the emphasis on refugees being able to make a full contribution to the interchange.

There is some convergence between policy and academia on the multi-dimensionality of integration in that it cannot be fully understood without exploring the full range of factors involved and their interconnections. But a framework for exploring integration has yet to be put into operation. In addition it is agreed that there are factors which can negatively affect the integration process, so that there is a need to consider the negative as well as the positive. However, whilst some commentators see asylum policy itself as one of the negative factors (see Refugee Council, 2006), the Government's declared negative indicators are essentially to do with racism and harassment. The Home Office makes no link between the way asylum has been politicised, the media's scapegoating of asylum seekers and public attitudes to asylum (Hubbard, 1995; Huysmans, 1995).

There is consensus that the development and use of indicators is useful and desirable and is an important means to understanding the position of refugees in relation to the host population. While it is recognised that integration encompasses 'soft' outcomes, more functional outcomes through education and employment are also recognised as being highly important. However, in the policy arena functional aspects of integration are given precedence, with employment and the development of English language skills as Government priorities. This emphasis on employment is shown by the move to develop a specialised employment function as part of the new national integration service.

The role of education and training, and employment, in the integration process

Academic literature and policy documents both emphasise the importance of empowering refugees to achieve their full potential as members of British society, contribute to the community and have access to the services they are entitled to (Ager and Strang, 2004; Home Office, 2005). This clearly includes having access to education and training provision and the labour market.

Little attention has been paid to engagement in education and training but nonetheless these areas are crucial for enhancing social integration and improving English language ability (Kershen, 2000; Pithers and Lim, 1997; Schellekens, 2001). The little research that exists documents the difficulties refugees experience when trying to learn English and the obstruction to the integration process caused by the lack of language skills.

A great deal of attention has been given to the problems refugees experience when they try to gain employment. As with education and training, the importance of the relationship between employment and integration is much emphasised (cf. Bloch, 1999, 2000, 2002; Coussey, 2000; Knox, 1997; Robinson, 1998; Valtonen, 1998). Employment is recognised as a key aspect of resettlement (Joly, 1996; Robinson, 1986; Srinivasan, 1994). There is evidence to suggest that economically independent newcomers adjust more easily to their new surroundings (Finnan, 1981). Feeney (2000) states that the inability to locate work is the single most significant barrier to successful integration of refugees into British society and that it can have a damaging effect on the person's well-being.

Research suggests that employment brings a whole raft of benefits for new-comers. It enables interaction with hosts, increases opportunities for learning English, creates the opportunity to build a future and to regain confidence and self-esteem whilst providing economic independence and identity (Bloch, 2000, 2002; Joly, 1996; Valtonen, 1998). Despite the importance of em-ployment for refugee integration and resettlement, and the fact that many newcomers are skilled and highly motivated to work (cf. Bloch, 2004; Carey-Wood, *et al*, 1995; Phillimore and Goodson, 2002; mbA, 1999; Peabody Trust, 1999; Pile, 1997), most newcomers experience unemployment or under-employment. This chapter explores the literature around access to ETE, to-gether with the associated problems newcomers face in relation to their 'functional' integration (Zetter *et al*, 2002).

Without doubt the introduction of the national dispersal programme under the 1999 Asylum and Immigration Act has added to the complexity of issues facing many neighbourhoods in which newcomers have settled. There has been growing concern over the increased volume and diversity of migrants and the impact of large numbers of newcomers on these areas and on the attitudes and behaviour of members of the settled community (Zetter *et al*, 2006).

Newcomers in dispersal areas have been conceptualised as both a challenge and an opportunity (Phillimore and Goodson, 2006). In both academic and policy circles these concerns have led to growing debate about the implica-tions of dispersal. This book focuses on the effect on the integration process of dispersal issues and access to ETE. They are the key factors in the quest for social cohesion and inclusion.

Like integration, social exclusion and social cohesion are contested terms. There is no consensus about the exact factors or agency responsible for them or how they can be measured successfully (Beauvais and Jenson, 2002; Forrest and Kearns, 2001; Hills *et al*, 2002; Home Office, 2003; Jenson, 2001; Kearns and Forrest, 2000; Pahl, 1991; Woolley, 1998). Social exclusion has been described as feeling 'excluded from the mainstream', a feeling of 'not be-longing' (Power and Wilson, 2000). The UK Government recognise some of the complexities of social exclusion and describe it as:

> ...a shorthand term for what can happen when people or areas suffer from a com-bination of linked problems such as unemployment, poor skills, low incomes, poor housing, high crime, bad health and family breakdown. (ODPM, 2000: 1)

Despite ongoing debate around the meaning and definition of social exclusion there is some agreement that there is a strong relationship between education, employment and social exclusion, especially in racially segregated areas (Power and Wilson, 2000; Social Exclusion Unit, 2001; Wilson, 1998). Two issues of concern arise concerning the relationship between the labour market and social exclusion and between unemployment and low paid or marginal employment.

Wilson's (1998) report for the Social Exclusion Unit, *When work disappears*, outlines the impact in the United States of the disappearance of work from poor, racially segregated neighbourhoods and how joblessness has affected both individuals and the social life of neighbourhoods. The shift from ethnic minorities being poor but working to being unemployed en masse is termed the 'new urban poverty', to which Wilson attributes many of today's problems:

> Today's problems in America's inner-city ghetto neighbourhoods – crime, family dis-solution, welfare, low levels of social organisation and so on – are in major measure related to the disappearance of work. (1998: 2)

The relationship between unemployment, social exclusion and the down-ward mobility of neighbourhoods has been recognised. Difficulties in gaining work can lead to high levels of economic inactivity, and this has become the reality for many newcomers to the UK. With no obvious way out people begin to feel trapped, become depressed and lose initiative: this results in frustra-tion and negative behaviour.

The impact of low income levels is further perpetuated as demand for local shops and services is reduced, and has a knock-on effect on the number of job opportunities created. The effect of unemployment thus moves beyond the individual and the present moment, and has an impact on the future trajectory of an area since:

> ...these clustering impacts on people's life chances and on neighbourhood condi-tions have wider consequences. Being poor in an area with many poor people and poor conditions generates a gradual loss of confidence in the system. (Power and Wilson, 1998: 8)

There is some evidence to suggest that as the character of an area changes its residents become less attractive as job applicants. Furthermore, it has been argued that employers make discriminatory assumptions about inner city ethnic minority workers and screen them out in a selective recruitment pro-cess (Wilson, 1998). Thus, for some, locating employment and breaking the vicious circle becomes even more challenging. Chapter Seven takes up the issue of employment opportunities and the job market.

Issues and effects of marginalisation

The link between the availability of employment and social exclusion is not as straightforward, as Wilson (1998) suggests. Several authors highlight the importance of considering the quality of job opportunities made available in order to have a positive impact on localities. Critics of US systems say using labour market flexibility to create jobs does little to reduce social exclusion if those available are marginal jobs which lack security, a decent wage, training and promotional prospects. Rather than reducing social exclusion, such employment ends up widening the gap between those at the bottom of the earnings scale and the overall average. However, if such work can be viewed as a stepping stone to something better the situation may not be so bleak (Atkinson, 1998).

There is a complex relationship between employment and social exclusion: success depends on whether the work restores a sense of control, acceptable relative status and prospects for the future (Atkinson, 1998). Evidence suggests that when refugees do find work, their jobs rarely meet these criteria. A key issue therefore must be how refugees, who are often marginalised by state policy (Zetter and Pearl, 2000), can be integrated into dispersal areas without becoming permanently socially excluded. How can this happen without exacerbating poverty and deprivation at individual and neighbourhood levels?

The costs of marginalisation: Government responses

The report by the Social Exclusion Unit (2001) observes that social exclusion is something that can happen to anyone, but acknowledges that certain groups who are disproportionately at risk (cf. Castles *et al*, 2002; Dorr and Faist, 1997; Richmond, 2000). The process of seeking asylum means that individuals can find themselves in one or more of the vulnerable positions that the Social Exclusion Unit identify as risk factors such as living in a low income household, being from an ethnic minority community, being homeless, being in care and non-attendance at school. They also identify the huge costs of social exclusion to individuals and society. At an individual level, under-achievement in education and employment, low incomes, poor access to services, stress and ill health are potential dangers. A key cost to society is the threat that structural inequalities bring to community cohesion (Cantle, 2005), and the associated problems that inequality may lead to, such as higher levels of crime and fear of crime, greater stress and reduced mobility.

The promotion of good community relations between migrant and settled communities has been a key policy objective of the UK government for many decades (Miles and Cleary, 1993; Schuster, 2003; Schuster and Solomos, 1999). As a response to growing concerns about social exclusion and as a way of addressing the perceived threat posed by newcomers, the Government has prioritised the need to build social cohesion (Commission on Integration and Cohesion, 2007). Failure to build cohesion will hamper new communities in their integration efforts and pose severe threats to communities (Favell, 1998; Zetter *et al*, 2006). How to promote and maintain social cohesion has become an important challenge for the UK Government: this is reflected in the publication of *Our shared future* (Commission on Integration and Cohesion, 2007). Since September 2007 it has become a statutory requirement for public bodies to promote social inclusion, just as they have a duty, underpinned by law, to further racial and since April 2007 gender equality.

The drive to promote social cohesion reflects a wider European agenda that emerged in the late 1990s. It wasn't until early 2000, when the European Commission (2000a, 2000b, 2001) and Council of Europe (2000a, 2000b) promoted cohesion in integrationist terms in order to tackle the risks of social and political disturbances, that the notion of cohesion resonated with the UK's stance and found support from UK policy makers (Zetter *et al*, 2006).

Zetter *et al* argue that the explicit promotion of social cohesion as a key policy objective marks a shift away from the promotion of multicultural race relations. The settlement and integration of newcomers became problematised in policy terms because of the view that patterns of new migration challenge notions of 'national identity', as they might undermine supposedly commonly held norms and values which are said to underpin the foundations of social solidarity, citizenship, belonging and identity (Anderson, 1983; Soysal, 1994; Weiner, 1995). They maintain that in recent years the mainstreaming of cohesion policy and the development of the refugee integration strategy has encouraged a shift away from accepting and celebrating difference and towards a greater emphasis on inclusivity and assimilation. They further argue that it is the relationship between new migration and cohesion which has heightened public concern, and driven policy making in this direction.

However, much literature is critical of the dearth of joined-up policy making on the settlement of refugees (Castles *et al*, 2002; Dorr and Faist, 1997; Richmond, 2000) and of policy coherence at national level. This has led to uncertainties at local level and to competing tensions between national and local agendas (Craig *et al*, 2004). It seems that promoting cohesion at the same time as enforcing restrictionist asylum policy sends mixed policy messages and creates confusion.

Restrictionalism in relation to the provision of ETE

As with social exclusion, the relationship between community cohesion, education and employment is not straightforward. Different types of provision may promote or undermine cohesion. Education and training is an important policy objective for remedying the breakdown in social cohesion (Gradstein and Justman, 2002; Green *et al*, 2003). However, the 2002 Nationality, Immigration and Asylum Act introduced a number of policies with far-reaching implications on ETE for newcomers, including the withdrawal of subsidies to help pay for certain kinds of training and the removal of the right for asylum seekers to apply for permission to work. These restrictive policies which remove the right to work or to develop work skills are counter-productive and increase newcomers' long-term exclusion from the labour market and society.

They enforce reliance on benefits and state-provided housing and threaten community cohesion in dispersal areas through making asylum seekers visible consumers of state resources. It is important to explore newcomers' rights, entitlements and access to ETE to understand how they can become self-sufficient and can contribute to their local area.

Access to education and training is as a fundamental need for asylum seekers and refugees so, despite their restricting policy on access to employment, the Government until recently allowed free access to many courses for those in receipt of benefits or National Asylum Support Service (NASS) support. The Home Office in *Full and Equal Citizens* (2000) stressed the importance of access to English language training and later legislated to oblige refugees seeking British citizenship to take English lessons and be able to demonstrate tangible improvement in their language proficiency before citizenship was granted (Home Office, 2002). The *Life in the UK* test (Home Office, 2004) incorporates both English and knowledge of citizens' rights and responsibilities in the UK.

The importance of education to integration has long been recognised in academic circles. Research by Harrell-Bond (1988) showed that participating in education in the new country enhanced self-esteem, whilst Schaffer (2001) has argued that it equips refugees with some of the tools they need to negotiate the systems of their new country, with English language acquisition being crucial. However, little research has explored the extent and quality of refugees' access to education and training and how they link with education and employment or the refugees' aspirations. The rest of this chapter looks at entitlement to education and training and considers provision.

Educational funding and entitlement in schools

Entitlement to education for newcomer children under the age of 16 is relatively straightforward. Refugee and asylum seeking children are entitled to attend and benefit from schooling. Local Authorities (LAs) have a legal duty to ensure that education is available which is appropriate to their age and ability. The Education Act 1996 places LAs under an obligation to provide education to all children in their area regardless of their immigration status.

Schools have access to additional funds from the Department for Children, Schools and Families (DCSF) to support the extra education costs for asylum seeking and refugee children dispersed to cluster areas under NASS arrangements. However, the quality of provision and access to English for speakers of other languages (ESOL) for children varies by LA and indeed by school, and may depend on the experience that a school has in teaching children for whom English is an additional language.

Further Education (post 16)

Whilst in theory at least, migrant children's access to education should be the same as that of UK born children, adults' access to education varies according to their status. There are no legal restrictions to adults studying in the UK providing they can meet the frequently subjective entry requirements of the course in terms of qualifications and English proficiency, can pay for the course and support themselves whilst studying. The next part of this chapter sets out Government policy in relation to payment of fees, and support for adults in education. Chapter Four explores the impact of these policies, including entry requirements, on the ability of newcomers to access education and training.

Until 2006 there was no limit on the number of free ESOL classes that a newcomer could access at a Further Education (FE) college, if they were running and if they could meet the entry requirements of the level for which they were applying.

This situation has changed markedly with the announcement of 'new priorities' in FE, implemented in the 2007/8 academic year (LSC 2005, 2006a). The original policy announcement had stated the intention to exclude all asylum seekers from ESOL and to make access to free ESOL means-tested for all other migrants. The policy was said to have emerged from the unprecedented and unsustainable demand for ESOL classes from new migrants, particularly economic migrants from A8 countries, a situation acknowledged to be problematic in the NIACE review of ESOL provision (Grover, 2006). This policy shift was widely condemned, at a time when the popular press was calling for migrants to speak English and for the reduction of investment in translation services. Following a campaign by, amongst others, the Universities and Colleges Union, the policy was reviewed so that migrants on low incomes and asylum seekers who had been in the UK over six months were permitted to access free ESOL classes.

Access to other FE, that is, post-compulsory education for those over the age of 16 studying below Higher National Diploma (HND) level, is at present free to asylum seekers and refugees between the ages of 16 and 18. They can also access the Learner Support Fund to help to pay for some of the costs of studying, such as books and materials and travel. Those refugees aged between 16 and 19 and studying full time for 'A' levels, Advanced GNVQ or NVQ 3 can apply for an Educational Maintenance Allowance if they come from a financially disadvantaged background. Access to FE is more restricted for those over the age of 18. Asylum seekers now have to wait until they have been in the UK more than six months before they can attend any Learning and Skills Council funded course. Traditionally the ability to access such courses has been dependent on the ability to speak and write English.

From 2007 the number of newcomers able to access such classes was expected to reduce. Asylum seekers cannot access any support or hardship funds, nor any course or support that is funded by the European Social Fund (ESF). This is because ESF funded courses are aimed at those who are involuntarily excluded from the labour market, and asylum seekers are not entitled to work.

Newcomers who are in receipt of benefits can access any part-time course, requiring contact of less than sixteen hours per week at concessionary or free rates. Department of Work and Pensions' rules mean that any individual in receipt of Jobseeker's Allowance is not allowed to study for more than 16 hours per week. This restriction is problematic for skilled or professional refugees who wish to re-qualify or adapt their skills to the UK labour market. Following the evaluation of the ASSET UK programme, which sought to help newcomers gain access to the labour market, Aldridge *et al* (2005) recommended that Jobcentre Plus (JCP) should apply Jobseeker's Allowance availability criteria more flexibly, to enable claimants to participate in full-time training and work experience for the long-term benefit of both themselves and the UK economy.

The implications of this ruling for newcomers trying to locate employment commensurate with their skills are explored in later chapters.

Higher Education

Support for enrolment in Higher Education (HE) has been slowly withdrawn for all residents in England over the past decade. At the same time students have been expected to make a contribution to their fees. Until 2006 this was a fixed fee which had to be paid upfront but since September 2006 Universities and Colleges have been able to charge top-up fees, a policy that was controversial because it excludes those from financially disadvantaged backgrounds from Higher Education. Unlike the previous fixed charge fee, students have to repay the borrowed top-up fee when their earnings reach a certain level rather than paying their fees in advance.

Funding is available through student loans awarded by an individual's local authority. Discretionary Awards can be awarded to those most in need but this seldom happens in reality. HE institutions offer hardship funds to the students judged to be most in need. However, asylum seekers are not entitled to these awards and those with refugee status are only eligible if they have lived in the UK for three years before the start of their course. In addition, these groups may have to pay fees at the much higher overseas rate, although Universities can exercise discretion and either waive fees or charge 'home' fees. Those with refugee status can pay home fees and can apply for discretionary funding. Individuals wishing to take Postgraduate courses can apply for a Career Development Loan to cover a proportion of course fees.

Postgraduate courses are charged to all who apply, although fee levels vary depending on whether a student is classified as a home or overseas student. It is possible to apply for awards from the UK funding councils. Awards are offered on a competitive basis and cover both fees and maintenance.

To be eligible an individual must have refugee status and have a good first degree.

Re-qualification and accreditation of prior learning

There is no national database on the qualifications, skills, experience and training of refugees. Surveys indicate that a sizeable proportion of refugees arriving in the UK have high levels of skills and education (Aldridge and Waddington, 2001), and many refugees and asylum seekers are highly qualified people. The Home Office's survey (Bloch, 2002) found that a third of refugees had degrees, postgraduate or professional qualifications. Two thirds of those who had held jobs in their own countries had worked as professionals, as managers or in business.

Kirk (2004) found that 23 per cent of refugees who provided details of their occupation before coming to the UK had worked in skilled professions and a further 22 per cent were managers or senior officials. This compares to 12 per cent skilled and 15 per cent managers in the host community.

A range of research has indicated that between 80 and 96 per cent of asylum seekers want to work once they are legally entitled to employment (Aldridge and Waddington, 2001; European Commission, 2001; Home Office, 2001; mbA, 1999; Scottish Refugee Council, 2001). However, many struggle to prove their skills because they lack employer's references or certificates. Those who do possess certificates often find that the National Academic Recognition Information Centre (NARIC) system of assessing UK equivalence either does not recognise their qualification or downgrades it.

In addition, employers are said not to trust non-UK qualifications because they do not understand them. The outcome of all this is that skilled and professional refugees struggle to return to their fields of expertise or gain employment commensurate with their skills. NIACE has warned that without high quality advice and guidance and access to a means of re-qualification the majority of refugees end up in a low pay or no pay cycle.

Accordingly it has been argued that a system of vocational re-orientation or accreditation of prior experience or learning (APEL) is required (Aldridge *et al*, 2005; Phillimore and Goodson, 2001; Phillimore *et al*, 2007). At present provision for APEL is limited to the occasional professional programme, such as the Refugee Doctors programme run by Refugees into Jobs in North London, which is funded by regeneration or community cohesion funds rather than through the mainstream education budget (Phillimore *et al*, 2006). Although the National Vocational Qualification (NVQ) system can in theory be applied as an APEL system – the way in which FE is currently funded – on the basis of contact hours plus outputs, means that refugees can not be assessed for an NVQ without either attending a college course or finding an employer prepared to help with their assessment. Financial imperatives or Jobseeker's Allowance regulations mean that it is difficult for refugees to attend lengthy vocational training courses. Clearly a change in the system is required to take account of the needs of new arrivals in the UK. The types of system that might be developed are discussed in our concluding chapter.

The process from relative helplessness and neediness towards greater self-sufficiency and improved self-esteem is what Tomlinson and Egan (2002) call 'resettlement'. They argue that English language learning is a vital part of this process. In addition to the clawing back of free ESOL classes, significant problems have been identified with the current ESOL system. The demand has increased enormously since dispersal. Even before the introduction of the Citizenship Test made English language competence a pre-requisite for gaining citizenship, refugees sought to learn English because they needed proficiency to communicate generally and more specifically to gain work (Bloch, 2002).

As demand increased, some commentators expressed concern about a deterioration in the quality of provision and the lack of availability (Griffiths, 2003; Steels and England, 2004). Others highlighted the need for ESOL providers to take into account the varying needs and abilities of newcomers and suggested that more flexible and specialised provision should be introduced (Bloch, 2002; Steels and England, 2004). Furthermore, there has been concern about the fitness for purpose of ESOL provision in helping the new arrivals to achieve a level of language competence that enables them to find employment (Aldridge *et al*, 2005; Griffiths, 2003). Some of the barriers they face when they seek to develop their English language skills are explored in Chapter Four.

Clearly, access to education and training is complicated for new arrivals. The complexity in provision and entitlement is difficult to comprehend. Whatever learning a newcomer seeks, good information, advice and guidance (IAG) is critical to the identification of appropriate courses and support. Studies show that newcomers tend to seek advice from friends and family rather than from professional advisers (Bloch, 2002; Shiferaw and Hagos, 2002).

IAG is often touted as the key to orientating newcomers about both education and the labour market (Aldridge *et al*, 2005; Phillimore *et al*, 2007c; Waddington, 2007). Tomlinson and Egan's (2002) research into provision found that those offering IAG often referred to 'empowerment' when describing their work. It was argued that advice gave refugees knowledge that, unlike their homes, families and material possessions, could not be taken away from them. However, the reality was that the advice offered to newcomers was frequently disappointing and disheartening. Honest advice about the realities of accessing training and employment often led to demoralisation, and recipients of this negative advice tended to view organisations as unhelpful – which explains their reliance on friends and family. A further difficulty with mainstream IAG is its generalised nature (Aldridge *et al*, 2005). Whilst Jobcentres and FE colleges can offer refugees information quickly and free of charge, their knowledge of the needs, aspirations, abilities and rights of refugees is often patchy: they tend to stereotype new arrivals and point them towards ESOL and low-skilled work.

Shiferaw and Hagos (2002) found that respondents who had attended specialist guidance training courses such as the Refugee Education and Training Advisory Service's (RETAS) Job Search and the Refugee Assessment and Guidance Unit's (RAGU) APEL programme had more chance of finding temporary or full-time employment than those receiving more general guidance. Individuals who had been in the UK for some years were more likely than recent arrivals to request advice from JCP, colleges or local council advice services.

Specialist refugee-focused IAG provision has been identified as the most able to engage with and transform the prospects of refugees. Where staff possess in-depth knowledge of the issues facing refugees, and have links to national organisations which give them wide-ranging and up to date knowledge about rights and opportunities, the chances of successful engagement are higher than via mainstream IAG provision (Aldridge *et al*, 2005; Phillimore *et al*, 2007). Tomlinson and Egan (2002) also argue that the shared identification of user and provider, which means involving people from refugee communities in advice work, and the ability to offer a wider range of advice, typical of Refugee Community Organisations (RCOs) rather than more specialised access points, enable them to deal with underlying issues such as homelessness, which may prevent people from accessing training or work. The capacity of RCOs to provide advice, guidance and services is explored in Chapter Six.

Experiential research into accessing and providing ETE for newcomers

There has been little academic or policy research exploring refugees' access to and experience of learning. The discussion of the existing literature shows that access is difficult, provision patchy and entitlements complex. But little is known about how these problems impact on newcomers and how they negotiate their way through the system. This book examines the ways in which newcomers access learning, what they hope to gain from their courses and what they need to achieve their aspirations.

It also considers the challenges faced by providers in dealing with a relatively new cohort of students. Whilst we explore the experiential aspects of learning we also seek to explore how new arrivals are accessing learning and the difficulties they experience. For new migrants, the desire to learn is often inextricably linked with the desire to work. Before moving on to examine the research on which the main part of this book is based, we consider newcomers' access and attitudes to work.

Employment policy

In theory, newcomers' access to employment should be a lot more straight-forward than to education. Non-EU economic migrants with work permits are entitled to employment as set out in their documentation. This may specify a particular skills shortage area or, in the case of students or highly skilled migrants, allow access to any line of work, or restrict employment to a certain number of hours in total. Migrants from the European Accession countries can seek work providing they have registered themselves under the Workers Registration Scheme. Asylum seekers are not permitted to work. Refugees are entitled to work in the UK, although not in certain civil service jobs.

It has become increasingly clear in the last five years that refugees are struggling to access employment despite relatively free access to the labour market. The National Integration Strategy, *Integration Matters* (Home Office, 2005), stresses the importance of service provision in helping refugees to reach their full potential. Specifically, language training, contact with JCP, and opportunities for work experience and re-accreditation were identified as being of key importance.

The new initiatives included the SUNRISE support workers, personal integration plans, a Refugee Integration Loan and increased emphasis on citizenship. The Department for Work and Pensions' *Working to Rebuild Lives* (DWP, 2005) was also released. Building on Integration Matters, this document stressed the importance of sustainable employment for refugees. It called for a strengthening of the links between JCP and refugees, help for refugees to understand the labour market and to improve their employability and collaborative work to meet the needs of refugees and their local communities. It also highlighted the need to work with and support employers in areas of skills shortage.

The Government recognises that employment is a key factor in the integration of refugees. Employment support is an important part of the government's National Refugee Integration Agenda. The NRIF Education Training and Employment Subcommittee met quarterly until 2006 and took up a series of issues relevant to employment. These included monitoring the progress of employment strategies, improving the use of JCP by refugees, ESOL, permission to work documentation, equivalence of qualifications and access to National Insurance Numbers (Tait, 2003).

JCP has introduced a refugee marker which it hopes to use to collect data to aid both the assessment of refugees' progress generally and to contribute to the development of techniques for collecting information about refugee clients so it can track individual outcomes and trends.

This increase in emphasis on improving the employability of refugees stands in stark contrast to the policies that forbid asylum seekers to work and legislate against employers who utilise illegal labour.

Withdrawing the right to work for asylum seekers: background and implications

It has been argued that allowing asylum seekers to work immediately upon their arrival to the UK could save money for the taxpayer by reducing the financial support needed to sustain them during their application period (Tait, 2003). However, present government policy works on the basis that allowing them to work would be an additional 'pull' factor in attracting more asylum seekers, and economic migrants 'posing' as asylum seekers, to the UK.

The withdrawal of the concession to work happened without consultation in July 2002 and was followed by protest from refugee agencies and organisations promoting refugee employment. The Government's argument at the time was that speeding up of asylum claim processing would make the concession to work unnecessary. Although processing has been accelerated, there are still significant numbers of asylum seekers whose claims are not processed within six months. There is a backlog of people who have been waiting years for a decision and believe their claim has now simply been lost in the system. Prolonged periods of unemployment have been seen to impact on motivation and mental health whilst contributing to the de-skilling of professionals (Tait, 2003).

Recently EU policy compelled the UK Government to consider a concession to work if an asylum claim has taken more than twelve months through no fault of the applicant. There is little knowledge amongst refugees of how or where to apply for permission to work and considerable fear that to do so would bring their case to the attention of the authorities and possibly increase the likelihood of a negative decision.

Furthermore, the introduction of on the spot fines for those employers taking on asylum seekers, failed asylum seekers or illegal immigrants has made employers wary of taking on legitimately employable refugees.

The literature on integration contains considerable academic evidence of the key role of employment in integration. Under the New Deal Programme, established in 1997 (Hasluck, 2000), the Government aimed its policies at creating initiatives specifically for historically excluded groups including ethnic minorities, women, young people and the long term unemployed.

Research by Bloch (1999, 2000) suggests that the refugees who are working adjust more easily to the host society than those who are unemployed. In particular women who were able to work experienced significantly enhanced psycho-social well-being compared to the unemployed (Shields and Wheatley Price, 2003). Indeed it has been argued that:

> ... for a refugee, who has been powerlessly dependent on the benevolence of the receiving country, the psychological value of obtaining a job will be greater even than for an indigenous worker ... a job will often provide a context where the refugee can improve language skills and come to terms with the social environment of the receiving country. (Robinson, 1998: 155)

Refugees share many difficulties in entering the labour market with other immigrants. Both groups can be hampered by language difficulties, lack of qualifications, skills and experience relevant to the labour market and discrimination on ethnic or racial grounds. Voluntary economic migrants will be mentally prepared for job searches, may have timed their arrival to coincide with a demand for labour and will be informed to some degree about the opportunities and challenges involved. Refugees, on the other hand, are not migrating as a result of labour demand, and the decision to accept them for resettlement is taken on humanitarian grounds rather than on the basis of labour market demand (Field, 1985). Many have no idea of what awaits them or in some cases which country they are going to.

The theoretical underpinning of Government intervention

Whilst the emphasis on the employment of refugees has undoubtedly increased, there is little evidence except for the SUNRISE programme that there has been much investment into mainstream initiatives to increase employability.

Field (1985) outlines three possible models for the role of the state in the resettlement process.

- 'front-end loading', which recognises that resettlement is a costly and difficult process, and seeks to make substantial initial investments in human capital to avoid sustained dependency

- 'short-term dependency', which assumes that relatively minimal expenditures are needed to convert the refugee into a taxpaying citizen

- 'sustained total or partial dependency', which provides refugees with sustained welfare benefits.

45

This third option is currently favoured in the UK. It is the cheapest option in the short term but arguably has the most costly social and economic implications in the long run. Field (1985) argues that while long-term support for unemployed and under-employed refugees is hugely expensive, it requires no high profile policy initiative and therefore no separate budget needs to be put aside.

Given the media and public attitudes to asylum seekers and refugees, it has not been politically expedient since dispersal to devote large sums of money to refugee-specific initiatives. Hence almost by default, and certainly because of the politicising of asylum, the UK Government has opted for the dependency model to avoid the political discomfort of introducing separate policy initiatives and justification of a special budget against other spending priorities. This model is problematic from economic, social and humanitarian perspectives.

Developing indicators of integration in relation to employment

The inability of refugees to locate work is arguably the single most significant barrier to their successful integration into British society (Feeney, 2000). They struggle to find employment commensurate with their skills and their efforts at integration often entail downward professional mobility (Sargeant and Forna, 2001; Mestheneos and Ioannidi, 2002).

Mestheneos and Ioannidi (2002) suggest that there is potential for objective indicators to be developed which assess the extent to which refugees have become integrated into society by comparing their position to the dominant majority.

Employment statistics for refugees

Existing data clearly demonstrates that large numbers of refugees are excluded from the labour market. Recent research (Bloch, 2002; Haque, 2003) found that migrants generally fair worse than other people in terms of locating work, with those from industrialised countries doing better than those from poorer countries. Employment disadvantages existed at all qualification and skills levels but the situation was better for those from English-speaking backgrounds. The 2000 Peabody Report focusing on London, found that 51 per cent of those who had been in the UK for five to eight years were unemployed (cited in Midlands Refugee Council, 2001). The situation for the most recent cohort of asylum seekers was even worse. Bloch (2002) found that only 29 per cent of refugees were working at the time of her survey and that they were employed in low-paid, temporary and unskilled work. A literature search undertaken by mbA Consultants for the Refugee Council (1999) found that unemployment rates varied between 75 per cent and 90 per cent. Other authors have found rates between 57 per cent (Feeney, 2000; Sargeant and Forna, 2001) and 81 per cent (Walters and Egan, 1996).

The situation is particularly serious for refugee women, with mbA (1999) data showing that only 7 per cent of refugee women were employed. A recent report on refugee women in London (Dumper, 2002) found that they had high levels of skills but were amongst the most excluded from the labour market because they lacked access to the conventional support systems available to women in the UK.

The picture for refugees across the country is uneven. No data exists which explores the different unemployment rates across dispersal areas but Carey-Wood *et al* (1995) found that prior to the establishment of the dispersal programme refugees were far more likely to be employed if they lived in the South East of England. Furthermore, little data exists to demonstrate the extent to which refugees are underemployed. Such high rates of unemployment are remarkable given a national average of 4.7 per cent (ONS, 2005), and given the high levels of skills possessed by refugees and the skills shortage currently existing across Europe.

Factors relating to employability and underemployment

Research to date has demonstrated that refugees are in a poor position in the labour market in relation to both the general and the ethnic minority populations. There is clearly a wide range of variables that affect a new migrant's employability. Ethnicity, age, gender, and type of work sought all affect the likelihood of entering the labour market and the level of entry. Although there is variation between these factors it is clear that, regardless of these factors, all refugee groups are struggling to access employment. Some of the barriers preventing refugees from gaining employment are common to all newcomers: others may be gender or vocationally specific. Large-scale survey work underpins much of the research exploring barriers to employment.

A survey undertaken for the *Working to Rebuild Lives* (DWP, 2005) strategy found that a third of the respondents saw their poor English as the main barrier to gaining work (Dunn and Somerville, 2004). The levels of literacy in a refugee's own language influences their ability to learn a new language. Language and literacy skills vary by country of origin and depend on whether the colonial past means that English was taught in schools. Whilst language barriers are acknowledged to be problematic, little is known about how they affect access to work or learning, and there is scant information about the particular problems that asylum seekers and refugees experience when seeking to learn to speak English. Newcomers' access to, and experiences of, ESOL classes are explored in Chapter Four, as are the ways in which language barriers impact on newcomers' ability to work and learn.

Kempton (2002) argues that the principal factor influencing migrants' labour market outcomes is education. Qualifications obtained in the UK are generally more highly valued than those gained overseas. Sargeant and Forna (2001) give the example of refugee doctors, of whom there are up to 2,000 in the UK: they cannot practice medicine because their qualifications are not automatically recognised by the General Medical Council (GMC). Less is known about the situation of other skilled and professional newcomers. This book looks at the extent to which newcomers can use their qualifications in the UK, their ability to access proof of qualification and employers' attitudes to overseas qualifications.

Employers' attitudes and work experience issues

Little empirical evidence exists to indicate the extent to which employers view imagined or anticipated problems as barriers to employing a refugee. Employers' attitudes to refugees or the lack of compatibility of newcomers' skills and experience are often cited as major barriers to employment. One factor often mentioned is the lack of UK work experience or of references from an employer. Monti (2005) found that potential employers rarely asked refugees at interview about their achievements or their employment record before reaching the UK.

Waddington (2005) argues that UK-based work experience placements help refugees to re-orientate their skills to UK work methods but few such placements are available. Little has been written about the use of work experience to enhance employability and there is a dearth of systematic research exploring the availability of work experience or its efficacy in improving the employability of refugees. The wider employment literature indicates that work experience was found to help overcome fears about the perceived risk of leaving benefits, particularly for those who had been unemployed for a long time. Work placements gave an individual the opportunity to undertake a job and increased their self-confidence (McQuaid *et al*, 2005). Only by providing the opportunity to demonstrate skills and experience can prior knowledge or experience be given a performative value for employers (Flanagan *et al*, 2000: 361; Nikolau-Walker and Garnett, 2004; Sargeant and Forna, 2001).

Most of the sparse research looks at barriers to employment from the perspective of refugees and fails to examine employers' attitudes to issues such as work experience. Chapter Seven explores the impact on refugees in dispersal areas of having no UK work experience or references from the perspective of both refugees and employers.

Several studies have shown that unfamiliarity with the expectations of UK employers', application systems and requirements and the latest occupational developments greatly disadvantage newcomers seeking employment (Aldridge *et al*, 2005; Sargeant and Forna, 2001; Shiferaw and Hagos, 2002). The European Union Good Practice Guide, a website for issues of Structural Funding, has maintained that fear of culture clash, more than language problems, are the reason why employers are disinclined to hire refugees. The length and nature of the asylum process is another factor. This is partly because asylum seekers are prevented from working so when they finally gain the right to work they tend to have been long-term unemployed (Shiferaw and Hagos, 2002).

Waddington (2005) asserts that the lack of opportunity for purposeful activity during the waiting period has an impact on eventual employability. The effects of long-term unemployment have been mentioned but little is known about the less functional barriers to employment, largely because of the dearth of qualitative research in dispersal areas aimed at understanding the barriers and how they interact. It is important to explore how self-confidence and self-esteem affect employability, and how the asylum process affects newcomers. These issues are also explored in Chapter Seven from the perspectives of both newcomers and employers.

There has been little research exploring employers' attitudes to hiring newcomers, and what little exists has largely been undertaken in the South East (Hurstfield *et al*, 2004). On the spot fines have diminished employers' willingness to employ refugees. The onus is on them to demonstrate that their employee has a legal status to work; this and the burden of bureaucracy discourage them from employing refugees (Dunn and Somerville, 2004; Sargeant and Forna, 2001). Research into the reasons why refugees thought they were struggling to gain employment raised concerns that they were being discriminated against (Bloch, 2004; Monti, 2005).

Once again the views of employers themselves are missing from the literature, as are refugees' stories of discrimination. It is important to explore the extent to which xenophobia or stereotyping influence people's willingness to employ refugees or to place them in good jobs. More information is needed about employers' attitudes to employing refugees, the information they have and the support and information they require.

Actions and agency: whose responsibility?

While it is argued that the actions of the state or employers have an impact on employability, the agency of newcomers themselves is overlooked. Much of the research into newcomers' employability makes generalisations about the key barriers to employment and whilst quantitative data is used (for example Bloch, 2004) to indicate differences in employment rates or ability to speak English between ethnic groups, little consideration has been given to the variation in experiences, aspirations and opportunities from the perspective of the individual. There are variations in employability based upon age, gender, length of residence in the UK, the amount of time taken to get a positive decision, the socio-economic conditions within dispersal areas and the ability to move to find work.

Attitudes towards migration, and whether this is viewed as a temporary or permanent move, affect levels of labour market participation. Attitudes to fleeing, to their homeland and to the country of refuge all affect the settlement outcomes for newcomers, as well as how they view the likelihood of political stability in their country of origin. An intention to return to their home countries implies a degree of transience (Bloch, 2004) and can make them reluctant to invest in employment and training opportunities, whereas those who plan to remain and seek family re-unification are particularly keen to find work so they can demonstrate to the Home Office that they can support their family. The factors underpinning refugees' choices and decisions are as important to explore as are the employers' attitudes. The job market too must be considered.

The availability of jobs: UK labour market shortages

Review of the literature demonstrates that although large numbers of refugees want to work they face numerous barriers to employment and their unemployment levels exceed those of the most disadvantaged in the host community, amounting to more than ten times the national average. That under-employment is the norm for refugees is not well documented (Aldridge and Waddington, 2001; Bloch, 1999, 2000).

At a time of increased globalisation of competition for skills, recruitment of skilled personnel has become a struggle for many organisations in Europe. Whilst there are regional and sub-regional differences in labour markets, in the present economic climate the issue is not a lack of skilled job opportunities. Menz (2002) identifies two types of skills shortage in the EU: highly-skilled, and low-skilled or seasonal work.

Whilst Europe is moving from an internal to an external labour market based on the work permit system, the supply of jobs still massively outstrips the supply of workers to fill them. The final part of this chapter examines the skills shortages that exist in the UK and the role that new migrants might play in relation to the economy.

The Skills in England 2002 (DfES, 2003) report outlines a range of skills shortages likely to exist in the period leading up to 2010. Key areas of shortage include health professionals and various types of associate professionals, teachers, carers, salespeople, administrators and transport-related occupations, amongst many others. In 2001 Reed Recruitment, a leading UK employment agency, reported that three-quarters of companies were trying to cope with skills shortages (Sargeant and Forna, 2001).

The Learning and Skills Council's National Employer Skills Survey (2003) paints a detailed picture of the extent of skills shortages in the UK and the implications for the economy (see Figure 2.1 overleaf).

Among employers who were looking to recruit, around a quarter could not find applicants with the skills they required. Problems recruiting the right employees can lead to extra costs for employers, from the need to increase recruitment and advertising expenditure, to offering higher salaries, or to up-skilling existing staff. Some 270,000 unfilled vacancies were considered by employers as 'hard to fill', largely because of insufficient applicants with appropriate skills but also because of generally low levels of interest in certain posts (LSC, 2004). Sometimes applicants who did apply were deemed unsuitable for some of the reasons that refugees are rejected from jobs: they were not able to demonstrate that they possessed relevant documentation, skills, work experience or qualifications.

There is variation between the regions in the proportions of skills shortage vacancies (SSVs), but they exist throughout England. London (16%) and the South East (17%) accounted for the largest number of SSVs closely followed by the West Midlands (12%) and the North West (12%). A wide range of skills was found to be in shortage. With so many vacancies there is considerable scope for skilled newcomers to contribute to the UK economy, providing their skills can be matched to the wide range of opportunities.

Sector	Total employment	Total unfilled vacancies	Total unfilled vacancies as a % of employment	Total HtFVs	Total HtFVs as a % of employment	Total skill-shortage vacancies	Total skill-shortage vacancies as a % of employment
Weighted base	2,275,559	56,388		21,011		9,966	
Unweighted base	21,877,288	679,072		271,413		135,295	
	%	%	%	%	%	%	%
Agriculture, etc	0.3	0.2	2.5	0.3	1.2	0.3	0.8
Mining and quarrying	0.2	0.1	2.2	0.1	0.8	0.1	0.2
Manufacturing	14.2	8.1	1.8	8.9	0.8	11.0	0.5
Utilities	0.5	0.4	2.2	0.1	0.3	0.1	0.2
Construction	4.5	5.2	3.6	7.7	2.1	9.9	1.4
Retail and wholesale	18.0	16.2	2.8	14.6	1.0	13.1	0.5
Hotels and catering	6.4	11.9	5.7	12.6	2.4	8.0	0.8
Transport and communications	6.3	5.6	2.8	5.9	1.2	6.1	0.6
Financial intermediation	4.2	3.7	2.7	1.9	0.6	2.1	0.3
Business services	16.2	17.8	3.4	16.3	1.2	21.3	0.8

Sector	Total employment		Total unfilled vacancies		Total unfilled vacancies as a % of employment		Total HtFVs		Total HtFVs as a % of employment		Total skill-shortage vacancies		Total skill-shortage vacancies as a % of employment	
	%		%		%		%		%		%		%	
Public administration and defence	5.0		3.6		2.2		2.1		0.5		2.1		0.3	
Education	8.4		6.0		2.2		4.2		0.6		4.9		0.4	
Health and social work	10.5		13.3		3.9		16.7		2.0		12.8		0.8	
Other services	5.2		7.9		4.7		8.6		2.0		8.2		1.0	
Total	100.0		100.0		3.1		100.0		1.2		100.0		0.6	

Figure 2.1 Summary of vacancies analysed by sector (LSC, 2004)

Economic contribution by newcomers

Little is known about the current economic contribution of asylum seekers and refugees in the UK, as existing data sources do not distinguish between refugees and other migrant groups (Tait, 2003). Recent studies have produced some findings regarding the contribution of migrants generally. A report for the Home Office estimated that migrants contributed £2.5bn more in taxes than they consumed in benefits and services in 1999/2000 (Gott and Johnston, 2002). There is yet more potential for contribution, if new migrants are given the opportunity to raise output by expanding the supply of labour and filling difficult to recruit posts (Kempton, 2002).

Implications for employment policy

A combination of skill shortages and a complementary skills mix can enable sectors to expand and make more efficient use of assets. At the higher skilled end, migrants play an important role in certain professions, accounting for 27 per cent of health professionals and 9 per cent of teaching professionals in 2000 (Labour Force Survey, 2000). Migrants can indirectly generate economic activity elsewhere, through knock-on effects; create jobs by employing people; and also help to develop new sectors and new ideas, resulting in some restructuring of the economy.

The international evidence shows that migrants do not have negative effects on either wages or employment of the domestic workforce. Immigration is found to have a positive effect on the wages of the existing population. Using the most robust data source available, Dustmann *et al* (2003) found that an increase in immigration equivalent to 1 per cent of the non-migrant population resulted in nearly a 2 per cent increase in non-migrant wages. This positive effect will be undermined if the growing numbers of refugees settling in the UK are unable to access employment or use the skills they have brought with them to any effect.

Yet studies suggest that asylum seekers and refugees have higher than average educational, skills and qualification levels, and strong motivation to work. Many have degrees or experience as professionals, managers or in business. The majority are young men of working age. Refugees and asylum seekers, like other migrants, have a great deal to offer the UK if initial obstacles can be overcome.

The available data suggests that migration does not have a significant impact on overall unemployment amongst the existing UK population. There are plenty of jobs in the UK. Migration, particularly since dispersal, has meant that there is a pool of labour that is as yet largely untapped. The key challenge is how to link newcomers to the vacancies. Clearly employers expect applicants to be able to demonstrate skills, experience and qualifications.

This book goes on to explore the potential of new migrants, and refugees in particular, to take an active role in the economy. It looks at what they have to offer, what support they need to get into training and education, how their existing skills and experience can be evidenced and what mechanisms can be put in place to demonstrate to employers, and society as a whole, the opportunities that newcomers offer. The mechanisms employed to research these issues are the focus of the next chapter.

3

Exploring new migrants' experiences of education, training and employment: methodological considerations and research approach

Research into the lives and experiences of asylum seekers and refugees spans many fields from economics and epidemiology to history and anthropology. Each discipline brings with it research traditions and methodological approaches which shape how research about newcomers might be undertaken. Whether or not there is a separate discipline of refugee studies is a matter of debate. What is clear however is that there are some issues around research into new migration that are worthy of consideration. One of the main criticisms of research in this area, which this chapter seeks to overcome, is that many researchers are insufficiently explicit about how they collected their data. This lack of transparency is particularly problematic in preventing other researchers from making judgments about the findings, evaluating the conclusions or learning from the approach employed (Jacobsen and Landau, 2003).

This book draws on a variety of research studies. Before exploring the methods employed in these studies, we consider the role and function of research into new migration, issues regarding subjectivity and bias in the research process and some of the difficulties with sampling strategies and data availability. The overall purpose of this chapter is not to provide a review of the methodologies employed to research refugees and asylum seekers in the UK, but to set out clearly the methods employed in the several empirical studies that are the source of data for the rest of the book. Consideration of the challenges of researching new migration, issues around conceptual clarity, sampling and data availability will help develop a context to the discussion of the approaches adopted.

Challenges of working with new migrants

In reviewing the field of refugee studies, one of the key conclusions that can be drawn about research in the area is that few studies into the experiences of refugees and asylum seekers end without making policy recommendations (Black, 2001; Castles, 2003). Perhaps this policy orientation emerges, as Jacobsen and Landau (2003) suggest, from researchers' experiences of working with refugees, and from an awareness of the horrific nature of some of the personal histories and background, which make it hard for researchers to simply report on people as if they were statistics. In fact, much work in the education, training and employment (ETE) field has emerged from NGOs, who wish to expose the difficulties faced by new migrants with a view to pressurising governments into softening their deterrent stance on immigration, asylum and associated policies (e.g. in the UK, RETAF and the Refugee Council).

As the field evolves and questions and concepts become more complex and obscure, a concern arises that the more academic and scientifically rigorous research becomes, the less relevant it is for policy and practice (Jacobsen and Landau, 2003). They describe the situation where research is intended both to be scrupulously academic and also to generate a policy evidence base aimed at improving the situation of new migrants as the 'dual imperative'. Research has greatest potential to impact upon policy by demonstrating scientific rigour. However, in many instances, a lack of objectivity and rigour is demonstrated by researchers who already have an *a priori* agenda and use research as a means to validate the main issues and concerns on that agenda. Jacobsen and Landau (2003) call this type of approach 'advocacy' research because its primary goal is to provide evidence for change in policy or for funding regimes rather than the pursuit of knowledge in its own right.

The issues of bias and subjectivity in research are by no means unique to refugee studies. They are two of the most commonly articulated criticisms of qualitative research generally (Denzin and Lincoln, 1998; Kincheloe and McLaren, 1998). From a positivist research perspective researchers should be able to transcend subjectivity and disconnect knowledge from everyday life and their own personal ideologies in order to ensure that their research is scientific.

There has been growing criticism of this stance from post-positivists, in particular those who position themselves in an interpretivist paradigm. They argue that the quest by positivists for objectivity is based on the subjective generalisations of a small group of people with the power and prestige to be able to call themselves 'scientists' (Code, 1993). We suggest that values, politics and knowledge are interconnected rather than hierarchical, and thus there is need for sufficient reflexivity in research writing to enable the reader to explore the knower's values, politics and biases in order to make judgements about those aspects of self that impact on the research process and knowledge (re)creation (Alcoff and Potter, 1993). Essentially we are talking about methodological transparency, about how choices of research methods, sampling and analytical frameworks are made, with some consideration of the researchers' subjectivity and its impact upon the choices made.

Another feature which impacts upon research methodologies, including the type of questions and methods employed, is project sponsorship. While Research Council funded research generally allows researchers value freedom and encourages the use of academically sound approaches, all discussed within detailed methodologies, the luxury of such sponsorship is not available or viable for the vast majority of researchers. In the UK, the largest sponsors of research into issues surrounding new migration are statutory bodies. Generally they enter negotiations with researchers with some fairly fixed ideas of the types of topics they wish to see addressed and in some cases even the kinds of questions and methods they wish to see employed. This was certainly the type of sponsorship used in most of the research discussed in this book. As researchers and the authors of this book, becoming more and more immersed in research about new migration, we admit that we have, over the years, adopted an increasingly advocacy orientated role in the ways in which our research findings have been used and disseminated. We have nonetheless sought to maintain the academic quality of our studies because we are first and foremost working in an academic environment. The nature of our jobs means that we face the dual imperative of producing research that is academically rigorous and can be published in peer reviewed journals, whilst being policy relevant because of the nature of the research sponsorship upon which our ability to fund the research depends. In addition we believe that sound research can strengthen rather than undermine the potential for advocacy.

The nature of the research projects

The first type of research reported here was sponsored by bodies including three Learning and Skills Councils (LSCs) with a clear interest in post-compulsory education and training; two local authorities; a sub-regional Jobcentre Plus (JCP); and a city based statutory SRB employability project. Steering groups from a wide range of bodies oversaw all of this research. Although constrained in the topics we were researching, we had the freedom to explore whatever dimensions of each topic we considered important, and to construct research tools and analyse the data in a systematic way.

The need to temper conclusions is a concern, an area of heated negotiations for many academics undertaking state sponsored research. In these projects we were fortunate in that we were free to write up our findings without the need for any substantive editing. Indeed the presence of a wide range of experts on the steering groups, including refugees, gave us a sounding board with which to ensure our research tools and sampling strategies addressed the research aims in a rigorous and scientific manner, while being comprehensive in terms of perspectives.

The second type of research discussed in this book offers more potential for advocacy or subjectivity. The EQUAL funded review of employability initiatives, whilst match funded by the Home Office, had no constraints whatsoever on aims, objectives, research questions, research tools or sampling, other than that our funding was offered on the basis that we would explore refugee employability. This strand of work entailed a European dimension and through a formal EQUAL transnational partnership known as MEET.

The third stream of work, a Joseph Rowntree Foundation funded review of ESOL in the West Midlands, emerged from a refugee community led request to explore why ESOL was not working for asylum seekers and refugees in the West Midlands. This piece of research was undertaken by a team of trained refugee researchers and was explicitly aimed at advocacy, but as shown in the later discussion of the methodology employed, we sought to adopt a rigorous approach through the triangulation of methods and perspectives.

The importance of conceptual clarity
Categorisation of newcomers

A further concern about refugee research is the lack of clarity around definitions, and the operationalisations of key concepts such as *refugee* itself. Few studies define the term refugee in technical or legal terms. The contentious question 'When is a refugee no longer a refugee?' is rarely considered in empirical studies. If we are not clear about what is meant by the terms refugee, asylum seeker, and other new migrants for that matter, we will struggle to locate appropriate respondents and to make the comparison between groups. Throughout the book the terms 'newcomer' 'new arrival' or 'new migrant' are used interchangibly to denote the general asylum seeker and refugee community. However, there are occasions when the experiences of the system, rights and entitlements differ because of status. When this is the case the terms refugee or asylum seeker are used specifically to denote where the discussion relates to those with or without legal status.

In practical terms refugee refers to anyone who, having applied for asylum in the UK, has been given recognised refugee status (Thomas and Abewaw, 2004). This includes anyone with Indefinite Leave to Remain, Exceptional Leave to Remain, Humanitarian Protection or Discretionary Leave. The term asylum seeker applies to those who have applied for asylum and have not yet had a final decision on their case. Those who have exhausted the appeals process and received a final negative decision are described as failed asylum seekers. Many come from countries to which the UK government is unlikely to deport them. Our definitions are based on the legal definitions of the term and are the definitions we use in all the studies we have undertaken.

The point at which a refugee moves from being a refugee, in identity terms rather than legally, to becoming a regular resident, clearly depends on their own perspective and possibly that of others. Some prefer to avoid the label altogether, while for others being a refugee will always be part of their identity.

The research on which this book is based is focused on the West Midlands. Some of the urban centres which became dispersal areas had little experience of accommodating asylum seekers and refugees, while others had a history of hosting people seeking sanctuary. In a bid to bring some comparability to the main LSC studies and to identify a cut-off point beyond which individuals may no longer require intensive support, we consulted our steering groups about whether to introduce a date based definition of refugee. It was agreed that the starting point for the research should be asylum seekers who had arrived after the Balkan troubles in 1991. Their arrival was seen as the beginning of a turning point for the West Midlands, where asylum seekers began to be dispersed to the region through programmes, through the actions of local authorities in the South East and eventually by the National Asylum Support Service (NASS).

The use of the separate terms asylum seeker and refugee to denote difference is somewhat arbitrary. The UK Government feels that making the distinction between those who have and have not been granted status is important because of the different set of policies that applies to each (cf. Home Office, 2005). From a refugee perspective the term asylum seeker can seem superfluous since they are aware that they and their peers, irrespective of their legal status, have been through similar experiences of flight from persecution and then seeking sanctuary. Because of this they can find it a struggle to comprehend why Immigration Officers, other people and institutions treat people differently (Phillimore *et al*, 2007).

In refugee studies outside the UK, and certainly in the main refugee receiving countries close to the sites of conflict or disaster, a refugee is defined as someone who is displaced from their country of domicile. No distinction is made between those who are displaced because of economic, climactic, or political reasons. While these arguments have a logic, the policy focused nature of this book and the research on which it is based means that we need to distinguish between the two terms.

A further complication is that there are several thousand people who have entered the UK as EU citizens having gained their refugee status overseas, for instance, large numbers of Somalis previously settled in the Netherlands and Scandinavia. But, for the purpose of this study we shall include them as refugees because there are commonalities in their needs and experiences and those living in refugee communities do not make any distinction between people with EU citizenship or UK refugee status.

A final complication was whether to include the families of those who have come to the UK through family reunion. For the purpose of our studies we opted to include them because we believe that their needs and experiences have much in common with their peers. Rather than waiting to see if they can stay in the UK as they were processed through the asylum system, they have had to wait elsewhere, often in a refugee camp, while their family members sought the resources, agreements and documents required to enable them to enter the UK, a process as uncertain as the asylum system itself. The inclusion of all these categories of people in this text could make for some terminological difficulties as we discuss the different groups. So we have opted to use the terms 'newcomers', 'new arrivals' or 'new migrants' to cover all the above categories, and will specify a particular term only where a distinction needs to be made.

Definitions: education, training and employment (ETE)

For this research, education and training (ET) relates to any types of post-compulsory learning that a newcomer is able to or would like to access, and all their past learning experiences both within and outside the UK, be it statutory education or training.

The term employment covers any paid employment, self-employment, unpaid or paid work in family businesses, subsistence farming and employment in the grey economy. In taking such a wide definition of work we were focusing our attentions on the types of skills and experience that newcomers may have acquired through engaging in an activity which had some relationship to income generation.

Sampling

Having defined our terms we need next to consider the issues around sampling in refugee studies. We found a tension in the literature between a positivistic natural science based approach, which prioritises the production of 'hard', quantifiable data, and the interpretive stance focusing on experiential data from an insider or 'emic' perspective in a bid to uncover the most authentic accounts associated with the refugee experience.

Jacobsen and Landau (2003) express their concerns about the small sample sizes often used in refugee studies. They argue that while qualitative research gives rise to a great deal of rich data which can help in the development of hypotheses that can be tested by larger scale studies, and can help shed light on, for example, little known refugee experiences, it produces data which cannot be generalised. They believe that the kind of samples selected do not easily lend themselves to comparative work, either between different groups or across time. Accordingly, they advocate the use of random sampling techniques, whereby every person in the target population has an equal chance of being interviewed, and claim that unless random sampling is employed, findings cannot be representative so the power to generalise about the refugee experience is reduced. They acknowledge that randomisation is an ideal, given that in most refugee situations the size and whereabouts of the population is not known, which means there is often no comprehensive sampling framework to select respondents from.

There is an over-reliance on community organisations for selecting respondents. Once some respondents have been identified there is a tendency to identify others by using a snowballing technique. Over-reliance on snowballing can be problematic. The likelihood of skewed or biased research increases when the respondents engaged are similar, as is often the case when utilising community groups. In addition, those who are not part of the common group are likely to be excluded. However, the need to use small samples, to snowball and to work closely with refugee organisations may well be the reality of refugee research. If so and if non-systematic sampling techniques are employed, the limitations of the approach need to be considered and made explicit.

Hynes maintains that: '...whether refugees are themselves the experts of the refugee experience is also a contested idea dependent on ontological position' (2003: 11). She considers the issue to be more one of authenticity and validity of data than of sampling strategies. Hynes expresses concern that the disempowering nature of the refugee experience is in danger of being repeated if we treat refugees as research objects who are merely units in a sampling strategy, rather than as experts about their own experience.

Since the 1980s there have been calls for refugees to be given more of a voice in the shaping of research agendas (Indra, 1989). This call has been reiterated specifically with regard to UK policy research, with Beresford (1996) claiming that the research agenda has failed to reflect the interests of refugee service users. Baker (1990) also calls for refugees to be considered as experts in their own fields: 'the refugee experience'.

Hynes (2003) argues this is not possible in the UK because there are such high levels of mistrust between refugees and the state. If we are to take the stance that refugees themselves are experts on refugee experiences, Hynes asks how we might facilitate their meaningful involvement given the loss of trust that accompanies the refugee experience. Refugees in the UK are trying to overcome numerous obstacles to make a new life and, Hynes argues, the state offers little support, in effect further disempowering individuals.

As asylum seekers have no political rights and are required to answer questions 'correctly' if they are to gain leave to remain in the UK, they are likely to feel vulnerable within the research process. Treating them as units in a sampling strategy adds to their disempowerment. Yet trying to engage refugees less passively may make them feel they have to behave in a particular way or portray themselves in a certain manner to present a particular image.

It takes time to build trust and to get to know a community or its members well enough to be able to tell if there are inconsistencies in data caused by respondents telling the researcher what they think they want to hear, or delivering a political message they feel might most benefit them or their community.

Jacobsen and Landau (2003) ask why a refugee would want to tell an interviewer anything that was not in their own interests and are concerned that the validity of the data could accordingly be threatened. The same question could be asked of any social research. There are well documented cases, employing the most rigorously randomised surveys, where respondents have sought to present a particular image, notably the over-reporting of involvement in crime by young men keen to appear 'hard'.

Taking a different perspective on validity, Hynes argues that 'there is layer upon layer of mistrust that is part of the refugee experience' (2003: 14). Lack of trust between researcher and the researched casts doubt on whether the refugee is willing to provide accurate information. However, this is not a reason for failing to undertake the research; rather a reason why research should be undertaken with refugees rather than on them. Particular care also needs to be taken to ensure that confidentiality is offered and understood, to clarify the nature of the research, who it is funded by, what the relationship is between the research and statutory bodies and what it hopes to achieve.

Ideally trust can be built through trusted gatekeepers. Like Jacobsen and Landau (2003), Hynes (2003) warns of over-reliance on key community organisations. Instead she quotes Bloch (1999) and Castles *et al* (2002) who suggest that a wide range of organisations and gatekeepers should be engaged. Often we researchers are so reliant on gatekeepers that we treat them as agenda-less, whereas in reality they can be quite powerful within their own communities and may wish to promote a particular message. Awareness of all these issues and the ability to analyse how they affect the research process will ultimately determine the quality and rigour of the research.

The debate seems to imply polarity both between qualitative and quantitative research, and between the role and influence given to refugees themselves within research programmes. Such dualism is artificial. The reality is that a multi-method approach, one which tries to gain rich experiential data from the point of view of refugees whilst linking this approach with survey work or large scale secondary data sets to allow generalisation, is both possible and desirable.

In our studies we have sought to triangulate in terms of methods and perspectives. Surveys and questionnaires were used to help us make some generalisations but we have also talked with refugees, education providers, employers and statutory and non-statutory support organisations in a variety of settings to understand some of the processes underpinning our survey findings. Pulling together data from a wide range of sources and perspectives allows us to identify inconsistencies and to generalise where convergence in the data indicates strong trends.

Ethics and interpretation

A rarely discussed issue in relation to the methodologies of new migrant research, is the constraint of language and its impact on the validity of the research and upon trust between researcher and researched. The use of inter-preters and translations is a fact of new migrant studies. Interpreters are frequently hired on the basis of language ability and availability, with little consideration of their ability to ask questions in an appropriate manner, something most social researchers are trained to do. In his candid discussion of his experience of working with interpreters in Tunisia, Guy Jobbins (2004) describes how he came to realise that the interpreted responses he received to his questions bore little relationship to the answers given by the inter-viewee. Interpreters, despite constant reminders, were extremely reluctant to translate responses word for word and instead offered a summarised, sani-tised version.

One common approach to overcoming this problem is to team up with researchers who share the same language as members of the communities in question. But, unless *verbatim* translations from tape recordings are avail-able, and this is an expensive business, it is difficult to ascertain whether the questions posed were presented as required and whether the responses given represent a full and accurate translation.

Confidentiality and reciprocity are also issues. Respondents may be con-cerned not to portray their true feelings if they fear the information might be divulged to others in their community. Researchers from the same country may help to overcome language barriers but there is no guarantee of allegiance. Whether they are 'countrymen' or from opposing sides in deeply sectarian countries, there is a risk of over-familiarisation or active dislike, or both. Either way such issues can influence the quality and validity of the data. We consider the issues around interpretation and translation in our dis-cussion of in-depth interviews.

Other ethical issues in research with newcomers warrant attention. Asking asylum seekers and refugees to recount painful events can cause distress. Revisiting early feminist writings on social research we find suggestions that researchers should be prepared to act as a friend or adopt the role of therapist rather than objective observer, and take some responsibility for ensuring they support the respondent to get through the experiences their research might trigger (Stanley and Wise, 1993). This contradicts Jacobsen and Landau (2003) who maintain that even greater objectivity is required. We argue that this poses ethical questions, such as how we deal with respondents who want us to help them. And once we begin intervening in the lives of our subjects are we not changing those lives?

Within our projects we sought to avoid issues that were potentially emotional, although even asking someone what they used to do for a job inevitably stimulates memories. Though we lacked the resources, time or expertise to counsel individuals ourselves, we did direct them to other services and actively sought information for them if we could not immediately answer their queries.

A final concern sometimes raised in social research is whether or not researchers should turn a blind eye to illegal activity. Within our research we came across respondents working illegally or housing failed asylum seekers. Since confidentiality was always assured we were ethically bound to honour this, so did not see it as our duty to take any action about such matters.

We move on to consider the availability of data on new migration in the UK, before discussing how we overcame some of the problems around accessing information to build a picture of the newcomer population in the West Midlands.

Availability of data

Accessing data about refugees is particularly difficult because once they gain leave to remain they become part of mainstream society. Ethnic monitoring systems, commonly used as the basis for national surveys, and for monitoring the profile of service users by the majority of statutory service providers, do not seek to record immigration status, so data sets relating specifically to refugees' experiences generally do not exist. The situation in the UK is particularly challenging because we have no national data set to help us monitor the progress of refugees. Many of the Scandinavian countries and Canada have such information (Phillimore *et al*, 2005). In the UK it is very difficult to disaggregate the refugee population from the wider ethnic minority population and 'this lack of baseline data hinders research and policy and service development considerably' (Heyworth and Peach, 2004). Census data is problematic because there is no marker for refugee status and as refugees are so transient they are more likely than the general population to be missed. Newcomers are also reported to be reluctant to reveal themselves to official bodies or to declare their correct country of origin (Employability Forum,

2006). An additional problem we encountered was that the only available census data on ethnicity at the time of the research was from 1991, and this pre-dated dispersal.

Locating information about the populations and whereabouts of asylum seekers is more straightforward. NASS collects data which details the age, gender, country of origin and postcode of every asylum seeker they support and sends quarterly reports detailing this information to the Regional Asylum Manager. Without the right contacts this information can be hard to access. It is also notoriously difficult to comprehend and somewhat unreliable (Hynes, 2003).

More newcomers were dispersed in large numbers from the South East to the regions, by local authorities seeking to reduce housing and other support costs, and to reduce the alleged pressure on local services in the south. This was pre-NASS or Interim Arrangement. Many receiving local authorities were not informed about these placements, as contracts were arranged directly with private landlords. While they may have anecdotal evidence, or a rough estimate of the number of asylum seekers who fell into this category, they have no accurate data about the numbers or locations of these new arrivals. The local authorities who placed them will have statistics on the number of asylum seekers they support in the regions, and have to be approached individually. It is at their discretion whether or not they choose to release such information. And there is no information about the number of people entering the regions through family reunion or of refugees who arrive ad hoc from elsewhere in the EU.

In April 2004 JCP introduced a refugee marker, which identifies those refugees who have come into contact with the organisation and elected to disclose their refugee status. Obviously, this marker will only give a picture of those who have registered at the Jobcentre since 2004 and will exclude all those who have not had contact with the organisation. All our LSC studies were carried out before the implementation of the refugee marker.

Enquiries by the Employability Forum (2006) revealed that by 2006 some 70,000 refugees had been identified nationally, a third of them women. Some 7,000 clients had been identified in the West Midlands. Because of Data Protection issues it is not possible to gain access to any spatial aspect of this Department for Work and Pensions (DWP) data, or postcodes, for example, to help identify populations of refugees and where there are high concentrations of unemployed refugees who may require focused support. The problem of identifying and locating the subjects for our studies provided the content for a major research project in the West Midlands.

Locating the newcomers, a methodology for the West Midlands

The deficiencies in UK asylum and refugee data are well recognised (Stewart, 2004). We undertook studies for three different sub-regional LSCs in 2002, 2003 and 2004 and sought to identify the main areas in which asylum seekers and refugees were living. Within these studies we sought to map the populations of newcomers in the sub-regions and to use the population profiles we produced to develop a sampling strategy for the qualitative research and household surveys that were to form the key parts of those studies. This task was not completed for the fourth sub-region, Stoke on Trent, because the LSC in that area did not commission a study.

In 2005 we were asked to undertake an analysis of all existing data around newcomers for the West Midlands Regional Housing and Spatial Strategy (Phillimore and Goodson, 2005). We employed the same methodology as in the previous LSC studies, but introduced an element of population forecasting in a bid to provide some mechanism to aid spatial planning in the region. Rather than explore the methods used for each separate study we can demonstrate the technique used to develop a picture of the newcomer population in the West Midlands, a picture that formed an important evidence base for the region.

To identify asylum seeker populations and assess the current numbers, locations and ethnicities living within the region, we collated and combined NASS data on subsistence-only cases and supported asylum seekers together with the Refugee Council Emergency Accommodation data set, and wrote to all local authorities known to have been supporting Interim cases. Interim asylum seekers are those who were dispersed to, or accommodated in, the regions between December 1999 and the formal introduction of the NASS dispersal programme. They are supported by the local authority that dispersed them.

Once collated, this data provided a fairly complete picture of the locations and numbers of asylum seekers in the region, assuming that NASS data is accurate. It can only be described as 'fairly' complete because of the conjectural nature of the data but also because censuses undertaken in NASS properties suggest that data provided is not always accurate. Asylum seekers move from, within and between accommodations without notifying NASS. Some accommodation is illegally occupied by overstayers who may be refugees or failed asylum seekers, or legally occupied by failed asylum seeking families who under current arrangements must be housed until removal. Nevertheless this methodology produced data which was considered sufficiently reliable for identifying appropriate categories and locations of newcomers to be included in our study.

In order to fill out this data, to flesh out the model, a further study was initiated. We sought a profile of the refugee population by writing to all the local authorities covering the main dispersal areas requesting information on the number of refugees housed in their stock and the numbers presenting as homeless, where possible seeking information on ethnicity, age and location. We requested the same information from Housing Associations where large-scale voluntary transfer had taken place, and also Supporting People units. The then West Midlands Consortium (WMCARS) and Refugee Council were also asked to provide estimates of the numbers of refugees in the region. Analysis of CORE database returns indicated the number of refugees housed by housing associations in the West Midlands, and key Refugee Community Organisations (RCOs) in the region were asked to provide data regarding the number of refugees they were serving.

All the data collected was mapped according to a geographical information system (GIS). This enabled the locations of asylum seekers and refugees in the region to be identified. Through discussions with local authority officials we

Table 3.1: Refugee data collected for the West Midlands Regional Housing Study

Area	Type of data and indication of availability of refugee data			
	Supporting People	Housing Allocations	Homelessness	RCO
Birmingham	Yes	Yes	No	No
Coventry	Yes	Yes	No	No
Dudley	Yes	Yes	No	Yes
Sandwell	No	No	No	No
Staffordshire	No	Yes	Yes	No
Stoke	Yes	No	Yes	No
Telford and Wrekin	No	No	Yes	No
Walsall	No	Yes	Yes	No
Warwickshire	No	Yes	Yes	No
Wolverhampton	Yes	Yes	No	Yes

sought to identify the number of EU citizens in the region who had refugee status.

A total of 9,604 asylum seekers were found to be living in the West Midlands at November 2004, most of them placed in the central sub-region. The largest asylum seeker populations were located in Birmingham (3,792), Sandwell (1,354), Coventry (1,225), Wolverhampton (936), Stoke (731), Dudley (711) and Walsall (552). The amount of data we were able to collect regarding refugee numbers and locations is much lower than the estimates from regional bodies so we treated it with caution. We located data on 3,110 refugees living in the West Midlands, of whom 1,639 were housed under a Supporting People programme. The majority of refugees were living in Birmingham (1,486) across some 34 wards. There were also significant refugee populations living in Coventry (705) across 16 wards and in Wolverhampton (521) spread across 12 wards. Of the remaining authorities only Dudley had a sizeable refugee population (216). The locations of refugees and asylum seekers living in the West Midlands are illustrated in Figures 3.1 and 3.2.

At one end of the scale, the Refugee Council (Midlands) estimated that there were currently 13,000 refugees in the region. They arrived at this number by adding up their estimates of the numbers of refugees from the main refugee sending countries: Vietnam (4,000), Bosnia (2,000), Albania/Kosovo (300), Somalia (1,000), Iran (1,000), Afghanistan (1,700), Iraq (1,000) and West Africa (2,000). They sought to be conservative in their estimates, citing the minimum number of individuals from each of those sending countries. They expected a further 2,300 individuals each year to become refugees or clients with status.

The WMCARS estimate was at the other end of the scale. They calculated there were 76,530 refugees in the region by adding the total number of NASS clients dispersed to the region and granted leave to remain (18,780), to Home Office estimates of the numbers of refugees moving into or out of the region. Home Office data suggested that 25 per cent of all refugees from other regions come to the West Midlands and a small percentage (6%) leave. This amounts to 39,073, representing the appropriate proportion of all positive decisions granted since dispersal began. They added on a figure of 8,678 dependents, calculated at 15 per cent, and a further 10-15,000 refugees who had entered the region as a proportion of 177,070 positive decisions made between 1990 and 2000. The figures in the WMCARS estimate are based on Home Office data. No data was available on secondary migration into the UK. Evidence from Home Office research has been cited by the LGAs for years; however the

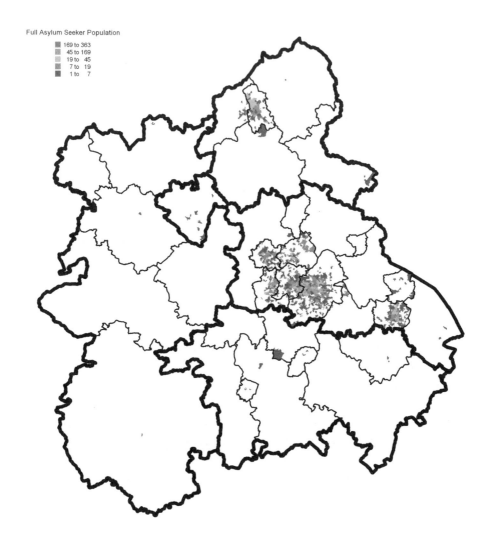

Figure 3.1: Locations of asylum seekers across the West Midlands

report has never been published and attempts to gain access to the data have always failed, although WMCARS had a particularly close relationship with the Home Office so could ask questions about the report to help inform their strategic planning. The estimates we received from organisations we asked to help us calculate the refugee population of the region were far higher than the numbers identified in the mapping exercise.

Refugee Population
Total Number

- 37-86
- 14 to 37
- 7 to 14
- 3 to 7
- 1 to 3

Figure 3.2: Refugees living in the West Midlands

We also developed our own approach to estimating the number of refugees in the region and provided projections from 1990 to 2007 using existing figures for asylum seekers and Immigration and Nationality Directorate (IND) determination rates (see Home Office quarterly statistics). If we assume that, after appeals, 34 per cent of applicants are given the right to remain (based on mean determination rates 2003-04), and that once asylum seekers are given a decision on their case they leave their accommodation and are replaced by asylum seekers newly dispersed to the region, then 6,439 bed spaces would yield 6,030 refugees in 2004 (see Table 3.2).

		2000	2001	2002	2003	2004	2005	2006	2007
a)	NASS positive decisions to date (a)	3,000	5,000	7,100	-	-	-	-	-
b)	Interim cases (one off) (amnesty)	200	300	400	500	500	550	-	-
c)	Determinations since speed up	-	-	-	6,000	6,030	6,030	6,030	6,030
d)	Subsistence only (b)	300	500	700	1,200	1,117	1,117	1,117	1,117
e)	Somali (from Europe)	100	200	300	500	500	500	500	500
f)	Sangatte (one off				104				
g)	Incomers	540	900	1,275	1,246	1,222	1,230	1,147	1,147
h)	Out goers	-216	-360	-510	-499	-489	-492	-459	-459
i)	Notional figure for pre-interim cases (c)	7,000	-	-	-	-	-	-	-
Sub-total		**10,524**	**6,540**	**9,265**	**9,051**	**8,880**	**8,935**	**8,335**	**8,335**
Cumulative total			**17,064**	**26,329**	**35,380**	**44,260**	**53,195**	**61,530**	**69,865**
Total									**69,865**

a) based on estimates on the size of the asylum-seeking population, the speed of decision-making at that time and the percentage of positive decisions

b) based on estimated numbers of those on subsistence only, until 2004 when there were when actual numbers. A 34% determination figure is used.

c) based on Refugee Council and WMCARS estimates from 1990

Table 3.2: Estimate of the number of refugees in the West Midlands 2000-2007

Added to this is the number of interim cases (a one off figure as this scheme has ended) of 550; the influx of refugees from outside the region (estimated at 15% of total asylum seeker population based on HMRA research) (see row g Table 3.2); the number of Somali refugees arriving from elsewhere in the EU (e); those who are supported on a voucher only basis (34% of 1232) (d); and the estimated 6 per cent who leave the region (h). All calculations pre-2004 were estimates based on higher asylum numbers than 2004 but lower determination speeds. Children in emergency accommodation and unaccompanied asylum-seeking children (UASC) have been excluded due to the lack of accurate data. The exercise indicated that there were 44,260 refugees in the West Midlands at the end of 2004 and that the figure would increase to 69,865 by the end of 2007 (see Table 3.2).

This suggests that the Refugee Council figure, which covers the period from the Vietnamese Resettlement Quota Programme in 1979, is underestimating the number of refugees in the region, whilst WMCARS' estimate, which like ours only covers the period from 1990, may be on the high side. At a regional spatial study consultation event, sixty individuals from local authorities, private and social accommodation providers, and refugee organisations were invited to consider the three estimates. There was broad agreement that the middle range estimate most accurately reflected the newcomer population in the region.

Household surveys

The first LSC (Phillimore *et al*, 2003) study was undertaken in the Coventry and Warwickshire sub-region and the methodology developed was applied to two further studies in the Black Country and Birmingham and Solihull sub-regions. The steering groups were eager that a household survey should be undertaken as part of the methodology for this study because they were keen to have data that could be quantified and from which some generalisations might be drawn. They wanted to compare the findings of their General Household Survey (GHS), which explored a wide range of issues around ETE, with a newcomer sample.

Although constrained by the fact that the GHS had already been designed and implemented, we were able to use comparable questions and add extra questions to explore additional areas. We had no funds to create a separate control group but the findings from the GHS allowed us to make meaningful comparisons against the general population of the sub-regions. In this respect the findings would indicate how the newcomer population was faring relative to the general population, thus moving towards an indicator of integration in the areas of education and employment. The survey covered a wide range of areas including past, present and aspirational employment, economic activity, participation in learning, motivation to learn, locating learning, ESOL, integration and advice and guidance. The main difficulty was identifying a meaningful newcomer sampling framework.

Through carrying out the population profiling and mapping exercises we identified the ages, gender and country of origin of asylum seekers living in the three sub-regions and matched that information to postcodes. Information about refugees tended to be restricted to postcode. This enabled us to identify the main areas in which refugees were living generally, but not exclusively to locate those within social housing. In order to develop a sampling strategy for the household surveys in the three sub-regions, we calculated the proportions of the asylum seeker populations by gender and by country of origin, creating broad categories of Middle East, Africa, Central Europe, Eastern Europe and Other. We also sought to calculate the proportion of asylum seekers and refugees in each sub-region. Quota targets were set for each category.

Without a full list of every address housing a newcomer in each sub-region, we could not undertake random sampling. We could hardly knock on every door in the sub-region so we used the mapping exercise to identify the main areas where newcomers were living and asked the interviewers to spread out across the area and find no more than one respondent from each street, whilst seeking to meet our targets in terms of our key variables such as age, gender, country of origin etc. The multilingual interviewers were asked to identify the language requirements of interviewees if necessary, and to arrange for someone with the appropriate language to visit them. Interviewers were also asked to ensure that they knocked on doors at random times in the day time, evenings and weekends to make sure that the responses were not skewed towards those not in education, training or employment. A profile of the respondents from each area can be seen in Table 3.3.

We expected to locate a higher proportion of refugees in the Birmingham and Solihull study than to the Black Country study, largely because anecdotal evidence from WMCARS suggested that refugees were moving to Birmingham once they gained status. They thought this was because there were fewer established ethnic communities there than in Birmingham with its wide range of multicultural groups. This hypothesis was supported in a later Housing Aspiration survey, which showed Black Country newcomers expressing a wish to move to Birmingham and Birmingham residents who had moved there from the Black Country (see Phillimore, 2004).

	Coventry and Warwickshire	Birmingham and Solihull	Black Country	Total/ average
Sample size	374	610	613	1597
Asylum seeker %	75.1%	58%	72%	67.4%
Refugee %	24.9%	40%	27%	31.5%
EU nationals %	0	2%	1%	1.1%
Male	69%	79%	79%	76.6%
Female	31%	21%	21%	23.4%
Number of country of origins represented	31	49	50	

Table 3.3 Profile of the respondent

The Coventry study reported in this book was undertaken in 2002 at a time when asylum claims were being processed very slowly and there were far higher numbers of asylum seekers than refugees. Over time there was a shift in the newcomer population from asylum seekers to refugees as decision-making speeded up and the rate of new arrivals in the UK slowed down. Although not all interview recruitment targets were met, variance was less than 10 per cent. The main difficulties were identifying European respondents and locating sufficient respondents in the Walsall area of the Black Country. The use of the asylum seeker database to frame the sample for both asylum seekers and refugees also had its difficulties. There are no guarantees that the profile of those gaining leave to remain matched that of those being dispersed to the West Midlands. No detailed information is available about the results of asylum claims made by people living in the region. The difficulty in identifying European refugees might relate to their being less likely to be granted leave to remain because the so-called Balkan crisis was deemed to have been resolved prior to 2002. Conversely, Europeans may have been harder to locate because they had longer established communities in the region, and might have moved to be closer to communities outside the main cluster areas.

Restricting the door knocking to the newcomer cluster areas could also be seen as problematic in terms of findings because newcomers living outside the main multicultural areas were not included. They might have moved because they wanted to integrate with the local population, had found employment in another part of the city or had moved to be with relatives. The findings from the survey could therefore only tell us about the individuals who live within cluster areas in the main urban centres. These findings are discussed in Chapters Four and Six.

Exploring the experiences of refugees: parameters and challenges

The household survey could tell us how many respondents were unemployed or engaged in ESOL but not why they were in that position. We conducted in-depth interviews with newcomers, to explore the experiences and processes underpinning their present position and future aspirations. In this part of the study we wished to explore how newcomers' aspirations and needs varied according to their skill levels, gender and asylum status. We tried to interview people across different ages. Whilst we realised that there were likely to be major differences in people's needs according to their length of time in the UK, ethnicity, religion, former education and class we did not have the resources to undertake sufficient interviews to take account of all these variables. Instead we tried to cover some of these factors by making sure that, for example, we had a good spread across gender and different age groups; that we covered the main countries of origin identified within each urban area; and that we interviewed people from a range of educational and occupational backgrounds within these countries.

The next difficulty was how to recruit respondents. We asked gatekeeper organisations to assist. These included accommodation providers, Refugee Community Groups not serving one particular ethnic group, local NGOs, Connexions, JCP, Local Authorities, leisure clubs and ESOL providers. In addition, a question at the end of each of the household surveys asked if the respondent would like to take part in further research. We compiled a list of possible interviewees and selected those who met our criteria. An incentive was offered to each interviewee to cover the costs of travel or childcare.

In total 66 interviews were undertaken for this study: 26 in Coventry and Warwickshire and 20 each in Birmingham and Solihull and in the Black Country. A profile of the respondents is given in Table 3.4. In Coventry, the earliest study, the majority of interviewees were asylum seekers, but by the time of the later projects most were refugees. This reflected the shift in the status of new arrivals in the region. Over time we found that the response of asylum seekers was fairly homogenous whereas that of refugees, who actually had the right to work and study, was much more varied. The in-depth interviews were conducted by researchers in the newcomers' first language or with the aid of interpreters sourced locally through refugee centres.

In addition to the in-depth interviews, we held a series of focus groups with newcomer students, women and unskilled workers. In Coventry there were three sets of focus groups. We looked at how the learning experiences of thirteen students identified through local colleges compared with those in their country of origin and what might be improved for them in the UK. We also looked at the specific experiences of eleven new migrant women, their aspirations, constraints and opportunities. Finally, we recruited eleven un-skilled newcomers to explore with us the issues underlying the aspirations of newcomers working in low skilled employment.

In Birmingham too we ran a focus group with students and recruited women and low skilled workers via stakeholders in various organisations from NGOs to statutory providers and also through word of mouth via the in-depth inter-viewees.

The focus groups differed from in depth interviews in that although they were intended to explore particular issues in depth, they could also locate the main commonalities and differences in experience between participants. This ap-proach worked well for women and students, enabling them to find common ground and generate synergy within the group. It was less successful for the unskilled workers as their experiences and backgrounds were very diverse. Another significant difference to the one-to-one interviews was that the focus groups were convened in English with the use of some interpretation by the participants themselves or a multilingual facilitator. The profile of parti-cipants in the focus groups is set out in Table 3.5.

The methodology for the ESOL study

The findings of a Joseph Rowntree Foundation study into newcomers' ex-periences of ESOL are also reported in this book. The research for this study was undertaken in 2006 by *community researchers*. There were fifteen, all of them new migrants recruited via an RCO network to receive accredited train-ing in social research skills at the University of Birmingham. The training pro-vided was essentially the same as the qualitative research methods training delivered to post-graduate students, but taught through action and discus-sion, and assessed through carefully observed and mentored research activity.

Each student received a minimum of 50 hours research training, twelve hours of which was on a one-to-one basis. The researchers were then employed by the university to undertake semi-structured interviews exploring newcomers' experiences of ESOL lessons and how these might be improved. Each student

Sub-region	Country of origin	Gender	Age	Asylum Status
Coventry and Warwickshire	Kurdish, Iraq (9)	Male (21)	16 (1)	Asylum seeker (17)
	Sudan (2)	Female (5)	17-18 (3)	ELR (3)
	Central African Republic (2)		19-24 (6)	Refugee (5)
	Afghanistan (1)		25-30 (9)	
	Angola (1)		31-35 (2)	
	Bosnia (1)		36-40 (2)	
	Burkina (1)		41-45 (1)	
	Cameroon (1)		56-60 (1)	
	Ethiopia (1)			
	Pakistan (1)			
	Rwanda (1)			
	Somalia (1)			
	Ukraine (1)			
	Uzbekistan (1)			
	Yugoslavian (1)			
	Zaire (1)			
Birmingham and Solihull	Kurdish/ Iraq (7)	Male (10)	16-19 (1)	Asylum seeker (5)
	Congo (2)	Female (10)	21-24 (3)	ELR (10)
	Somalia (2)		25-34 (9)	ILR (4)
	Sudan (2)		35-44 (6)	EU (1)
	Afghanistan		45+ (1)	

Sub-region	Country of origin	Gender	Age	Asylum Status
Birmingham and Solihull (continued)	Croatia Eritrea Iran Pakistan Palestine Rwanda			
Black Country	Afghanistan (2) Albanian (2) Angola DR Congo Eritrea Iran (3) Iraq (2) Polish Rwanda (2) Saudi Arabia Somalia (3) Sudan	Male (10) Female (10)	21-24 (2) 25-34 (13) 35-44 (5)	Asylum seeker (2) ELR (7) ILR (11)

Table 3.4: Profile of case study participants

Characteristic	Low skilled workers Coventry	Women Coventry	Students Coventry	Students Birmingham
Age:				
18-20	-		1	1
21-26	3	3	2	1
26-30	5	5	5	2
31-35	2	2	3	2
36-40	-	1	2	1
41-45	-		-	1
46- 50	1		-	1
country of origin:				
Albanian		1		
Afghani	2	1	1	2
Angolan			1	
Burundian		1	1	
Cameroonian		2		
Colombian			1	
Congolese			2	1
Ecuadorian				
Estonian	1			
Guinean			1	
Iranian	1	2	3	2
Iraqi	4		2	2
Polish				
Russian	3	1		
Romanian		1		
Sierra Leonian			1	
Sri Lankan		2		
Somali				2
Length of time in UK:				
6 months or less	2	1	3	
7mths – 1yr	-	6	1	5
13mths – 2yrs	4		6	4
25mths – 3yrs	5	4	2	
37mths – 4 years			1	

Characteristic	Low skilled workers Coventry	Women Coventry	Students Coventry	Students Birmingham
ASR status:				
Asylum seeker	6	10	8	
ELR	4		3	2
ILR	1	1	2	7
Marital status:				
Single	9	4	11	4
Married – spouse in UK	1	5	1	3
Married – spouse outside UK	1	2	1	2
Dependants:				
None	11	4		5
Outside the UK		1	1	
Inside the UK		6	1	
Employment status:				
Currently working or training on New Deal	7	0	1	0

Table 3.5: The focus group participants

was asked to contact ten newcomers from their personal networks in Birmingham who had attended ESOL classes at some point. Community researchers represented different countries of origin and they were encouraged to interview in their first language then translate the findings and enter them into a data analysis table. Each community researcher was encouraged to write their own individual report based on their findings. The research team also analysed and wrote up the combined data set. The profile of the interviewees can be seen in Table 3.6.

Some individuals interviewed friends or colleagues from a wide range of backgrounds, in some cases holding some interviews in English when this was their common language. When they discussed sampling with the authors, they generally agreed that the findings were probably skewed towards those who had achieved more in ESOL than the average, because a proportion of their interviewees had been interviewed in English. Nonetheless, the community researchers were able to reach a wide range of

Country of origin	Age	Employment	Gender and status
Afghanistan (11)	17-18 (9)	Employed (25)	Male (77)
Albania (5)	19-24 (19)	Self-employed (2)	Female (44)
Burkina Faso (1)	25-30 (29)	Unemployed (91)	ILR or HP (119)
Burundi (2)	31-35 (29)		EU (2)
Cameroon (9)	36-40 (25)		
Chad (1)	41-45 (6)		
Congo (12)	50-55 (1)		
Egypt (1)	Missing (3)		
Ethiopia (1)			
Iraq/ Kurdistan (17)			
Iran (10)			
Iraq (4)			
Ivory Coast (1)			
Kenya (1)			
Kosovo (5)			
Rwanda (10)			
Somalia (14)			
Sudan (13)			
Syria (1)			
Yemen (1)			

Table 3.6: Profile of ESOL interviewees

respondents, for example single parents who would have been hard to reach by the University because they had no relationship with any community organisation. Certainly the scale of the work: 138 interviews, 121 of which were valid, across 20 different countries of origin, would not have been possible without the involvement of community researchers.

Standardisation and verification

In order to triangulate the data collected by the community researchers we sought to interview ESOL tutors. These interviews were aimed at gaining their perspectives on the efficacy of ESOL and exploring issues around drop-out and success rates, so we could understand inconsistencies in the LSC achievement data, which was also analysed for the ESOL project. Eight ESOL tutors were contacted via colleges and the ESOL tutor network. All tutors were interviewed by a researcher from the university with the assistance of one of the community researchers. We interviewed tutors from three different colleges in permanent and contract posts, as well as one line manager. This small-scale study was intended to provide a sounding board for us to assess the validity of the community research data. It worked effectively, demonstrating that the issues raised by tutors were very similar to those raised by students.

All of the above interviews and focus groups required a topic guide, which was agreed with each funding body before piloting. Similar topic guides were used across all the studies to allow as much comparison as possible, although additional questions were added as necessary or appropriate to particular geographical areas. The research team on the Joseph Rowntree Foundation project prepared the ESOL tutor questionnaire. The ESOL topic guide was devised collaboratively between all the community researchers and the research team. All the interviews were conducted using the same topic guide, which comprised of open questions that gave researchers the freedom to probe issues as they arose.

Exploring ESOL achievement through secondary data analysis

We used a quantitative method to analyse access and success rates within the further education system, when we looked at recorded information about ESOL students. The LSC in the West Midlands provided us with their enrolment, success and completion data for all LSC funded ESOL courses in the region for the years 2002, 2003 and 2004. The data is compiled by the colleges and aggregated by the LSC.

Importantly, although the LSC identify asylum seekers via their fee remission they do not identify refugees. So to categorise a refugee cohort we used the refugee countries of origin identified in the asylum seeker and refugee reviews we had conducted for the LSC between 2003 and 2005. We included only the mainly asylum seeker sending countries, such as Rwanda and Afghanistan, and excluded those that were a significant source of economic or other migrants such as Pakistan, Brazil and South Africa. By excluding those countries we have omitted some refugees (for example about fourteen asylum seekers arrived in Birmingham in 2003 from South Africa and 25 from Pakistan), but there are likely to be some migrants from the key African countries who were not refugees. Thus we cannot claim that 100 per cent of the cohort in our refugee database were refugees or that it includes all refugees attending ESOL classes in the West Midlands.

Give or take these small opportunities for error, the figures arrived at showed that between 2002 and 2004 some 23,861 refugees and asylum seekers had enrolled in ESOL courses. The numbers and proportions of refugees and asylum seekers gaining a certificate for the different levels of ESOL qualification were then established. We also calculated drop-out rates and examined the varied numbers enrolling in classes at different ESOL levels over the three year period, to assess whether students were progressing to higher levels over time. Analysis of these findings is documented in Chapter Five.

Investigating the role of statutory and non statutory agencies

We also wanted the LSC commissioned studies to explore the statutory and non-statutory organisations providing information, advice and guidance and services to newcomers. We sought to investigate the range of services available to newcomers, the challenges faced by providers in meeting newcomers' needs and the resources required by the organisations to build their capacity to meet needs and to develop in order to support future needs. This information was gathered in two phases in each LSC study.

The first phase involved a postal questionnaire to statutory agencies and NGOs in each urban area. Databases of possible respondents were obtained from a wide range of organisations including those with a newcomer focus, such as the Refugee Council and local refugee centres, and others such as the LSC who had a community learning focus. We also used a snowballing approach, asking organisations we identified to provide us with their own referral databases. Eventually all the databases were merged and questionnaires dispatched using mail merge. Sixty five questionnaires were dispatched in Coventry and Warwickshire and 44 (68%) were returned following telephone reminders. A further 262 questionnaires were posted to organisations in Birmingham and 103 (39%) returned. Return rates were low in Birmingham. At least 50 organisations were impossible to contact: some of them had moved on or were no longer in operation. In the Black Country, 75 out of 181 were returned (42%). Across the three sub-regions, non-statutory providers returned a total of 222 questionnaires. Once questionnaires were returned they were analysed and a profile drawn up of those providing services to newcomers.

In the second phase, we carried out site visits to a sample of respondents, twelve in each of the three areas. Organisations were selected on the basis of their size, the extent to which they dealt with newcomers and whether they were statutory or non-statutory. Another criterion was whether or not they had been recommended as a site of good practice in supporting newcomers with their ETE needs. We sought to achieve some geographical spread so in the Black Country we covered the four main urban areas, and in Birmingham the main newcomer cluster areas. Each site visited included an interview about the nature of provision, organisational successes, difficulties encountered, plans for the future and capacity issues. A tour of each organisation was laid on, during which questions which emerged from our observations could be addressed. Interviews with twelve statutory providers were conducted, four in each sub-regions. All the questionnaires for these as well as topic guides were produced by the research team with the support of the steering groups.

Survey of employers

Much has been written about employers' attitudes to employing newcomers but empirical evidence is lacking about what employers actually say. This stage of the research sought to interview a range of employers who had staff shortages, to explore their attitudes to employing newcomers. Three separate employer surveys were undertaken. The first followed a review of skills gaps and shortages in and around Wolverhampton and was used to develop a profile of 'employer types' to help target potential local employers for interviews. Key criteria considered when developing the profile included: sectors reported to have good growth prospects and areas where increased output, jobs and productivity were predicted; areas identified as having low skills and occupations, where there had been difficulties in recruiting workers and filling vacancies. This research was undertaken for JCP in Wolverhampton in 2002 (see Goodson and Phillimore, 2002). The main target sectors and occupations identified as offering a range of opportunities for low level and higher level qualifications included computing services (word processors and computer aided design), retail/customer care (sales assistants, receptionists), crafts and related occupations, health and social care (doctors, nurses, care assistants, nursery nurses), education, hospitality and catering. Based on these target sectors and occupation types, a range of organisations were selected from a local newspaper search of job vacancies. Fifty employers who had recently advertised for new recruits were sent a letter to inform them of the research and ask for their co-operation in the study. Follow up telephone calls were made and face-to-face interviews were secured with ten local employers.

The second was undertaken for the LSC in Birmingham and Solihull. One hundred employers were located through various means. Those who were considered to be open to employing refugees were selected from the committee of the Institute of Asian Businesses; those currently experiencing re-cruitment difficulties in sectors with key skills shortages were selected from information provided by the Chamber of Commerce; those with skills shortages in the sub-region's expanding retail sector were selected from a list of organisations sited within the Touchwood Retail Centre in Solihull; and a range of others in skills shortage sectors were identified as having multiple vacancies from advertisements in the *Evening Mail*, the most widely read local paper. Twenty five employers agreed to take part in a twenty minute telephone interview.

The final employer study was undertaken as part of the EQUAL funded MEET European study of employers' attitudes to newcomers. The research team at the University sought to identify the main skills shortage sector in the region by looking at the LSC (2003) report on sector skills shortages. We identified employers who were regularly advertising in local papers, and conducted nine telephone interviews. Regardless of the study, each interview explored these employers' perceptions around the ETE needs of newcomers as well as their own training needs in relation to newcomers; issues of routes to employment and questions of legislation. We also looked at employers' attitudes to the kinds of workers they felt newcomers might be and the sorts of support they as organisations would need to help them employ newcomers.

Investigating attitudes of education providers

Having sought newcomers' perspectives on their education and training experiences, needs and requirements, it was important to triangulate and consider the views of education providers. A two-stage process was undertaken in each of the three LSC areas by researchers at NIACE and overseen by the University of Birmingham. NIACE were in fact associate partners in all three LSC studies. They have comprehensive databases of all statutory providers across the UK. In the first instance NIACE sent a postal questionnaire to all providers in the area to explore existing provision and future plans. The NIACE database was used for each sub-region, plus also data collected from the LSC and local organisations. Questionnaires were thus sent to all the learning organisations in each sub-region, whether private, community or statutory based. A total of 137 questionnaires were dispatched in Coventry and Warwickshire and 70 returned (51%); 65 questionnaires were dispatched in Birmingham and Solihull and 36 returned (55%); and finally 75 were dispatched and 31 responses received in the Black Country (41%). Once training and education provision was identified, face-to-face interviews were conducted with providers to explore their perceptions of working with newcomers and examine ways in which provision can be matched to newcomers' needs and aspirations.

In each area a range of providers currently working with newcomers was identified on the basis of size, location and type of provision. Each organisation was invited to attend a face-to-face interview, although a few requested a telephone interview. The interviews explored providers' perceptions of the aspirations of newcomers in terms of ETE, the barriers they face in realising aspirations, what could be done to overcome barriers, types of provision and learner support, funding and future plans for development. Twelve interviews were held in Coventry and Warwickshire, fifteen in Birmingham and Solihull and fifteen in the Black Country.

Review of employability initiatives

The final piece of research is a Europe wide study of migrant focused employability initiatives. This piece of work was undertaken in 2004, as part of the Progress GB EQUAL project, to explore good practice across the European Economic Area in enhancing the employability of migrants. The object of this research was to develop an employability model to implement as a pilot in the UK.

A database of organisations working to enhance migrants' employability was constructed from the combined databases of a wide range of organisations and through Internet searches. Some 556 organisations were identified, 227 based in the UK and 329 elsewhere in Europe. A questionnaire designed by the UK research team was piloted with partners in the Netherlands, Germany, Spain and Italy and then translated either by these partners or by professional translators and dispatched to all organisations on the database.

All questions were closed except the final one which requested the names of other organisations working with migrants that might be contacted. A total of 144 further organisations were identified in this way. The responses were analysed and 36 organisations providing employability support were telephoned and asked for a brief interview to explore their services in more depth.

Those who undertook activities aimed at enhancing the employability of skilled migrants were asked to host a site visit. We visited 28 organisations across Germany, the Netherlands, Norway and the UK to interview project managers and their clients about the types of work undertaken in the project and the policy framework that underpinned their work. This employability initiatives study helped us to develop our ideas about how newcomers could be better helped to gain access to the labour market and the type of policy that could facilitate enhanced employability. Some of these ideas have helped to formulate the recommendations set out in the conclusions in Chapter Eight. Having explored some of the challenges associated with researching refugees and set out the methodological approaches used to examine the situation of new migrants in the West Midlands, in the next chapter we consider some of the findings in relation to newcomers' access to learning.

4

The exclusion of new migrants from learning

We are educated back home, but here we are nothing. (Kurdish Iraqi man, 23)

Although it is argued that new migrants can bring social, cultural and economic benefits to wider society the reality for many newcomers, particularly asylum seekers, is a lengthy struggle to reach the point of feeling that they have some role in UK society. Learning English is the main priority for many. Once they are proficient they may want to learn new skills or to get existing skills recognised so that they have evidence of their knowledge and experience to bring to the labour market.

From a policy perspective it is important that newcomers can access the learning they need to facilitate their integration and inclusion in their new communities and the wider economy. This chapter is concerned with newcomers' experiences of accessing and undertaking learning in the UK. We set the context with a profile of newcomers' educational backgrounds in both their countries of origin and in the UK, before examining some of the problems they face when they seek to engage in learning.

The newcomer population is made up of diverse groups of individuals with a broad range of aspirations and experience and the barriers to their learning differ widely. Data in this chapter is based on responses from 44 focus group respondents, 187 one-to-one interviews and 1597 quantitative interviews conducted as part of household survey enquiries. All interviews explored similar themes concerning attitudes and experiences of learning. The study looked at women, professionals, young people whose education had been interrupted, people who had received no schooling and those with a trade background.

Their experiences, common issues and some group-specific problems are considered before possible policy responses are outlined.

Newcomers' educational backgrounds

Assessing and documenting the educational background and qualifications of newcomers and trying to assess the UK equivalence of what they learned in their country of origin is a difficult task. Our research demonstrated that there were significant cultural differences in ways of communicating achievement in education and learning. In addition, the only database available for translating overseas qualifications to UK equivalents, the UK National Academic Recognition Information Centre (NARIC) system, favours broad generalisations which are hard to match to the certificates held by newcomers.

Data from our quantitative surveys revealed that on average 80 per cent of newcomers had been in full-time education in their home countries and 43 per cent had received some type of qualification. Qualifications that could be translated ranged from school certificates to PhDs. Twenty three per cent of the qualifications of newcomers were at Higher Education level. Their achievements included degrees in medicine, engineering, architecture and electronics, diplomas in teaching and nursing, law and management.

Comparing the qualifications of newcomers with those of the general West Midlands population was difficult, as not all the qualifications had a UK equivalent. In addition, many newcomers had completed lengthy apprenticeships that did not culminate in a formal recognisable qualification, but could well be equal to a high level in our National Vocational Qualification (NVQ) system. Our findings must be viewed with caution as the levels of newcomers' achievements may have been underestimated because of these difficulties.

Overall our data suggests that newcomers hold lower qualification levels than the general population in the region but that nearly a quarter of those with qualifications were at degree level. On average, 69 per cent of newcomers had no proof of their qualifications and only 20 per cent of them had tried to get their qualifications converted. Of those who had sought to gain proof of equivalence through the NARIC system only a handful had succeeded.

New migrants' views and experiences of learning and ESOL

Just over half the newcomers (56%) had engaged in some form of learning since leaving full-time education and most of these (90%) had done so since arriving in the UK. Learning English was predominant. At the time of our research, findings indicated that exactly half (50%) of all new migrants were engaged in ESOL classes. Of those who were engaged in learning, 73 per cent anticipated that it would lead to a qualification and 82 per cent of these expected this to be in ESOL. A small number were working towards other qualifications: one or two were engaged in GCSEs, NVQs, BTECs, A-Levels, City and Guilds, CLAIT or courses that led to European Computer Driving Licence certification. Even fewer newcomers were studying for university diplomas or degrees, or vocational certificates in areas such as food and hygiene. Fifteen per cent of them had already gained a qualification of some kind in the UK, mostly through a Further Education college. The most common qualification was in ESOL, although some had gained CLAIT, GCSEs and NVQs.

Even amongst those who had had little or no formal education in their country of origin, learning was considered most important in helping them to settle, improve their future prospects and enhance their ability to integrate into society. Most were keen to learn. They wanted to return to the specialist subjects they had pursued in their countries of origin, while those with little prior learning wanted to study a new subject area.

They described learning as an opportunity that could open 'a whole new world', and a chance to improve their current education in order to secure 'decent' employment in the future. Most newcomers were unable to begin any academic or vocational learning until their ability to speak and write English improved. Mahmood, a 25 year old Iraqi, exemplifies a newcomer keen to continue with his education. He graduated with a Diploma from a Teacher Training Institute in Iraq, with a specialisation in Mathematics. When we met him he had been in the UK for three months and had devoted his time to learning English. He was spending 14 hours a week attending ESOL classes and supplemented these by watching television and listening to the radio with a notebook and pen in hand to pick up new words and phrases. He said he felt it was imperative to acquire a good command of the English language to help him feel at home, to mix with local people and to be able to continue with his education. He hoped to be able to study for a university degree and later a Masters degree in Mathematics. He also wanted to enrol on an IT course to help improve his immediate employment prospects. Mahmood ultimately wanted to be a mathematics teacher but, like many newcomers, he was prepared to take any job available in the short term to make ends meet.

Many of the new migrants who were working were keen to study. They hoped that continuing their learning would help them to improve their medium to long-term employment prospects. Many wanted to learn a trade, or work towards an occupation that was likely to provide them with secure work, or an opportunity to progress beyond working in low-skilled and poorly paid jobs. Professionals viewed training as critical to helping them begin the process of returning to their former professions.

The motivation of the children who were accompanied by their parents was strongly affected by the parents' attitudes. Many parents were keen to encourage their children's learning progression and viewed learning as the key to improving both their children's lives and the future prospects of their family. Only a few were as interested in extending their learning beyond improving their English. This lack of motivation to learn was related to complex personal problems around family and housing rather than a disinterest in learning *per se*.

Many newcomers saw ESOL lessons as providing a vital link with the outside world and recognised that learning English was the main factor that would enable them to learn not only UK culture, values and norms but also to learn in the wider academic and vocational sense. They believed that without a good grasp of English their prospects and future employment trajectories would be restricted to low paid work. Those who had no prior English language education considered ESOL the main priority. Even those with good spoken English were keen to access language support to improve their reading and writing. The acquisition of English was clearly seen as crucial in the development of self-sufficiency and self-esteem and in the struggle towards social inclusion (see Tomlinson and Egan, 2002; Bloch, 2004). For those who wish to build a future in the UK, language competence is now even more important in the light of the new citizenship legislation.

Newly arrived migrants often located ESOL classes through informal networks such as friends, family and other community members. They were only likely to use other sources of information to locate provision, such as Jobcentre Plus (JCP), Learn Direct, council asylum teams, professionals such as solicitors or interpreters, or voluntary sector organisations when they had found their feet. More confident individuals searched through libraries, the Internet and the local newspaper, as well as approaching colleges directly to identify what courses were available. Locating advanced ESOL and finding out about wider learning opportunities was more challenging. It is apparent that misinformation about learning spread rapidly within groups with close social ties and that whilst word of mouth offered opportunities to access information it could also be problematic if this information was inaccurate. Some asylum seekers, for instance, had heard from their peers that they were not entitled to access ESOL so had not even tried to enrol despite wanting to learn English.

Those who had engaged in learning were on the whole positive about their UK learning experiences. They enjoyed their courses and felt they had received appropriate levels of support. However, those engaged in classes other than ESOL found that getting to grips with the UK education system took several months. Education in the UK differed from their experiences of education in their countries of origin as it was based upon doing, or independent reading, rather than on rote learning, and assessments were based on assignments rather than on exams.

Newcomers particularly welcomed the opportunity to meet English people through their courses because this provided an excellent opportunity to speak English. Not all had positive experiences while engaged in learning. They reported incidences of being treated differently by tutors and students because of their status. Some tried to avoid revealing their status because they feared prejudice. They tried to conceal any dealings they had with the asylum system lest other students shunned them:

> Some people see you differently as an asylum seeker and they would keep a big distance from us or not be friendly. (Albanian woman, 32)

> There is racism among people. People don't accept refugees. White areas don't accept. (Iraqi Kurdish man, 30)

On the whole those attending college considered that the opportunity to learn was extremely valuable. Since many were recent arrivals in the UK, their college course provided the structure for their day and was the main focus of their lives. Consequently they took their studies very seriously. They were perplexed and frustrated by the behaviour of some UK students and could not understand why they had opted to attend college but were not serious about their studies and showed no motivation to learn.

Experiences of ESOL were also mixed. Some students had very positive experiences and reported how they found that their classes had given them the confidence to speak English and that they had then been able to engage with other courses or to find work. As well as improving future prospects, the immediate gains of attending ESOL lessons were that their sense of well-being developed and that they could overcome their feelings of isolation:

> I have gained lots of success with my English language. I can solve most of my problems now. I am more independent because I can speak ... that is quite good for me. I can go to doctor without interpreter and I do shopping by myself. Before I always had to ask my wife but now I do it by myself. (Afghani man, 40)

Apart from learning English, ESOL courses provided a social space for new-comers to make friends and meet people from different countries and cultures. Although they spoke of their desire to practice English outside the classroom, the reality was that few had much chance to converse in English outside the college environment. The mix of people with different first languages in ESOL classes provided opportunities both for socialising and learning. English was often the only common language and was therefore their only way of communicating. ESOL offered a rare opportunity for new-comers to break their isolation and helped them to understand and feel part of British society. Through meeting other asylum seekers and refugees in their classes they built friendships, provided each other with support in and out of the classroom and began to feel more accepted into society.

One Congolese refugee described ESOL as 'the only institution that accepted me'. Others confirmed the importance to them of the classes:

> I have gained lots of experience in ESOL in terms of understanding UK culture and other newcomers' culture. (Somali man, 36)

> I have received lots of things from that course about life here, about the law and order and about UK constitution and a lot of other thing. It is good to learn from different people's culture as well. We could learn a lot from them ...There were some times each student was speaking about their cultures and their life, what sort of life they had back in their country. We learned a lot from that ... I learned about different culture and different customs that was quite helpful to me. (Afghani man, 40)

While newcomers welcomed the social relationships they built with other students they particularly appreciated the pastoral support provided by tutors which often went well beyond tutors' standard teaching responsibilities. Many tutors spent a generous amount of their time offering assistance by translating letters or making telephone calls on behalf of their students. This support impinged on teaching time but was important and should not be underestimated:

> The teachers care about individuals and are always available to help us with our homework and other problems...that make a big difference not only for me but for the others in the class as well. I had big problems with my house and I don't know where I would have be if I did not get help. (Kurdish man, 23)

Barriers and constraints to ESOL

Although attending ESOL classes brought many benefits, a significant number of students were dissatisfied with the quality of their lessons or their speed of progress. Gaining access to ESOL was a problem because of the lengthy waiting lists for classes at all levels. There was no system at local or sub-regional level to direct newcomers to colleges where there were vacancies or at least shorter waiting lists. Indeed little information about waiting times or options is given to students seeking to enrol:

> When I came to this country, I didn't know anybody and had lots of problems. I went to register to a college but the college didn't accept me and they asked me to come next year. From that time I go to college. Over one year I was waiting for the course. (Afghani man, 17)

> The college puts everybody on the waiting list, even if it is not realistic, even if they have to wait for a year. They do not direct them to another college so you are stuck. (Woman from Ivory Coast, 34)

Amount and quality of provision

Before 2001, many colleges in the English dispersal regions that now have key roles in language provision had little demand for ESOL. The arrival of thousands of asylum seekers meant that colleges were under great pressure to put language programmes in place quickly. This left many struggling to identify and recruit qualified tutors, which exacerbated the problem of long waiting lists (Griffiths, 2003). By 2006 the ESOL system was in crisis. Despite the millions of pounds being pumped into the system by the DfES, waiting lists continued to grow and many migrants progressed slowly in their language learning. The arrival of hundreds of thousands of A8 migrants since 2004, many wanting to improve their language skills, has placed further pressure on the system.

Concern about lack of progress provided the rationale for the Joseph Rowntree Foundation research which specifically looked at refugees' experiences of ESOL. Refugee Community Organisations (RCOs) in the West Midlands have long been worried about the inability of ESOL students to converse in English, even after several years of tuition. The research we carried out for the Learning and Skills Councils also revealed problems.

A number of students did not enjoy their classes and had changed provider, were on the waiting list for another provider or had dropped out altogether. Around 40 per cent of students attending ESOL classes dropped out, although drop-out rates varied between providers. Students had different expectations and aims from their ESOL classes. Their aims fell into three separate areas: to learn basic conversational English in order to communicate, to improve their language ability to access work and to improve their language to the point where they could access Higher Education (HE). The extent to which newcomers were able to reach their personal goals varied: those who sought basic conversational English were satisfied (45%), those wanting workplace English (16%), or English for HE (22.5%).

Dissatisfaction and low levels of achievement were partly linked to the fact that classes were not streamed by ability, which meant that students were often placed in mixed ability classes. The more competent and motivated students were left feeling unchallenged and in some instances 'held back by those who did not take it [ESOL] seriously'. Changing classes could be problematic so some students opted to leave their ESOL courses rather than 'waste [my] time' in lessons where they could not progress:

> Every time I attend the classes, I found out that I have gone beyond that level ... sometime the teachers would just teach the same thing...it was difficult to learn anything new. So I stopped going. (Ethiopian man, 34)

Being placed in mixed ability classes was only one factor that impeded progress. Some learners had difficulty understanding course content and many found the course materials inadequate because they were repetitive or too basic. A number of them said that working with, or socialising with English speakers or watching English TV had progressed their English far more than attending ESOL.

There was evidence that in some colleges class sizes were too large for the classrooms provided. Students spoke of having nowhere to sit in class because there were not enough chairs, and of having problems seeing and hearing the teacher.

The question of assessment is worth considering. Some newcomers reported instances where they had enrolled on an ESOL course and received no initial assessment, whilst others considered the level of assessment to be poor. Once they started attending their classes they found they had been placed at the wrong level, more often than not in a class they considered to be well below their capabilities.

Beyond basic levels of ESOL

In 2006 NIACE were appointed to undertake a systematic review of ESOL (Grover, 2006). Findings from this review shed some light on the difficulties new migrants faced in accessing higher level ESOL courses. Provision above basic levels was found to be patchy, largely because colleges were not funded to provide courses above Level 2. This may explain why there is a greater supply of low level courses and why learners who want to improve their English to obtain work or to continue to HE struggle to find appropriate provision. Aldridge *et al* (2005) found that the majority of jobs required a level of English which was considerably higher than Level 2.

Our research indicated a 'one size fits all' approach to delivery, which was problematic for many students. New arrivals in the UK have diverse ethnicities and educational backgrounds with corresponding differences in educational attainment levels. Steels and England (2004) found that advisers struggle to assess students accurately and refer some individuals to ESOL who have extremely poor basic skills. Students who could not read or write in their own language were severely hampered in their ability to engage in the most basic of lessons, whilst others with high levels of educational attainment languished in courses way below their level. Students in this study felt that assessing individuals according to their language ability alone was insufficient and that factors such as their wider skills and aptitude for learning should also be taken into account when determining which level ESOL class is appropriate.

Concerns were also expressed about the lack of vocational courses for new migrants. For those in work wishing to progress in their job, or those wishing to return to their specialist area, opportunities for learning specialist English were limited. As one Cameroonian man explained:

> ESOL alone can't help me. I am an Engineer by training. ESOL qualification can't help me much. (Cameroonian man, 37)

Some people told us that they had managed to locate courses for only a few hours per week but found that this was not enough. Most students wanted to continue with ESOL when they found employment but struggled to fit the courses around their jobs because most courses ran during the day. Finding appropriate courses was particularly problematic for those working in jobs with unpredictable hours. And many said they would be reluctant to attend courses after work if they were held in the workplace as this would separate them from their work mates and emphasise their immigration status, which they did not wish to do. It was clear that working newcomers needed flexible mainstream provision.

The standard of ESOL teaching was also an issue. Students identified a range of good and bad practice. They appreciated friendly and supportive teachers who gave extra support with their learning and pastoral issues. But the main criticisms were about the poor quality and lack of study materials, inappropriate venues where learners were often disturbed, the high turnover of tutors, boring lessons and inexperienced, unenthusiastic and unprepared teachers:

> Give us a teacher who can teach us English ... because when they are there they seem they want to finish their time and go home. (Rwandan woman, 27)

The inconsistency of experience and training between classes and teachers was a major concern. So was the struggle to understand the course content when tutors had heavy accents that impeded students' ability to determine correct pronunciation:

> I find it very difficult to understand accents from different people, even the teacher has a different accent which does not help us to learn ... I think it makes it much more difficult ... I know the other students think it is hard to pick up what he [tutor] is saying. I learned much more from the teacher before, she was clear. (Burundian man, 18)

The variation they reported in teaching quality is supported by findings from the Adult Learning Inspectorate and the Office for Standards in Education (Ofsted), who also reported inconsistencies in the quality of ESOL teaching. Our research showed that the initial experience of being on an ESOL course was very important, as it was difficult to transform negative experiences into something positive once someone lost faith in the system. Those who left ESOL rarely returned to give lessons another chance.

Many students wanted full-time or intensive courses as they felt they would learn much more quickly if they were immersed in language learning. However, in order to comply with Jobseeker's Allowance regulations they were not allowed to attend lessons for more than sixteen hours per week. Full-time courses were out of the question for newcomers claiming benefits. The sixteen hour rule created a vicious circle whereby those who could not speak English properly struggled to find work, but if they were unemployed and in receipt of benefits they were not permitted to study English for the hours needed to become proficient enough to apply for work. Even the students not constrained by JCP rules found provision limited to only two hours per week in some colleges. A critical mass of time was needed to facilitate progress; a few hours a week were of little use.

Barriers and constraints to wider learning

This section looks at the experiences and difficulties of new migrants in accessing wider learning opportunities. Whilst ESOL was often the first step of the learning journey for new arrivals to the UK, many aspired to progress ultimately to vocational or academic courses. The barriers students encounter when trying to move beyond ESOL learning into Further and Higher Education are a cause for concern. We have seen how important language competence and the function of ESOL is in the overall integration of new migrants into society and the labour market. Language plays a pivotal role in enabling an individual to access wider educational opportunities.

Language was considered to be a key barrier to tapping into generic and specialist courses. As one newcomer said: '...once you speak the language all opportunities are in front of you'. Several of them were keen to engage in a whole range of learning opportunities but were discouraged by their poor English language skills which they thought would prevent them from being eligible for courses. With so few courses offering integrated ESOL support many struggled to see how they could succeed in mainstream provision. Some had been discouraged by the long waiting lists for courses they were eligible to attend such as ICT training; others said they had been discouraged from taking courses by their tutors, who maintained that their language ability would hold them back. Akam is a twenty year old Iraqi who, although encouraged by his tutor to engage with wider learning, found that his English combined with several other difficulties, such as cost of transport and course fees, constrained his learning.

Akam had been living in the UK for two years. He originally wanted to work in medicine but his plans were interrupted when he was forced to leave Iraq to flee persecution. Although unable to fulfil his original dream of becoming a doctor he could work towards his new ambition of working with computers. He had attended ESOL classes since he arrived in the UK, and was encouraged by his ESOL tutors to enrol onto a City & Guild's computing course.

Travelling to college was expensive and time-consuming as he had to change buses several times. He also struggled to study because of the constant noise in his shared house. His poor command of English made it a struggle to make friends on his computing course or outside his own ethnic group. All these problems held back his progress on his course.

Akam was also working as a night porter in a hotel. This job helped him to practice his English and to earn a living while studying. Without his wages it would have been difficult for him to study:

> ...not everyone can afford to pay for the course, many of us on the course are on a low income or not working ... There are so many people who would love to study. But they are not able to work to pay for this course and they don't know how to find the right course to suit them. So how do they get on it? Without some help it is difficult to make a good decision...

Akam eventually wants to work in a bank, or to develop translation pro-grammes for Kurdish speakers. But he was concerned that lack of advice and information about how to achieve his ambitions would hamper his chances of success.

Understanding the system: availability and access

The dearth of information, advice and guidance (IAG) about the availability of and entry requirements for courses affected many newcomers (see Chapters Five and Six). Many had no idea how the UK education system worked and would have benefited greatly from careers advice and guidance to help them access the right courses.

In the main, new migrants were keen to know how they could locate appro-priate training in their areas of interest at the level that met their needs. They wanted training that would lead to 'real' and 'decent' jobs. But such courses were said to be rare. In general newcomers found even greater difficulties gaining access to academic or vocational courses than to ESOL classes.

Misinformation or in some cases active discouragement from JCP staff was also reported. Confusion about their status and how it related to their entitle-ment to fee remission at Further Education (FE) level was common amongst newcomers. Whilst lack of appropriate documentation could prevent asylum seekers from gaining an ESOL place, there were also large numbers of asylum seekers who believed they were not allowed to study at all until they had been granted leave to remain. Consequently they excluded themselves from pur-suing any wider learning while their cases were under review, which could take several years. As well as the problems of accessing learning, some new migrants found their ability to learn hampered by other factors.

Inhibiting factors other than provider issues

Akam's case illustrates that housing conditions can have a major impact on newcomers' well-being and their ability to study. Living in shared accom-modation made studying particularly problematic:

> They put criminals to the same place with gentle people. The basic accommodation condition needs to be provided. If your life is quiet you can be successful. If not it is very hard to concentrate. (Cameroonian woman, 35)

Many said they struggled to focus on learning while living in temporary accommodation. Newcomers sharing houses with people who were not members of their family found that the lack of private space and the noise generated by housemates made it hard to study at home.

The transient nature of the newcomer populations also meant that friends or acquaintances of the other lodgers often stayed in the same property so that it became even more overcrowded and noisy:

> The social housing stock is dwindling, and refugees often find themselves in the oldest accommodation, plagued by damp and vermin... Somalis suffer a particular problem of overcrowding. ...Somali Muslims tend to have large families – to have six or seven children is not unusual. In addition, new arrivals often have difficulty finding somewhere to live, and take advantage of norms of family or clan obligations to move in with relatives. British housing is not designed for large households, and the health of members inevitably suffers. (Sudanese man, 43)

> The house is very old, it's really horrible and the neighbours [are] unfriendly...we keep ourselves to ourselves, there is fighting in the neighbourhood, a lot of trouble and sometimes racism on the estates so we stay in. I have even stopped going to college now. (Rwandan woman, 34)

Newcomers often have to live in areas with an excess of cheap housing. After gaining leave to remain, many stayed in these areas because they did not know of other options. Sadly, these areas were some of the most deprived. A whole raft of problems, from noisy neighbours to racial harassment, were coupled with poor housing conditions, including leaking roofs and vermin infestation and having no hot water or working cooking appliances. This was not conducive to study. The majority of asylum seekers living in poor and overcrowded conditions said their current living arrangements, combined with the uncertainty of the asylum process, affected their ability to learn:

> People who come to live here have some kinds of trauma in themselves. Some people are living here more than four or five years, but they still have problems ... Because they have no decision from the Home Office and they are living without any hope. They think every day that they might be sent by force to their countries any day ... I have some kind of mental health problem and my friend has the same sort of problems as me ... My progress was lower because of my personal problems. Psychologically I have a problem. When I come to this country, I was given one year leave to remain and that has been already ended, but I have no response from the Home Office for more than a year. I don't know what is going to happen to me. That became a kind of trauma on me. (Afghani man, 19)

> I was worried and anxious about my future in this country. I wondered if they were going to grant refugee status to me or deport me from this country. I will never forget the anxieties and the fears that I had when I was waiting for an answer and I will never forget those nights I could not sleep. All these things had negative effects on me. (Iranian man, 47)

Even individuals who had been granted leave to remain still suffered from the fallout from the experience of becoming a refugee and dealing with the asylum system. Pali, a 27 year old refugee from Rwanda, is an example of someone who has a lot to offer and who has used education to help deal with his trauma over the murder of his entire family.

At the time of interview, Pali had been in the UK for two years. Educational attainment had always been important in his family although being Tutsis made it difficult to access services in Rwanda. As a child he promised his father that he would do his best and now that he was living in the UK he wanted to honour his promise. Pali completed secondary school in 1999 having been sent to the Congo, against his wishes, to fight. On receiving his Diploma, he became a teacher and taught in primary school for twelve months.

Once in the UK Pali began a course in mechanical engineering. He enjoyed studying with British students and found the time he spent at college helped him to forget about his experiences in Rwanda for a while. Although flash-backs hampered his progress he was determined to continue with his learning as he saw his education as the most stable part of his life.

The emotional and psychological problems associated with being a refugee are immense. Health and emotional problems caused by the events that drove them to leave their home country, along with feelings of loss, loneliness, isolation and concerns about the well-being of other family members manifested themselves in a range of ways such as depression, anxiety, insomnia and post traumatic shock (PTSD):

> First of all the war I went through, the way people have been killed, the way a body is opened up from the stomach, it is not a story, I have seen it myself. What I have seen in my country it will never leave me. I had all those immigration troubles to add to my experience of war. Then I felt mentally ill and could not go out or do anything. (Congolese man)

The sum of such problems and the emotional pressure can powerfully affect people's ability to learn by draining their energy and making it hard to concentrate for long:

> I can no longer sleep well, I have insomnia, I dream that I am in war, I see what was happening and I have headaches. I am no longer able to concentrate on things as I used to be. (Congolese man)

Poor language skills exacerbated the isolation of newcomers from local communities and prevented them from accessing the clinical or therapeutic assistance they needed to deal with mental health problems: these in turn inhibited their progress in learning English. Asylum seekers and refugees often found themselves in a no-win situation. Although some education providers offered support services for their students these were not tailored to the specific needs and circumstances of refugees (see Chapter Five).

Students who could speak English were often unaware that they could access counselling or felt nervous about articulating their problems to a stranger. Women were also less inclined to seek support if the counsellor was male:

> There are many kinds of problems which you can not talk about in front of male, because culturally you can not talk to a male about a problem you experienced during the war. Then you choose to keep quiet, it means you live with your own problems. You can be angry inside and not talk to anyone…over time it gets worse. I developed very low self esteem, which I never used to have. I have always been confident, I always had high esteem, I used to like challenges and look forward to the future. (Burundian woman, 25)

On a practical level, getting to college was problematic because of the cost of transport, especially in the winter months and for those who could not walk there. Most newcomers attending college were in receipt of subsistence benefit and the few who were working had extremely low incomes. They did not even have enough to pay for travel:

> I did not have a bus pass and it was difficult for me to go to the college. They were saying that I should be more than three years to stay here and then I can be qualified to have bus pass. They did not accept to give at the end. I was receiving £32 per week and that was for my food and all the other costs. (Kosovan man, 19)

The cost and availability of childcare was equally out of reach.

Their low incomes also meant that they struggled to afford course materials and to pay exam fees:

> The main barrier for me was the financial problems. We were asylum seekers (my wife and me) and the life was very difficult with £30 which they were giving us. You have to buy books, pens, clothes and food. That £30 was not even enough for food … [I gave up the English course, because] I decided to work and earn money by myself instead of receiving from the government, because we couldn't survive with it. (Afghani man, 27).

Many felt compelled to seek any kind of employment rather than invest in learning that would improve their English proficiency. Their need for an income meant that they had to abandon their aspirations to pursue short-term goals and resign themselves to temporary, low-paid and unsustainable employment. In recent years Access to Learning Funds have been substantially reduced, making it difficult to access the financial support needed to study.

So far we have explored some of the general issues concerning ESOL and wider learning. But the newcomer population is heterogeneous, so it is important to examine the specific issues faced by different newcomer groups such as women, professionals, those with trade backgrounds and young people.

Newly arrived women

Refugee women in the UK face additional problems over and above those encountered by the men. Although there is research on the experiences of refugee women (Dumper, 2002; Refugee Action, 2006), there has been little consideration of refugee women's education and learning experiences in the UK and how they are affected by gender related issues. A range of gender specific problems were identified by the Greater London Authority (2004). These included gender-based persecution in their countries of origin, sexual and domestic violence, relationship breakdown in the UK, responsibility for childcare and all the responsibilities associated with being the primary carer for a family, including locating safe and suitable housing, accessing school places and locating appropriate health care. Many of these issues impacted upon the ability of women in our research to access learning, let alone reach their full potential.

Most of the women said that learning was critical to help them reach a point where they could build a future in the UK. Women's past experiences in their country of origin meant that some had limited experience of learning:

> I had very little formal education because of the civil war. My uncle taught us at home because of the civil war. Women got used to not going out because we could get raped. (Rwandan woman, 34)

Upon arrival in their dispersal areas many women were initially enthusiastic about the prospect of getting involved in learning. However, they rapidly discovered that they did not understand what opportunities were available or how to explore their learning options. Lack of knowledge was a problem for all new arrivals, but it was a particular issue for women because they were more restricted to the domestic domain so had fewer opportunities to access information, even via word of mouth. The women in our research struggled to locate any provision at all that met their needs, let alone gender specific provision that took account of cultural specificities. Many had problems in accessing and continuing learning, most commonly because of childcare.

The women often found that once they located learning opportunities that met their needs, no childcare facilities were available. Courses at training venues with childcare facilities were often over-subscribed and had long waiting lists.

Childcare was not free in all colleges, invariably excluding newcomers on low incomes. Women with children of school age could not be flexible about where and when they attended lessons because they had to fit classes around their children's schooling. Drop-out rates were higher amongst those who lived a long distance from their course. Many could not afford travel costs and could not walk long distances if they were accompanied by small children. Women were also reluctant to attend evening classes because they feared returning home after dark in areas they considered to be unsafe.

In some areas women were afraid of racial attack, and in some cases this made them withdraw from society. Nina illustrates the effects of racial harassment. A 32 year old Iraqi woman, Nina had to pass through a largely white social housing estate on her way to college. Whilst standing at the bus stop two white people swore and shouted abuse at her about her religion and for wearing the hijab. She was terrified and the incident undermined her confidence and made her reluctant to walk to college.

The Muslim women felt that global politics and the increased politicisation of Islam had led to rising resentment and mistrust, which had increased racism. The 9/11 attacks, the Iraq war and the 2005 London bombings were all believed to have increased tensions between Muslims and other communities. Symbols such as the headscarf have been associated with the stereotyped view that all Muslims are terrorists. Some respondents said that increased Islamophobia had a significant impact on Muslim women because of their dress code. Faced with so many barriers to studying, some women simply gave up.

Women migrants were particularly isolated in the UK and were more affected than men. As one Somali woman in her mid-thirties pointed out, '...women suffer much more, maybe because women stay most of the time at home ... we spend all of our time alone with no one to help us'. The loss of traditional social networks and the dearth of opportunities to develop new ones, made women feel vulnerable and exacerbated the problem of isolation (Goodson and Phillimore, 2008). They were predisposed to mental health issues, particularly in circumstances where isolation was compounded by domestic problems. These sometimes included domestic violence and the memory of traumatic gender specific experiences, such as being raped in their country of origin. Some were preoccupied with the possibility of having to return and were terrified of further persecution:

> Those who were raped back home, they are very afraid to go back home and face those who raped them. (Rwandan woman, 27)

Levels of depression were particularly high amongst new migrant women. Many took medication for their condition. Burnett and Peel (2001) argue that reducing isolation and dependence through spending more time productively in education and work is more effective than medication in relieving depression and anxiety. NIACE has called for the development of more courses tailored to the needs of female migrants (Aldridge *et al*, 2005; Waddington *et al*, 2005). Certainly, women in our studies wanted to access ESOL and be less isolated but while they recognised the potential offered by learning they felt powerless to overcome the multiple barriers to accessing it.

Professionals and newcomers with trade backgrounds

Newcomers with professional and trade backgrounds were keen to access employment as quickly as possible. Their employment experiences ranged from working in a family business or eking out a living in subsistence agriculture, to running corporations or achieving the pinnacle of a profession. Refugee professionals often held qualifications from their country of origin that were not automatically recognised by professional bodies in the UK. Those wishing to gain employment in the health sector, for example, had either to take further academic programmes or periods of supervised practice or follow an adaptation programme. Nurses had to complete the Overseas Nurses Programme to be registered by the General Medical Council. Acknowledgement of the needs of health care professionals has led to the development of a dedicated adaptation programme at the Faculty of Health, Birmingham City University (Peacock, 2006) but funds to cover the cost of course fees, childcare and travel are limited.

Recognition of their prior skills, overseas qualifications and experience is a huge problem as opportunities for new arrivals to access adaptation or accreditation of prior experience or learning (APEL) programmes are sparse. Addo's case is typical. In the Sudan Addo was a senior partner in a law firm and specialised in Shari'a and criminal law. He left Sudan after campaigning against resettlement and ethnic cleansing in the north of the country, arriving in the UK on Christmas Day 1999. But when interviewed in the summer of 2003, he was still awaiting the outcome of his asylum application. He had tried to re-qualify as a solicitor but was told by the Law Society that he must start university again. He was working in a hostel to save the money to pay his international student fees, as well as volunteering with two refugee community groups. If he is granted leave to remain he plans to specialise in immigration law. He is aware that to be successful he must re-train and is willing to start again because he is determined to return to his former career.

Most newcomers had anticipated that the UK system and work environment would differ from what they were familiar with and sought to engage in some kind of activity in order to get their skills recognised. They were often surprised to find that no systems were in place to enable them to validate their skills. Many were willing to undertake some form of further training to adapt their existing skills or acquire new ones but were held back by a lack of vocational ESOL, vocational orientation and APEL.

The dearth of opportunities for recognition meant that many professionals had little choice but to start again regardless of the length or breadth of their experience. Whilst some like Addo were prepared to do this, others, especially the more mature, felt they had neither the time nor resources to re-train. Several of the highly qualified newcomers in our research were frustrated at being told they had to 'restart at the bottom' when they were fully qualified, in one case with twenty years' experience.

Reluctance to start over again was in some cases a pragmatic decision influenced by age and circumstance. Jalil, for example, who arrived from Iran six years before being involved in our research, had worked for many years as a qualified accountant. In his mid fifties, he did not see re-training as an option but was keen to work as soon as possible, perhaps in the financial sector. Having exhausted his efforts to re-enter finance, he accepted a job in a warehouse and was working as a packer. Lazar, a Russian gynaecologist in his fifties, also saw little point in studying for four years when his career would continue for no more than a decade. Instead he tried to use his skills as a carer, and sought work in a care home for the elderly.

The prospects for professionals wishing to re-train in specialist areas such as the health service were poor because courses to convert qualifications were expensive, often requiring sixteen hours or more contact time, and rarely offered placements that would give them the work experience and employers' references they needed to gain work. Newcomers recounted being told by JCP advisers that their training and experience from outside the UK was worthless.

Conflicting advice from JCP and certain professional bodies about re-qualification also caused problems. Some who got places on courses that would enable them to re-train were then told that they could not pursue the opportunity because they would be in breach of the sixteen hour rule and their benefits would be withdrawn.

Often refugee professionals were actively discouraged by their JCP advisers from accessing courses that might aid their re-qualification. Several claimants told us how they had been advised to apply for any job in order to secure work in the short term and to forget their previous experience and start again at the bottom. Advice of this kind undermined their motivation to learn, as the case of a former medical student illustrates. Adel, a 23 year old Iranian, was told by his JCP adviser to drop two of his four A-Levels because he would not be eligible for Jobseeker's Allowance if he studied them all in one year. To remain eligible for benefits he must study the extra A-Levels the following year. Not only do these rules slow progress, but they inevitably keep refugees dependent on benefits for longer instead of earning their living. This aspiring doctor gave up medicine and opted for a career for which the university entry requirements were lower.

Many students had completed degrees in their country of origin but found that the UK NARIC system downgraded their qualifications – often to FE level. There were few mechanisms for these students to APEL their existing learning into credits for a UK degree. Instead of topping up their existing learning they had to study for an entire UK degree if they wanted a UK recognised qualification in their specialist area. Again, some were reluctant to go back to the beginning, especially those like Jalil and Lazar who had been working in their profession for some years and did not see re-qualification as a logical option at this stage. Some of the younger people were prepared to start again but were then thwarted by the insistence of some universities that they should be charged fees at the International Student rate, even if they had refugee status. The universities have discretion about charges yet many applied the higher rate to anyone who had lived in the UK for less than three years. This additional cost was an insurmountable barrier for most new migrants.

Lack of knowledge about learning opportunities was an issue even for professionals. They struggled to access information about university courses or any courses apart from ESOL and, as we have seen, ESOL provision did not prepare newcomers for HE or professional work. Over time the multiple stumbling blocks left them feeling hopeless and unconfident. In these circumstances the pressure to actively seek any employment often made them resign themselves to unemployment or low-skilled jobs, with the consequent loss of their professional identity.

Young people

Many young people arrived in the UK with incomplete qualifications, their education having been interrupted by civil unrest or persecution. They generally faced two issues. First, they had failed to qualify in their chosen occupation or profession and had no evidence of the progress they had made towards this goal. Second, they had little or no employment experience and no practical skills to equip them for employment in a particular field. Without the right qualifications or skills they feared being pushed into work that was of little interest.

Young people who spent some time in education in the UK struggled in the early stages of their engagement with the system. Improving their English language proficiency was considered the first step to engaging in the wider learning which was seen as the main gateway to employment. But young people adapted more easily to UK learning systems than mature students and those who had been employed in their countries of origin. They were pre-pared to work hard to make a place for themselves in the UK and were more likely than older newcomers to aspire to go to university.

Young people who spoke English in their country of origin adapted relatively easily to the UK system and had little difficulty in engaging with UK learning. People from former British colonies found some similarities in the UK edu-cation system and were able to integrate relatively quickly into classes. It was common for young people to find differences between the UK education system and those of their countries of origin, notably styles of teaching. The young people who did not speak English felt that UK education was more challenging but also more interesting. They appreciated what they saw as a plentiful supply of books, course materials and equipment.

Their stories illustrate a few of the difficulties the new migrants encountered when they tried to access further education. One young man who had entered the country at age sixteen had attended college part time, to learn English and computer skills. When he turned eighteen he was told, quite incorrectly, that his support would be withdrawn so he could no longer attend. A similar, frustrating experience was recounted by a seventeen year old girl who had started an NVQ course and then been told to leave because she was not old enough to enrol. Her earlier attempt to access a different course had been blocked because of uncertainties about funding. Other young people post sixteen reported that they struggled to find proper guidance. Inaccurate and conflicting information from differing services and the lack of coordination between them was particularly problematic:

> There is a lack of knowledge about who is responsible, a lack of coordination between NASS, Home Office, Social Services and Job Centre; I go from one to the other. (Somali man, 17)

Iva, a seventeen year old Yugoslavian, typified a young person who might easily drop-out of education if unable to access adequate support and advice. At the time of interview she had been in the UK for four months. She lived with and cared for her younger brother, aged fifteen. They had no surviving family. She had little experience of attending school, apart from four years between the ages of eight and twelve. Her brother was more integrated because he was attending school. Iva's life revolved around attending ESOL, which she enjoyed, and looking after her brother. She knew little about learning opportunities and lacked the confidence to ask for information. She was not aware that she could join a library, or ask about courses in cooking, the subject that interested her most. The only support she had received was an occasional visit by a social worker. Attending ESOL provided Iva with the opportunity to learn English and talk to other people. When her ESOL classes finished she did not know what to do next. Iva needed specialist support: although she wanted to continue learning, her poor language skills left her struggling to articulate her needs. She did not want to appear demanding but clearly needed guidance.

Like other migrants, young people awaiting an asylum decision found that their insecurity distracted them from their learning. Many were also worried about the asylum cases of family members who had travelled with them to the UK.

Conclusions and implications for policy

Our evidence shows that the learning needs of new arrivals are not being fully met. Their ability to engage in, or achieve, within education and learning systems was found to be constrained by numerous often interrelated factors. Furthermore, our existing qualification framework allowed few opportunities for new migrants to have non-UK skills and qualifications recognised. The dearth of initiatives to actively employ learning as a tool for integration such as those that exist in Northern Europe (Phillimore *et al*, 2005) means that newcomers have little chance to develop their employability, either as asylum seekers awaiting a decision, or once they have the right to work.

Motivation to learn and acquire new skills, in particular English language, was high amongst newcomers because they saw English as the most direct route to enhancing employability and future prospects. Yet access to ESOL classes was difficult and the quality of classes generally poor. In addition there was little specialisation or flexibility in provision. Few students had progressed through the entire system to the point where they had achieved employment level language skills. The majority of newcomers could not access the ESOL contact hours they felt they needed, because of the limited number of hours on offer or the JCP sixteen-hour rule.

Colleges should be encouraged to offer more intensive ESOL provision and the sixteen hour rule needs to be reviewed. It would make sense to allow new migrants to study as many hours as they need to improve their language and literacy skills to the point where they can access the workplace.

Furthermore, colleges need to offer smaller group learning. Improving initial assessments and streaming by learning ability, rather than simply language ability, would help to ensure that language learning needs are better met. More flexibility is required between different learning levels, whilst the building of review mechanisms into the learning process would help enhance movement between these different levels and help speed up the learning process.

At present most ESOL courses provide little opportunity for highly skilled migrants. The Level 2 ceiling for free ESOL courses creates a barrier that prevents them from progressing to advanced level English courses. It also creates an obstacle for highly skilled refugees to improve their English to the point where they can access employment. There is a clear need to increase the range of higher level courses to offer progression routes through ESOL and pathways into wider learning. Clearer links between ESOL courses and the International English Language Testing System (IELTS), which is required for health care professionals and entry into universities, would assist those wishing to move in this direction. It is hoped that the new policy of LSC to fund IELTS 6/7 and Cambridge Proficiency at national base may help facilitate this process (Grover, 2006).

There is also a strong case for providing more courses that go beyond basic conversation and teach the language and culture of the workplace. The need for more vocational ESOL was frequently expressed. New vocational courses aimed at specific sectors would improve the employability of professionals and those with a trade background. Those with experience in a specific area of employment would like to see more ESOL provision linked to wider vocational options to enable them to learn new skills or adapt existing skills to their specific sector, whilst improving their vocational language skills. The likelihood of employed newcomers engaging in any type of training depends on how such opportunities would fit around existing work commitments. More flexibility in the format and delivery times of existing training is required, as is the development of more work based learning opportunities to enable learning to become more accessible to all.

Access to HE is extremely difficult for asylum seekers and some refugees because of the high international tuition fees. Some people had been waiting for years for a decision about their asylum application. Eventually they exhausted all the affordable studying options because they could not progress beyond ESOL or FE level training. Although the Home Office has tried to speed up the asylum procedure there still appears to be much room for improvement. Expedition of the asylum procedure would help successful applicants engage with learning more quickly and prevent some of the problems associated with exclusion from education such as diminished confidence, isolation and mental health problems, lack of motivation, de-skilling, under-employment and unemployment.

Most new migrants, regardless of status, find it difficult to cover the full costs of learning. Women were far more likely to be excluded from education because of responsibility for childcare. Although the LSC made available £30 million in childcare for learners aged twenty and over, and a further £12 million to local authority led transport to remove the barriers for learners with disabilities and or those on low-incomes (LSC, 2006c), there is no standard approach to assessing eligibility for support. Few newcomers receive any assistance with their learning costs. The reduction in Access to Learning Funds in recent years has exacerbated this problem. Policy makers should be encouraged to increase subsidies or grants and to ensure that LSC funds for disadvantaged learners are accessible to new migrant learners to address their extreme levels of financial hardship.

Using education and training to provide opportunities for new migrants to integrate, whether they are asylum seekers, refugees or A8 migrant workers, is increasingly important in the light of the emphasis on social cohesion.

5

Providing learning for new migrants

...they [newcomers] always want to learn more, they are like sponges! They are very positive about learning new things and quite ambitious on the whole. We used to have groups that would walk five miles to class. (ESOL tutor)

The previous chapter showed how crucial access to learning opportunities is to the integration of new migrants. Most important for those of working age was to gain access to employment, achieve economic self-sufficiency and provide for themselves and their families (Somerville, 2006, 2007; Sriskandarajah, 2005). Education and training are a vital part of the journey towards securing sustainable employment.

Through accessing learning opportunities newcomers can be supported in the recognition, conversion and top-up of their existing skills, experience and qualifications, and the acquisition of new skills. And those who speak little English need to acquire adequate language skills before they can engage with any other forms of learning.

Another benefit of participating in education and training is the chance to learn about UK culture and systems. As we saw in the previous chapter, the learning environment offers newcomers the opportunity to mix with other students albeit in an institutional setting. Meeting a range of different people can help the process of settling in to a new country, reducing feelings of loneliness and boosting self-esteem and confidence but the world of learning, is hard for newcomers to access. Entitlements to learning are said to be confusing (RAGU, 2006), a problem borne out by the experience of the newcomers and information, advice and guidance (IAG) providers in our studies.

Looking at newcomers' experiences of education and training provision has helped us understand what they want, the extent to which their needs have been met and the barriers they face. It is also important to consider the challenges of meeting their needs from the perspective of those offering learning provision in an area in which there has been virtually no research. The research undertaken in the West Midlands provides an overview of the types of learning offered by education and training providers and to whom they are offering it. The data in this chapter is based on 137 questionnaire returns and 42 face-to-face interviews with education providers. Our research also explored the role of education and training in supporting integration, and as a purposeful, self-development activity during the waiting period. It looked at barriers to participation and delivery of learning provision, learner support, issues around retention and progression and reports on what has been achieved to date and what remains to be achieved.

Learning providers offering services to newcomers span the whole spectrum of adult learning providers in the UK system: Further Education (FE) colleges, private organisations, voluntary and community organisations and local authorities. All were included in our research. Very few of the providers surveyed were accessed by large numbers of newcomers. For example, just over 50 per cent of those who responded were providing for fewer than fifteen newcomers, whereas only 20 per cent of providers had more than a hundred newcomers in attendance.

The profile of new migrants accessing provision

Providers recorded socio-demographic information about their students and collected information through learners' self-declaration on their initial learner registrations or similar systems. This enabled them to provide at least partial profiles of their newcomer students. Unsurprisingly, the nationalities of individuals engaged in learning were as varied as those of the asylum seekers dispersed to the region. The main ethnic groups and nationalities accessing learning provision in the region were: Iraqi, Iranian, Congolese, Somali, Sudanese, Zimbabwean, Eritrean, Afghani, Chinese, Czech, Kosovan, Russian, Albanian, Turkish, Kurdish, and Burundian.

More men than women across the region accessed learning, unless the programme was specifically targeted at women. The majority of asylum seekers accessing general provision were male, whereas amongst those with refugee status, there was a greater mix of men and women. The balance between men and women depended on the type of provision and where recruitment took place. For instance, more men were taking part in a warehouse training course and more women than men were recruited through a Sure Start project.

Ages varied from those aged sixteen to twenty and adults of 21 to 44 age range. The number of older learners was comparatively low. The profile of learners in the study matches the general age and gender profile of asylum seekers and refugees in the region and in the UK generally (ONS, 2007; Sargeant and Forna, 2001). That fewer women were engaged in learning is exacerbated by the lack of availability of childcare for women newcomers with dependent children, as we saw in the previous chapter.

Learning provision

The majority of providers offered solely mainstream courses which were open to all students. Only six respondents of the 137 providers offered discrete provision for newcomers. Here the tutors could concentrate on the particular needs and circumstances of newcomers and offer a more welcoming and positive learning environment. Several providers argued however that mainstream provision was preferable because it encouraged integration with local learners. Some providers were anxious that offering specialist provision might make other learners think newcomers were given special treatment. In the main, providers believed that most newcomers preferred mainstream provision, although discrete provision was identified as suitable for certain groups such as women from particular cultures or for those who had arrived very recently. The newcomers themselves could certainly see the benefits of being engaged in mainstream classes because this offered one of the few environments where they could mix with members of established communities.

Less than half of the learning providers collected data about the provision being accessed by newcomers. Where monitoring information was recorded, the data mirrored the situation as reported in Chapter Four by newcomers themselves. Most newcomers were accessing basic education, including ESOL, literacy and numeracy. Far fewer were studying other subjects, mainly vocational courses such as art and design, business and administration, construction, engineering, hair and beauty, healthcare, hotel and catering/ hospitality, transport and ICT. Still fewer were studying academic subjects such as humanities, maths and sciences, perhaps with a view to entering higher level study in further or higher education institutions.

English for Speakers of Other Languages

In most cases newcomers attended existing ESOL classes although there were a couple of cases of demand being so great that discrete provision was specifically designed in response. ESOL was provided in different ways, most frequently as a stand-alone subject, but in some instances embedded into courses about British culture and living in the UK. ESOL with a vocational focus was offered by only a handful of providers, for example those who offered IT courses with ESOL integrated into the programme of learning. The type of provision on offer was limited by the availability of appropriate locations and accommodation and the levels of provision required.

Not many learning providers said they had waiting lists for their ESOL courses. Waiting times varied between two weeks and one term. This presents a very different picture from that described by a good many newcomers who reported very long waiting lists. Perhaps learning providers could simply not supply waiting list information as they did not monitor the situation. Tutors expressed concerns about waiting lists and how they were managed:

> The college puts everybody on the waiting list, even if it is not realistic, even if they have to wait for a year. They do not direct them to another college. (Tutor)

Some ESOL provision was available on a roll-on, roll-off basis and was therefore more flexible. But the vast majority of ESOL courses began at a fixed starting point, usually the beginning of a term, and required all learners to begin at the same point. This inflexibility may account for some of the long waiting times. In cases where they had missed the enrolment period students had to wait for a new course to start before being offered a place.

The range and levels of ESOL qualification on offer also varied. On the whole, provision reflected the experiences of the newcomers we interviewed in that most courses awarded qualifications only up to Entry Level 3, with a few providers offering higher levels, for example, up to Level 2. As we have heard, the skew towards basic provision is a major problem for newcomers. Most employment, except perhaps very low-skilled jobs, requires English at higher level (see Aldridge *et al*, 2005). Only a tiny number of providers delivered ESOL provision specifically focused on language for work, and it was felt that this was often too narrow in its focus so could be uninteresting and irrelevant to learners whose primary concern was to gain employment. Tutors expressed concerns that Entry level classes did little to help newcomers to communicate properly in English, let alone to progress their learning or get a job:

> They might have a certificate but it does not mean that they learned English. Entry 2 Listening and Speaking certificate does not mean that they can speak English. It doesn't even mean that they can read the Sun newspaper. It is a very low level. Entry level 3 means the English of average nine year olds in this country. (Tutor)

Perceptions about learning needs

In order to provide services to meet the needs of newcomers and to enhance their access to learning, learning providers have to understand those needs. While providers across the region were able to make some generalisations about the needs and aspirations of newcomers, they were conscious that new migrant communities are highly diverse and have many different needs. In some ways their motivation was little different from those of the general UK population: some were very focused, eager to progress and had clear goals, while others were less so.

The newcomers' pattern of learning differed according to their asylum status. Asylum seekers focused initially on learning English and then progressed to further education. Once a positive decision was received their focus moved to employability and courses that could enhance the likelihood of gaining work. Providers found that the length of time asylum seekers waited for a decision affected their motivation. Those who had spent months or years awaiting an outcome of their claim tended to be less motivated than new arrivals.

The main aspiration and need identified by providers was for newcomers to improve their English language skills. Providers were well aware that limitations in language ability prevented newcomers from fulfilling their aspirations to work in their original trade or profession or to move into a profession more suited to the UK labour market or to their new circumstances.

The new migrants who were highly qualified were usually the most motivated. There was widespread recognition amongst providers that newcomers with professional backgrounds were, however, likely to need intensive language training, study skills and assistance in seeking recognition for their qualifications. Providers were well aware that gaining employment was the refugees' main priority and identified a strong demand for vocational provision, especially for those who were less skilled or qualified or where adaptation was needed. Training that would lead to a UK qualification with established progression routes was much sought after, but as we have shown, not widely available.

Access to information about learning opportunities

We saw in the previous chapter that new migrants had difficulty in gaining information about learning opportunities. It was not readily accessible and the consequent reliance on friends or family meant they were too often misinformed. According to the learning providers' recorded information newcomers mostly found their courses by self-referral or 'access by themselves'.

All learning providers are meant to make information available about alternative provision if they are unable to provide it themselves. But information was seldom tailored to the needs of new migrants.

Information about courses was mainly in written format, so was of little use to people with poor language skills. Less than half (45%) of providers who offered learning to newcomers produced information in languages other than English – including Punjabi, Urdu, Hindi, Gujarati, Bengali, French, German, Spanish, Portuguese, Persian/Farsi/Dari, Arabic, Kurdish/ Sorani, Russian and Chinese (Mandarin and Cantonese). But these languages generally reflected the settled minority ethnic communities in the UK and providers recognised that few of the first languages spoken by the new migrants were represented. Whilst promotional materials aimed at raising awareness of learning opportunities amongst newcomers were widely distributed in public places such as libraries, voluntary organisations, Jobcentres, asylum support services or on the Internet, fewer than a quarter of providers, most of them in Birmingham, had used Refugee Community Organisations (RCOs) to publicise their programmes. Perhaps this tendency reflects the size of the city and its long history of inward migration, as well as the larger concentration of RCOs in the city than in the other dispersal areas.

Difficulties in attracting newcomer learners

Learning providers sometimes define groups as particularly hard to reach, yet 'hard to reach' is a contested concept. It refers mainly to the experience of mainstream providers and is generally rejected by voluntary and community sector providers, who are closer to the target groups and may engage more readily with newcomers and other 'hard to reach' groups. However, it was evident from the colleges participating in our study that they viewed some groups of newcomers as particularly challenging to provide for. They pointed to women, those with health problems, physical disabilities, or special educational needs and older people. Providers acknowledged that people with mental health problems often felt isolated and were particularly difficult to engage.

The providers identified the factors they believed underpinned the challenges in reaching certain groups of newcomers. They found traditional forms of marketing learning opportunities to be less successful with newcomers than with other potential learners, because the college was advertising its services in the wrong place or the wrong language. Providers identified cultural factors particularly saying that some women might feel uncomfortable participating in a mixed gender class. They also assumed that UK styles of delivering learning might be very different from that in countries of origin and possibly not as accessible. They recognised the need to offer courses to help newcomers understand how the UK college system works. Both learning providers and potential learners struggled to understand the funding regulations and entitlements for newcomers, and this prevented some from engaging in learning. Keeping up to date with current policy around new migrants' entitlements to learning and frequent policy changes were described as 'difficult' and 'confusing' (for example, LSC, 2006).

Retention and barriers

We heard from newcomers about their struggle to maintain attendance on courses and how some dropped out when they felt they were not making satisfactory progress. Retention rates varied greatly between providers with anything from 10 per cent to 80 per cent of newcomers failing to complete learning programmes. Many tutors reported that drop-out was a major problem:

> We constantly lose students and receive new students. The profile of students changes enormously in six weeks ... There is a very high turnover of students and it is difficult to keep records. (Tutor)

> For asylum seekers and refugees, relative to other students, success and attendance rates were lower. They rarely finish the whole academic year. (Tutor)

The Learning and Skills Council (LSC) monitors retention and achievement rates within the ESOL provision they fund. Access to this data allowed us to calculate the drop-out rates across the West Midlands (see Table 5.1) and found these bore little relationship to the patterns of engagement described by providers and tutors. LSC data indicated a low drop-out rate and a relatively small difference in those between asylum seekers and refugees. This, combined with tutors' conviction that drop-out rates were far higher than those recorded, warranted further investigation. With positive determinations for asylum seekers resting at around 25 per cent after appeal (Home Office, 2006), and therefore 75 per cent of all asylum seekers no longer eligible for ESOL, we would expect asylum seeker drop-out rates to be far higher (perhaps around 75%).

Colleges were concerned about their ESOL drop-out rates because they are one of the key means by which their performance is measured by the LSC. The LSC data is collected by means of a census. Colleges could enter data for all students enrolled on their courses, but inputting it is an onerous task. It is probable that colleges are only inputting the data of those students 'on the books' at census times. They are not going to be paid for the students who dropped out after a few weeks so there is no incentive to include them in the statistics. It is also highly likely that if a learner drops out after generating only a small amount of funding, an institution may make a strategic decision not to submit the learner enrolment and write off the funding in order to show a better success rate. Certainly our interviews with newcomers suggested that many students dropped out fairly soon if they thought they had been placed at the wrong level. It seems that those who were recorded were the students more likely to stay on their courses.

With the student record data being so central to monitoring of the LSC it is important that it includes a full picture of all students so that high drop-out rates are quickly identified and research undertaken to explore the reasons why. This knowledge would certainly benefit tutors who want to take action to better meet the needs of their students and to improve retention rates amongst newcomer students.

	% Drop-out Refugees	% Drop-out Asylum seekers
1	19.1%	25.35%
2	17.2%	16.52
3	14.9%	34.21
Entry	15.6%	25.52
Unclassified	11.81%	1.21
Pre-entry level	0	0.24
Total	15.78%	18.52

Table 5.1 – LSC drop-out rates

There was uncertainty amongst the providers about why newcomers were not completing their courses. Little action was taken to follow up early leavers and they could only speculate about the reasons why newcomers stopped attending college:

> There are still a lot of unhappy students and we don't know why they are dropping out. (Tutor)

Other than those they believe had left because they had found employment, providers identified some of the reasons why newcomers were unable to continue their learning. Over time providers had become familiar with some of the common difficulties faced by newcomers and were aware of the transience and stress associated with the asylum process, the lack of financial support with travel and childcare costs and the wide range of competing priorities such as housing, family commitments, health and children's schooling, all of which could, as we have seen distract newcomers from their studies. Whilst newcomers complained about poor materials, tutors defended their position, but confirmed that colleges failed to provide appropriate resources:

> Very little resources are provided. It's hard to find the right resources. (Tutor)

Although it may be too early to identify any improvements in the experiences of ESOL students, some tutors felt that the Skills for Life packs issued by the DfES had markedly improved the quality of resources available to them and the students:

> Now the Government provides the ESOL material, which is great. You used to be stuck in the middle of nowhere with no resources. Now you can get detailed packs for each student. (Tutor)

Other reasons were given to help explain why ESOL teaching was so inconsistent. An extremely high turnover rate of ESOL teachers was a widespread problem. The fact that the majority of tutors are paid on an hourly basis with no job security beyond the hours they are allocated on a weekly basis was not considered to help matters. In the worst case scenario high drop-out rates meant that courses were cancelled altogether after a few weeks, leaving the tutor out of pocket. In addition, hourly paid tutors were not sent on training courses or, if these were offered tutors were not paid for attending. They were not invited to team meetings and were seldom told about new developments. Many tutors did not feel part of the overall teaching structure and complained that management of ESOL was poor and run by people who did not understand the system. They felt that compared to other departments in the college ESOL received insufficient investment, despite being lucrative for the college. Tutors said that over time they became disenchanted with the profession and sought more secure alternatives.

They expected the exodus of tutors from ESOL to accelerate following announcement of the LSC's new priorities: cessation of free ESOL for asylum seekers in the country less than six months, and means testing for other students:

> We are constantly losing good teachers as well due to lack of stability and job insecurity. One of my good friends decided to have training as driving instructor, as a result of the last changes. (Tutor)

Given the job's lack of appeal many experienced teachers left and were replaced with new recruits, some of them reported not to have the interpersonal skills to teach. Up to September 2003, anyone who had a standard of education equivalent to that required for entry into higher education and who had completed an English teaching course lasting four or five weeks full time, could apply for a job as an ESOL teacher. This level of qualification may be well below the learners' needs.

Since September 2003, a teaching qualification based on the Further Education National Training Organisation (FENTO) Standards for Teaching and Learning at Level 4 of the National Qualifications Framework or Subject Specification for Teacher of ESOL at Level 4 is required. However, there are no formal requirements for existing teachers to re-train or update their skills or teaching practice (Grover, 2006). One tutor had been seeking to retrain but could not join the course because, ironically, she did not have an ongoing ESOL class at the right level. She told us:

> If you have classes you don't have time to do the course and if you have time they won't allow you to do the course. (Tutor)

Also thought to be affecting retention was the incentive competition developing between providers. Some colleges were reported to offer incentives such as free bus passes, childcare or even cash to encourage students to enrol. The use of incentives was said to lead to competition between the providers rather than co-operation, and some newcomer students had changed provider to take advantage of incentives. While the stimulation of demand for learning among newcomers and removal of financial barriers to access is important, careful planning across sub-regions is needed to ensure that there is no unhelpful competition between providers and that asylum seekers should not be able to 'work the system', as reported in the case of some students who had enrolled, and received free bus passes, then stopped attending.

> Again due to the nature of these students, many hadn't attended an academic course before. They just didn't understand [the] discipline and commitment required. They would sign up for the course and do not carry on. I truly felt that a majority, if not the majority but a lot of the students, were there only to get a free bus pass. (Tutor)

Other providers put their high retention rates down to the fact that they only offered short courses, whilst a number of their students expressed the need for more intensive learning opportunities. Indeed, one college changed the enrolment period of a course from twelve to three months in a bid to increase retention rates:

> Now we enrol students for three months. This is to solve the problem with retention. (Tutor)

Other than tutors' comments, there was little acknowledgement of the problems raised by newcomers about poor quality teaching. But it was acknowledged that better assessment and ongoing support could help students to remain in learning and perhaps progress more effectively. The pace at which people developed their language skills was observed to differ quite significantly, with younger people generally learning most quickly. Many providers were aware that newcomers' previous experiences of education meant that some did not need to 'learn to learn' and were capable of learning quickly. These students would have preferred intensive courses, if they were available. Others, who had received little education in their country of origin, tended to have to start from the beginning:

> Albanians in Kosovo were out of education. So we had a group of young Albanians with little education. So they didn't have the tools to learn a new language. (Tutor)

While they recognised differences in learning ability, providers were also aware that good IAG that focused specifically on the needs of newcomers, including information to assist with social and vocational integration, were not always available in the college and learning institutions. The dearth of established and signposted progression routes within learning provider organisations meant that there was no clarity about progression. Providers recognised that the provision which did exist was often inappropriate. It was clear to some providers that, in the absence of suitable provision for newcomers within existing courses, more outreach and people-centred approaches were needed so that curricula were based upon identified need. In addition, progression routes, while obvious to tutor and student, were often constrained by college systems:

> Exams take place at a particular day and particular time. Some are ready to take the exams and move another level, but the college structure doesn't allow that. There should be on demand tests to move students flexibly, so that quick learners can pass to the next level without waiting to the end of the year...or else they get bored and leave. (Tutor)

Sometimes the barriers and drop-out reasons were beyond the control of learning providers. For example, as we saw in Chapter Four, some newcomers faced prejudice from the local community and employers, which made them reluctant to participate in learning because they were afraid of racism and discrimination. And as refugees themselves observed, the pressure on them, as on other benefit claimants, to gain paid employment as soon as possible exacerbated the conflict between short and long term goals. Providers could see that skilled and educated newcomers, once fully trained, would be able to contribute a great deal more to the UK economy than if they were removed from benefits in the short term to take a low skilled temporary job. But the providers, like the newcomers, were powerless to change the situation and were equally frustrated by the Jobcentre Plus (JCP) sixteen-hour rule.

Learner and learning support

After they located learning provision, newcomers needed advice and guidance to help them to select the learning programme that would be most suitable. And they required ongoing support to help them understand progression options or how they could link ESOL provision with wider learning opportunities. Yet newcomers, as we saw, received little or no guidance. Although most learning providers offered IAG during enrolment, initial assessment interviews by student services or through taster sessions, their IAG services were too general to be of much use to newcomers. They were aware that this was the case.

Some providers had built up a bank of knowledge and information over time so they could respond to their newcomer students, but this was purely as a result of their experiences of working with asylum seeker and refugee students and not due to any specific policy of their institution. Staff who gave IAG, whether initial and ongoing, included personal advisers, training co-ordinators, recruitment consultants, support workers, guidance workers, and trained tutors, usually ESOL tutors. Advice was usually given on a one-to-one basis, although one provider offered group advice and another delivered a specific training programme which offered extended IAG through learning in group and one-to-one sessions.

On the whole, providers believed that ongoing advice and guidance was delivered as an integral part of any course and that opportunities for additional support were available outside of the classroom. The quality of initial assessments was considered to be high on the whole and most providers were confident that they could help with personal and social as well as educational issues as they arose, adapting their response as required. These views conflicted markedly with those of the newcomers. This divergence in the views of providers and newcomers' perceptions of the usefulness of IAG could possibly be because there was no student monitoring, which might have helped determine satisfaction levels or progression rates. Some voluntary and community learning providers did not know what happened to their clients once they had assisted their entry into college, as they did not routinely seek or receive feedback. As we will see in Chapter Six, this was clearly an issue that other education or IAG providers were seeking to address by implementing better systems to record and understand the patterns of referral destinations amongst their newcomer clients.

Where college IAG staff were not specifically trained to assist asylum seekers and refugees, ESOL tutors often stepped in to fill this role. Providers found that their ESOL tutors were spending a great deal of time giving learning-related advice and guidance and assisting with other social and personal issues, at the expense of the ESOL lessons. As one ESOL tutors observed:

> One third of your time goes into teaching and two thirds goes to things like reading doctors' notes, phoning the Home Office etc, etc. (Tutor)

Whilst most providers believed their generic in-college systems were good, they recognised that there was room for improving the services offered to asylum seeker and refugee students and that specialist training was required for staff who dealt with them. They needed to know about issues such as financial and other support. It was widely acknowledged that structural support such as covering transport costs, childcare and funding for extra costs made a marked difference to newcomers learning experiences. A provider pointed out that:

> The educational maintenance money for 16-19 year olds leads to better retention rates, and if the learners are supported in this way, they do better. If you consider this as true then the reverse is also true: without the extra financial support it is difficult for learners like asylum seekers to do well and complete their courses. (Provider)

Many providers offered a range of learner and learning support for newcomers and thirty offered language support. Twenty-nine offered childcare facilities or support, much of which was provided free of charge. Several providers offered bus passes or help with travel costs. Some went the 'extra mile', as one provider put it, supporting asylum seekers and refugees through homework clubs and informal help to access services such as housing, form filling and applications, registering with doctors and dentists, and opening bank accounts. Another provider, as part of their contract, continued to provide up to thirteen weeks IAG support to refugees who had completed their course and gone on to work. Three organisations employed staff to assist refugees with CVs, job search, completing applications and work related tasks. Another ran a placement scheme, with 60 hours of learning plus a 35-hour work placement. This provider reported how work experience helped newcomers to move on and increased their confidence and knowledge of the system. The extent to which providers were able to offer general or work experience support was influenced by national funding policy or the availability of local funding.

It was not always possible to give personal support to deal with an individual's health and well-being, particularly with their emotional and mental health. The lack of support in this area affected some students' ability to engage appropriately:

> Some students may have emotional problems, trauma and low energy. This might be understood by inexperienced teachers as laziness. (Tutor).

Providers, in particular the private organisations, were sometimes expected to teach ESOL to people referred to their services who clearly needed mental health support before they could focus on learning. The providers felt inadequately equipped to deal with such situations:

> Many asylum seekers and refugees have a lot of emotional baggage which we are not able to effectively deal with; we are not equipped as tutors and providers. We need help that we can refer people on to, people who specialise in this area, not just more staff awareness of the issues. (Provider)

New migrants with particular learning support needs, such as dyslexia, were particularly hard to support because they needed intensive help that simply was not available. Newcomers' pre-occupation with the many difficulties they faced with no support rendered them unable to achieve their potential and provided a distraction for tutors and other learners. As one tutor observed: '...they have so many personal problems. They weren't ready to embark on an academic course'.

This was why one provider had chosen to provide bespoke courses which gave information about services that newcomers needed to know about, such as going to the doctor. A few providers suggested that cultural orientation programmes for newcomers should be developed, and that providers might have a role in raising awareness among local communities to dispel prejudice. Most expressed a desire to employ a member of staff who had the specialist knowledge to help deal with newcomers' problems – but all lacked the funds to make such an appointment.

On the whole, newcomers had access to the same learning resources as every other learner in the institution did. However, just as newcomers did not know about how to seek and understand help, they did not know how to access learning resources. A high proportion (80%) of learning providers offered newcomers access to ICT facilities including the Internet and computers.

Access to the Internet was especially popular. It enabled students to access new resources music or information in their own languages from their country of origin, and it helped them to maintain contact with family members or friends. Many providers offered newcomers access to library facilities and some to leisure and sport facilities. Some offered a variety of different resources including accommodation, a recording studio/theatre, medical services, counselling and welfare assistance, the use of laptop computers or careers advice and information. Staff working with newcomers tried to alert them to the resources on offer.

Public libraries were identified as another important resource, which a number of newcomers were believed to use on a regular basis to access computers and the Internet. Learning providers believed that newcomers visited their local libraries to use computers and access the Internet, and sometimes to gather information from books, audio and videocassettes, grammar books, bilingual dictionaries, newspapers and magazines.

Improvements and developments

Learning providers appreciated that the number of newcomers accessing their services was likely to rise and even those who were not working with asylum seekers or refugees at the time of our research were planning to develop provision for them. With provision for newcomers clearly at an embryonic stage it is important to plan how services might be developed.

Some learning providers thought that setting up provision in locations where newcomers live or in community centres where they felt safe would help to increase take-up, though research from other projects suggests that many refugees, particularly those with previous educational experience, are keen to study in established institutions and see this as more likely to lead to satisfactory and recognised outcomes (Gray *et al*, 2007; Waddington, 2007). Other providers talked about starting or increasing ESOL provision, offering intensive ESOL courses or English programmes suited to professional adaptation; expanding workplace skills provision; developing short work-focused training courses; and reviewing the suitability of all the courses on offer. In some areas providers were planning to explore whether Saturday or evening provision would increase access and were hoping to produce more documentation in a wider range of languages. Some intended adding art and design courses suitable for people with English as a second language and more bespoke programmes. Many of the suggestions the providers made took heed of the types of provision that newcomers indicated they were seeking.

Although they had the ideas and the will to provide the services they knew newcomers needed, the providers were thwarted in their ambitions by their inadequate resources. They argued that they could offer improved support where needed if they had more finance and resources. Learning providers needed funding for development work and one-to-one support as well as for covering course fees and subsistence. Access to Learner Support Funds needed to be increased to help secure greater participation and retention rates among newcomers.

The providers perceived that, in some areas at least, there was a shortage of qualified ESOL tutors experienced in working with asylum seekers and refugees. Providers from across the region suggested that a programme of staff training and support should be developed for existing staff to equip them to work more effectively with all newcomers. They thought that getting the timing right and fitting in ESOL, IAG and staff training with other staff commitments was difficult. The wide range of languages spoken by new-comers had increased demand for interpretation and translation services as well as bilingual tutors. The challenge of dealing with so many languages was expensive. Providers suggested that a free or inexpensive interpretation service was needed to assist in overcoming language barriers. Having a net-work of translators with the appropriate literacy and academic skills might also help. Overall, providers felt they had not had enough financial support to deal with the rapid changes in student need and were convinced that unless the true cost of supporting newcomers was acknowledged they would be unable to make the changes they knew were necessary to help all newcomers realise their potential.

As well as financial constraints, providers felt they were held back by the lack of co-ordination among agencies and organisations working with new-comers. They identified a need to establish a communications network be-tween providers and community groups and to work together to provide visible progression routes. They wanted to see more joined-up working be-tween all the organisations engaged with newcomers, and argued that all agencies, both specialist and mainstream, needed to be encouraged to work together more effectively. At the time of the interviews however, none of the organisations involved in our research had the capacity to take a lead in this area. Even providers who did not have new migrants accessing their provision indicated the need for staff training in this area as they anticipated that there would be demand for such provision in the future. Helping newcomers to assist themselves through the establishment of more self-help and support groups was seen as important and so was the role of refugee community organisations in providing a social setting where newcomers could meet. In the next chapter we examine the role and importance providers play in supporting newcomers access to education, training and employment and their wider integration.

Conclusions

Education providers undoubtedly have a key role in the integration of newcomers. They are the first port of call for most of the newcomers seeking to make a place for themselves in the UK and they provide a key social, as well as learning environment. Providers argued that they are the 'centre of gravity' in newcomers' lives, linking them to the outside world by giving them good IAG, providing relevant and appropriate learning opportunities, and by assisting with support to deal with wider issues. They considered their role to encompass the facilitator of integration as well offering as good learning provision.

Certainly many newcomers felt that colleges were the only places where they felt welcome, and saw learning as the key to their future. Yet there is plenty of evidence that newcomers encounter various barriers to meeting their potential, and that while learning providers are fully aware of these barriers, under the current funding regime they cannot dissolve them. Some barriers may reduce over time, for example, providers might address their inadequate knowledge about how to help newcomers with specific needs and develop staff training. While knowledge will eventually increase through experience, specialist training for college staff, or systematic mentoring relationships with experienced non-competitor organisations would speed the process and improve services for newcomers.

Our research findings point to the need for providers to increase and improve the quality of IAG offered to new migrants, particularly generic information on the availability and usefulness of courses. More specialist expertise is needed to help advise professionals and people with a trade background about possible career and training routes. Systems need to be developed to help convert and link qualifications to jobs and assistance, and personal action plans are needed to help set realistic targets and goals for newcomers to work towards. Newcomers who enter the country near or after the age of sixteen need learning opportunities to be better coordinated so they can access the most appropriate learning for their needs. They would benefit immensely from guidance related to their abilities and interests as soon as possible after their arrival so they become engaged in the system before they become de-motivated.

The politicisation of asylum, and immigration more generally, means that developing learning provision specifically for newcomers is fraught with problems, sensitivities and challenges. The lack of funding for development or specialisation means that at present newcomers' learning needs are not being properly met and there is little prospect of change. Learning providers believed that education and training provision for newcomers should place greater emphasis on training linked to qualifications and progression, and that there should be programmes at different levels, including work-based training so that short-term needs did not compromise long-term goals. Organisations which were in close proximity, should develop specialist provision and progression routes operating across a cluster of learning providers. Learning to speak English is the starting point of integration. This truism is recognised by newcomers, academics, policymakers and employers, yet the range of ESOL provision on offer was markedly inadequate.

In the previous chapter newcomers described how little chance they had to learn and practice English in real settings. More befriending and mentoring initiatives would not only offer opportunities for conversational English but would also assist newcomers' overall integration. Widening ESOL provision to include more programmes of cultural orientation and preparation for work would also be a significant improvement. Embedded and occupationally specific ESOL classes have been identified as vital in supporting the progression of newcomer learners, especially into appropriate employment (Gray *et al*, 2007; Phillimore *et al*, 2007b; Pickersgill, 2007). New programmes of vocational ESOL are currently being developed and it is hoped that the new ESOL for Work qualification launched in 2007 will help newcomers acquire appropriate language skills.

The funding of learning and IAG provision for newcomers should be sufficiently flexible to allow providers to meet their diverse needs. This could include paid time for development work, one-to-one support and outreach activity. Learning providers wanted not only an increase in Learner Support Funds but, ideally, ring-fenced financial assistance for the provision of childcare, fees, books and travel for those who were not entitled to access mainstream support funds. It was clear that providers were keen to continue their work and wanted to expand or improve services to newcomers. Better childcare provision in learning institutions is vital if more women are to participate in education and training.

Some providers in our research expressed ideas about how to improve services for newcomers, but others were isolated from knowledge about best practice in service provision for newcomers.

The review of ESOL led by NIACE in 2006 highlighted the importance of ESOL tutors in the lives of newcomers, their tutor often being the first trusted person the newcomer encounters in the UK (Grover, 2006). But although such relationships are highly valued by students, they are borne out of necessity and can be problematic. Until alternatives are established we need to think about developing good practice within existing provision.

Along with further resources and a change of policy around entitlements, two other factors can improve learning provision for newcomers. Both concern partnership. One is to involve learning providers in working closely in partnership rather than in competition. This would enable them to offer the optimal range of programmes and progression routes and together to improve the staff training on working with newcomers. The other responds to the issue that newcomers' needs are not confined to education and employment but encompass a whole range of factors that impact on their lives. In order to address these wider needs learning providers need to work closely with other organisations providing a raft of support services to help newcomers settle in the UK. Chapter Six examines the nature of the advice and support services offered by statutory and non-statutory agencies.

6

Supporting refugees into employment and learning

The personal skills of staff are important in all organisations. We need to raise awareness of the issues and train people to deal with newcomers in respectful ways. A lot of front line staff in the city are ignorant. (IAG Manager)

New migrants and education providers have stressed the pivotal role that information, advice and guidance (IAG) plays in helping them to access education, training and employment (ETE). Newcomers spoke about how the quality of support received affected success in the UK education system and labour market. So how well do organisations providing IAG meet the needs of newcomers? What more do they need to know in order to understand how gaps in provision could be filled? As well as looking at IAG provision offered by education and training providers, as discussed in the previous chapter, we also sought to explore the wider services which IAG providers outside the education system offered newcomers, the challenges faced by providers in meeting newcomers' needs and the resources organisations required to improve service delivery for newcomers. The data in this chapter is based on a total of 222 non-statutory questionnaire returns, 36 site visits to non-statutory organisations and interviews with twelve statutory providers.

IAG services for newcomers cover a broad spectrum of activity from advice on local job search to international tracing and messaging services. Institutions such as Jobcentre Plus (JCP) and Connexions and the organisations with whom they contract have a statutory responsibility to provide IAG around ETE. The West Midlands has a range of organisations with a statutory role. Employment agencies, Pertemps and Reeds Employment, are two of the main contractors. The non-statutory sector often helps newcomers to locate ETE, or helps support them with matters that affect their ability to study or work. The non-statutory sector is diverse and consists of Refugee Community Organisations (RCOs), Migrant Community Organisations (MCOs), local area specific community organisations, regeneration focused organisations and many more.

The majority of these organisations were operating on a small scale with modest funding. The Leitch Review (2006) acknowledged that services for adult guidance did not meet the needs of the population in general. Neither did they have the resources to make adaptations to service provision for refugees and other newcomers. New mechanisms aimed at quality improvement such as the Matrix Standard, a national quality standard for organisations delivering IAG for learning and work, had increased the professionalism of services. Currently all Learning and Skills Council (LSC) IAG providers must achieve accreditation against the matrix quality standard. This is the only quality standard designed to assess IAG provision. Clearly, further work was needed to create a service fit for purpose.

NIACE are currently leading a national consultation to explore what a comprehensive adult careers service might look like. We can expect to see such a service evolving within the next two years. With so many newcomers living, working and wanting to engage in learning across the UK any new advisory service needs to account for their needs.

We have discussed the numerous needs that impact on the ability of newcomers to access, remain in and achieve in ETE. Such complex needs require services to be delivered in a holistic manner. However under current policy and funding arrangements the organisations do not have the capacity and expertise to deliver integrated services. How they overcome the wider IAG issues whilst still continuing to provide advice and guidance on ETE is a major issue. This chapter explores some of the challenges faced by IAG providers in meeting the needs of newcomers. It begins with an overview of the ETE services for newcomers in the West Midlands looking at how both the statutory and non-statutory sector provide IAG for newcomers who wish to access education and employment. The ways in which organisations have responded to policy governing the delivery of IAG services, their current capacity to work with newcomers, the inter-linkages between the two sectors in service delivery and the ways in which the capacity of the sectors might be increased are all discussed.

The statutory sector

The main statutory providers involved in our research were Jobcentre Plus and Connexions. We also looked at several Birmingham City Council run Employment Resource Centres and other local authority services such as Steps to Employment, set up to help improve access to employment in the region. Each had a different remit for working with newcomers. JCP and Pertemps, a private sector organisation that held a number of DWP contracts, had a statutory role in dealing with newcomers in receipt of benefits, and Connexions in dealing with young people (under nineteen), but also dealt with newcomers of all ages on a self-referral basis. The study also included NetwERC, a collection of 25 independent employment advice and training centres that are part of the Employment Resource Centres. The Employment Resource Centres were tasked with trying to build partnerships with local providers to meet the ETE needs they identified at neighbourhood level. Refugees were entitled to access all the generalist services provided by these agencies.

Once refugees are granted leave to remain they are referred directly to JCP by the local authority or a private accommodation provider. At the time of our research all new refugees needed to apply for a National Insurance Number (NINO) at JCP. This has changed and the NINO is now automatically issued when refugees are granted leave to remain. However, most refugees continue to use JCP to access benefits or seek employment. Most unemployed refugees in our surveys were entitled to Jobseeker's Allowance (JSA). To be eligible for this benefit they, like all other applicants, must be able to demonstrate that they are actively seeking employment. Refugees in receipt of JSA are pretty much left to their own devices for the first eighteen months of their unemployment. Advisers may refer refugees to an ESOL programme or other provision, particularly if asked for assistance.

Once refugees have been unemployed for over eighteen months, or six months if they are under the age of 25, they are referred to New Deal. New Deal programmes vary enormously between JCP sub-regions. Provision is generally sub-contracted to private providers and typically comprises job search workshops and workplace orientation. Each person is assigned a personal advisor who remains their key contact throughout the programme. The personal adviser's role is to take the time to understand their client's experiences, interests and aspirations in order to prepare a personal plan to help get them into suitable employment. Everyone on New Deal must attend the programme weekly for a set number of hours, generally at least 25, and JSA is withdrawn if they do not fulfil this commitment. Unless a client can secure agreement from their JCP adviser, they will be forbidden to commence or continue any learning that clashes with their New Deal programme.

In some areas specific ESOL provision is available for migrants with poor language skills. Until recently this special provision was sub-contracted to private providers. Our findings indicated that JCP were the main referral agency to most of the services offered by other statutory organisations. In some cases this was a contractual arrangement such as that held by Connexions, who have an obligation to provide information and advice to young people, under the age of nineteen, to help them make decisions in the light of their mission statement: 'Get where you want to be in life'. Pertemps are similarly contracted to provide support to all those who have been unemployed over a specified number of months.

The kind of support that newcomers can expect from JCP has changed a great deal over the past few years, particularly with the rationalising of JCP staffing levels. There has been a significant shift away from one-to-one support to online advice and guidance. Any additional support before a New Deal referral is now usually signposted to non-statutory services or to further education colleges for ESOL classes. In most of inner city Birmingham an Employment Zone service, offered by private providers, is obligatory for people unemployed for over twelve months and is also offered to other groups such as lone parents on a voluntary basis. The underlying ethos of Employment Zone contracts is to enable jobseekers to benefit from expertise from the private as well as public sector. Attendance at an Employment Zone service is prioritised over all other learning in progress and claimants may be compelled to leave their courses.

The Employment Zone offers a variety of support to its clients. This includes one-to-one guidance to aid development of an Action Plan, skills assessment to help clients locate appropriate training, assistance with preparing CVs, application forms and interview techniques, help with job search, financial assistance with tools and clothing, loans or grants for equipment, and help with new business planning and business start up training and support.

The Employment Zone has 26 weeks in which to get their client into sustainable employment, defined as employment that they retain for more than thirteen weeks. The quicker they help a client get employment, the greater the remuneration to the provider. For example, if an agency can get someone into work within two weeks, the Zone provider keeps the equivalent of the individual's benefits for the remaining 24 weeks. This objective, of helping individuals to gain employment as quickly as possible, means that energies tend to be directed at those who are likely to gain work the fastest, and on low skilled work opportunities that are easily accessed. Interviews with JCP advisers revealed concerns that 'the Zone' rarely met refugees' needs because they were viewed as difficult clients unlikely to yield quick results. But there were examples when Zone providers managed to help refugees into self-employment by, for example, providing a loan to help with the initial costs of taxi hire so they could become self-employed taxi drivers.

Some of the organisations interviewed also provided specialist services to refugees. These were most likely to involve language classes but also they included interpretation services located within the provider's office on a regular basis. There was evidence that a few statutory providers were planning specialist services. One organisation was seeking to develop a mentoring scheme to help refugees into work; another offered a specialist programme for refugees that would offer business language training, work on self employment ideas and help with CVs, interviews and job searching. Only one of the statutory providers was offering asylum seekers assistance with locating training, schooling and voluntary work.

Statutory organisations encountered challenges when working with newcomers and found them a difficult group to assist. One of the main barriers said to prevent newcomers gaining jobs was employers' attitudes. All the organisations struggled with employers who did not wish to employ refugees. Some employers were so resistant to refugees that they refused to allow providers with offices in newcomer cluster areas to advertise their vacancies for fear of receiving applications from refugees or asylum seekers with permission to work. Newcomers were sometimes discriminated against on the grounds of their ethnicity or where they lived: some employers saw these as an indication that an applicant was a refugee or asylum seeker. And it was reported that some community-based organisations were reluctant to fund initiatives specifically for refugees and had effectively opposed the provision of specialist advisers.

Many of the concerns expressed by statutory organisations echoed those of the employers. This is discussed more fully in the next chapter. Essentially the reluctance was based on the belief that newcomers would have poor language skills which would inhibit them from being able to understand Health and Safety notices or basic instructions and from mixing with other employees and working effectively as part of a team. Although this was obviously not always the case, statutory advisers had observed that a significant number of their newcomer clients did experience language difficulties and commented on the chronic shortage of ESOL classes. Many newcomers could speak English but not write it. Recurring themes such as difficulty recognising qualifications, lack of UK work experience, a dearth of voluntary work places, loss of motivation, lack of child care and travel barriers had been picked up by newcomers, employers and advisers alike. Organisations supporting refugees to find work had to overcome some of these issues before they could realistically expect to place newcomers in sustainable employment.

Some advisers were concerned about problems they experienced at an organisational level which affected the nature of support provided. A few organisations were worried about the attitudes of some of their advisers towards newcomers. On occasion advisers reported experiencing 'belligerence' from refugee clients, so they tended to stereotype them as 'difficult' and would take only the minimum action required to provide them with a service. Consequently some refugees were not being offered the full range of services or were offered unskilled work rather than the training they needed to use their skills more appropriately in the labour market.

Also of concern was that advisers did not have the resources to deal with newcomers' complex everyday needs or the time to tackle the complex barriers that prevented newcomers from working. As one adviser put it: 'It feels like a problem without a solution'. Statutory providers confidently believed that with more time allocated for working with newcomers they would be able to help them more effectively. They were also concerned that if they planned for the long-term needs of newcomers they could not possibly meet their targets. They did hope that the failure to meet targets would galvanise management into action at a strategic level so that better data would be collected, particularly among certain communities, and more resources allocated. In the meantime they thought the situation would probably get worse rather than better.

The organisations involved in our studies struggled to identify ways around the difficulties they were experiencing. They recommended an employment strategy for each sub-region and hoped this might help to attract more resources. The issue of the negative attitudes of employers was considered extremely difficult to overcome unless specific measures were aimed at them, but this was seen as beyond the remit and resources of the statutory IAG sector. However, the provision of work experience programmes plus an organisation to arrange and oversee work placements, was seen as a way to challenge the attitudes of employers by giving newcomers the chance to show what they were capable of. Education providers felt that work placements could also help break down negative attitudes in the work place. They thought early mentoring for newcomers before they became de-motivated would safeguard newcomers' employability opportunities. There was widespread uncertainty about how the statutory sector could tackle the sheer scale of difficulties that newcomer clients experienced with the resources available.

With the exception of JCP, none of the organisations had received any advice from the Home Office, the DfES, or DWP (Department for Work and Pensions) about how to deal with refugee learning and employability issues. Statutory providers tended to rely upon local networks, RCOs, Asylum teams, the regional asylum consortium and JCP for advice on newcomer issues and supplemented this with information from the Internet. JCP did however receive advice from DWP and the directives sent to Regional offices and then out to the districts. They could interpret information about guidance at district level in accordance with the local needs of newcomer groups. Through careful interpretation of national policy two JCP offices had managed to identify some resources to provide specialist office based interpretation services. Interpretation was seen as a key element in providing successful services for newcomers. As one service manager asserted: 'even the best funded project will be diminished if good interpretation isn't available'.

Organisations identified several crucial key gaps in existing provision. Most frequently mentioned was the gap highlighted by newcomers themselves, namely, the lack of adequate and appropriate ESOL, ideally linked to vocational training. Statutory organisations also identified the shortage of any vocationally orientated support such as work placements, advocacy work with employers to help 'get them on board', and long term planning to assist newcomers to obtain sustainable work that suited their capabilities. A huge opportunity was being missed, it was suggested that the ideal time for a specialist service to assess and support refugees was surely during the 28 day transition period from asylum seeker status to refugee. Letting this slip was considered a major error, which they believed would undermine the employability of refugees in the long term.

Advisers saw a desperate need for specialist services for newcomers. Statutory providers argued that with greater support their own organisations could be developed to provide more focused and specialised services. But this would require an injection of funding plus better information about the newcomer population. In the absence of knowledge, capacity or resources to provide the support needed by newcomers the statutory sector was aware that a significant proportion of support, and particularly quality support, for newcomers trying to access ETE was being provided by the non-statutory sector.

Non-statutory provision

In an attempt to explore the types of organisations providing IAG and other forms of support to newcomers, we approached every organisation that could be identified as offering IAG, regardless of whether they were known to work with newcomer clients. Our findings indicated that most IAG providers were working with newcomers. Only 12 per cent of organisations had had no contact with new migrants at the time of our research. A few organisations were reluctant to provide specialised services to newcomers in the belief that their services should be open to all potential clients. Forty two per cent were providing services specifically targeted at newcomers, and 46 per cent had found that newcomers were accessing their wider provision.

There were various types of non-statutory organisations providing support to newcomers, such as RCOs, registered charities, faith groups and not-for-profit organisations. Central to the definition of RCOs is that they are established 'by' asylum seeking or refugee communities, or their pre-established communities, 'for' asylum seeking or refugee communities (Zetter and Pearl, 2000). It has been argued that the development of RCOs is a direct response to the difficulties refugees experience trying to access mainstream services (Carey-Wood, 1997) and that RCOs have a better understanding of refugees' needs than statutory agencies (Salinas *et al*, 1987).

One of the largest RCOs in our sample is a good example. Founded by two asylum seekers, who had begun by offering support to new arrivals in their own houses, it now provides specialist advice and guidance services to new migrants from many countries. The organisation has its own offices, employs eight full time staff and takes on a fluctuating number of volunteers. Eighteen languages are spoken by the advisers at this centre, clearly a huge advantage in helping to overcome the communication barriers experienced by so many support agencies working with newcomers. The manager, a newcomer from the Balkans and one of the founder members, maintains that the organisation's strength lies in its development 'by newcomers for newcomers' and the associated 'sensitivity and close empathy' with newcomers and their needs. It prides itself on the high level of trust developed with newcomer communities and on having managed to appoint staff who subscribed to the values of 'equity and fairness to all'. It derives additional strength from being well networked and working in a reciprocal way with its many partners at both local and regional level.

Whilst this organisation had successfully secured funding to gradually develop services and increase staffing levels, there were many examples of RCOs that had been less fortunate but which were continuing, against all odds, to provide support to their community. One such was an RCO established in 1999 to serve the Sudanese community. In recent years the organisation had gained charitable status but continued to be staffed entirely by volunteers, mostly from professional backgrounds. This RCO ran ESOL, dressmaking and IT classes as well as job finding workshops. It had actively sought to support a number of highly qualified refugees into professional employment in the UK. Although providing a valuable service, they struggled to access funding, and in spite of asking, had never been given feedback about their funding applications to help them learn how it might succeed.

The organisations involved in our research had been established for varying lengths of time ranging from a few months to decades or even over a century. Some were long established charities and community organisations, others were embryonic RCOs and voluntary organisations and a number had roots in movements such as the trade union movement. Some had been set up to cater for the needs of a single ethnic group, while others were open to all. Many operated on both a drop-in and appointment basis while others had no drop-in facility and operated on an outreach basis in community venues. Non-statutory organisations generally offered advice on learning and employment plus much else, such as immigration, housing, healthcare and welfare benefits.

Some organisations indicated that they had plans to provide specialist services for newcomers in the future. Others were keen to begin providing such services but did not have the financial and human resources. Funding problems were endemic in the non-statutory sector. Not all organisations received funding. Most of those who did were funded through a combination of statutory and non-statutory sources. Much of the statutory funding for learning and training advice was tied to the delivery of JCP equivalent provision on an outreach basis. Some providers operated entirely independently of JCP funds but had gained access to local funding tied to community cohesion or regeneration agendas.

Non-statutory organisations were rarely free to deliver services based entirely on the needs presented by their clients: funding was usually tied by contract to specific targets. A Christian faith based organisation, for example, depended on funding provided by a statutory contract to provide a variety of support services for newcomers and other members of the community. It was based in a former public house and since 1989 had been pioneering the re-engagement of hard-to-reach young people, irrespective of 'colour, creed or status', through Christian outreach and the provision of 'venues free from compromising pressures'. The organisation had a Youth Drop-In Centre and a restaurant which ran work experience programmes. It was involved in a partnership with a local college and the education service in a joint effort to address the needs of young people who were socially excluded and educationally marginalised. It was also a Connexions Access Point and an accredited IAG Centre, providing monitoring and guidance services through Personal Advisers operating in local community drop-in centres and supported housing. Through its broad remit this organisation had been able to support a number of young newcomers previously outside ETE into learning opportunities.

The potential for newcomers to access services varied geographically. Some organisations operated in rather narrow areas of perhaps just one or two wards while others provided services across a whole borough, city or region. Only a few operated nationally or internationally. New migrants' access to provision depended to some extent on where they lived. Services in central areas were available to anyone and those living in the main dispersal clusters could generally access specialist or discrete services. Those living in peripheral areas struggled to access help, because they were unaware of the existence of services, or were afraid to travel by public transport or could not afford to. However, some organisations offered outreach services or home visits to those who could not access their offices.

Another faith based organisation, established in 1999, exemplifies the type of organisation undertaking outreach. In the five years since its establishment it had dealt with 2,500 local people, 1,700 of whom were estimated to be newcomers from over 60 different countries of origin. It aimed to create an environment where people whose 'dignity has been damaged can have the self-confidence to take their place in the local community'. As well as visiting people in their homes it had a centre with ESOL and crèche facilities. The project manager explained how she had moved the organisation into the area to enable 'greater solidarity with local people'. The organisation's first premises, which opened in June 2003, were burned down in an arson attack. The project then secured much better premises in a parish centre and, with the aid of both volunteers and trained staff, now offers a crèche and English classes as well as citizenship courses and leisure activities.

Rather than organisations being established pro-actively in anticipation of the services that might be required to support those dispersed to the region, the approach to meeting newcomers' needs was entirely reactive. For example, a number of the RCOs, such as those discussed above, evolved in response to the emerging needs of newcomer communities that were not being met via the statutory sector. Often provision developed in an organic and somewhat *ad hoc* fashion as individual newcomers, perhaps those who had English and better understanding of UK systems, were approached by their peers for advice. Over time some RCOs developed their provision to respond to the increasing numbers of newcomers seeking access to their services, and to needs that required specialist attention. As organisations matured they applied for funds to support their work.

Some organisations that had been established to work in particular neighbourhoods had also begun to adapt their services to help newcomers. When newcomers first began to present themselves the organisations responded on an informal basis. As the numbers of newcomers increased they acquired funding to provide assistance as part of their core activity. Some organisations had responded to newcomers' needs when they became aware of the racially motivated crimes targeted at new arrivals, whilst others were motivated by concerns about the isolation of so many newcomers.

Few organisations in the non-statutory sector kept detailed monitoring records of the clients they worked with. In fact only 14 per cent of organisations recorded socio-demographic information, so could tell us how many newcomers used their services. Consequently it was impossible to assess accurately how many newcomers were using the services on offer. While some generic IAG organisations reported that they worked with newcomers on a small scale, it was not unusual for organisations working solely with newcomers to have hundreds of active cases. One specialist organisation estimated that it had worked with 1,500 refugees in the previous year alone. At the opposite end of the spectrum, one local community organisation was aware of working with only one asylum seeker in the same period.

Most of the newcomer client group were men. Nearly half of all organisations provided services accessed by men only, or by significantly more men than women. There was some specialist provision for women, with 14 per cent of organisations working solely with women, although not necessarily only with newcomers. In terms of countries of origin, the client population was similar to the demographics of the West Midlands newcomer population generally, except where specialist services were provided to pre-schoolers, teenagers and adults beyond working age.

Recently concerns have been expressed about the funding of single ethnicity projects. The emphasis has moved from multicultural provision to provision thought to foster community cohesion (Cantle, 2007). Our study revealed that only 5 per cent of organisations supported people of a specific nationality or ethnicity. All the others appeared to be serving clients from the full range of ethnic backgrounds living in the region. Newcomers presented with widely varying support needs, for example in the Chinese community, clients ranged from highly educated political activists seeking basic advice and guidance to help them through the transition period, to less educated people, perhaps from rural backgrounds, who required high levels of support because they had significant literacy problems, struggled with language learning and were experiencing cultural dissonance.

Some sections of the newcomer population were considered harder to reach than others. Like education providers, IAG providers found women, in parti-cular Muslim women and women with children, hard to reach. Other groups that were thought not to be accessing support services included young people, older newcomers, people with health problems and disabilities and newcomers living outside the major towns and cities. Refugees who were already working were also hard to support because they often needed help outside working hours. Community sector providers were less inclined to identify any group as being hard to reach, as they considered reaching all sectors of the local community their *raison d'etre*. Some organisations be-lieved that the newcomers who were particularly isolated because of mental health problems, or poor English language skills, were less likely to access the help they needed than those who were better networked and more confident. It seems there were several groups of newcomers who were not only failing to access learning but were failing to make even the most basic contact with IAG services. Unless some mechanism can be identified to reach these new-comers their prospects for integration and inclusion in both economy and society do not look good.

Supporting the diverse needs of newcomers

Despite their problems reaching some groups, non-statutory providers offered a wide range of services that were being accessed by newcomers. Our survey of IAG providers gives a broad indication of the type of services offered and the proportion of organisations providing each service (see Table 6.1).

Some 65 per cent of providers offered education and training services. The courses they ran ranged from community ESOL and IT to learning directed at self-employment or leisure such as dressmaking or creative writing. Some

Education and training	65%		Social	24%
Employment	37%		Counselling	23%
Youth	29%		Leisure	23%
Benefits advice	27%		Housing	16%
Services for women	27%		Legal/ immigration advice	15%
Health	25%		Other	29%

Table 6.1: Percentages of organisations by type of service provided

organisations were flexible and dynamic and sought to respond to the needs of newcomers as they arose. For example, one organisation worked with over 1,500 newcomers to offer education and training opportunities including a supplementary school for children. It organised cultural activities, maintained a website and circulated a newsletter. Employment related IAG, offered by 37 per cent of organisations, most commonly encompassed ETE assessments and skills audits, job search assistance, CV writing, presentation and interview skills, widening out to befriending and mentoring, work experience and advice on volunteering. Youth and health services, which were offered by 29 per cent and 25 per cent of organisations respectively, were often provided alongside benefits advice, (27% of organisations) and counselling (23%). Whilst health advice and counselling was widely available there was almost no specialist support to assist newcomers with mental health problems and little for helping drug misusers.

Other services were also available, for example translation and interpretation, and advice on social, legal, immigration and housing matters. But these were often provided piecemeal rather than within one organisation, so newcomers needed to navigate several organisations to find what they needed. Only a few organisations offered legal and immigration advice and support with housing, 15 per cent and 16 per cent respectively. Legal and immigration advice demands experts on the matter before it can gain the accreditation to offer immigration services legitimately. Organisations working with newcomers also offered support for victims of racial harassment, funding for childcare and provided clothing, food, furniture and other household items. Opportunities to join arts related and community leisure activities were provided by some 23 per cent of organisations and some provided opportunities for worship.

The services offered extended well beyond the normal parameters of IAG provision. Our findings revealed that non-statutory provision was far more diverse than the statutory sector. The inflexibility of statutory providers meant that they struggle to tailor provision to the requirements of newcomers. The offer of a wide range of services, often delivered in newcomers' mother tongue, attracted newcomers to services which had little to do with learning or employment. As trust slowly built between an organisation and its clients it became easier to help individuals to access learning. Statutory providers would benefit from working more closely with the more flexible non-statutory sector but the diversity of organisations operating in a fast evolving arena makes it difficult to keep track of what is available where.

Many of the organisations in our study served a variety of user groups but had only recently begun providing IAG to newcomers on a significant scale, following the influx of asylum seekers through the National Asylum Support Service (NASS) dispersal programme. In only a few years providers' awareness of the needs of newcomers had grown and so had their delivery of specialist services specifically tailored to meet them. The major challenge for service providers was caused by the constant changes in immigration policy, which left them struggling to keep up with newcomers' rights and entitlements. Also difficult were problems associated with the housing of newcomers in predominantly white areas and the racial harassment and anti-social behaviour that sometimes followed.

Another difficulty was gaining the confidence of people who had been poorly served by the asylum system. Many newcomers mistrusted the UK system and had become disillusioned by the quality and level of support offered by mainstream providers. Statutory support was generally viewed as lacking in continuity, whilst the voluntary and community sector was considered to be 'powerless'.

Organisations dealing with young newcomers spoke of the particular difficulties they faced when newcomers approached the age of eighteen because of the sudden change in their rights and entitlements. And many of these young people did turn to the providers for guidance.

Particular concerns have been voiced in policy and academic circles about the current state of RCOs in dispersal regions. Zetter *et al* (2005) have argued that more public funds should be allocated to help establish RCOs in the regions. They are 'doubly disadvantaged' as they try to establish services without a track record of provision, whilst having to depend on small-scale and short-term funding. The lack of funding and particularly core funding, was reported by all the organisations in our study. Without adequate funding, providers could not always meet the demand of their service users and sometimes had to turn people away. Staffing and resources were often unrealistic, and many organisations were operating in a 'state of crisis'. The dearth of trained staff in both statutory and non-statutory sectors meant there was little expertise, for example in ESOL, legal advice, interpretation and translation. Lack of materials in newcomer languages prevented newcomers from accessing the full range of support services.

Many organisations relied heavily on volunteer staff but although volunteering offered opportunities for newcomers to use their skills and gain some UK work experience, managers were concerned that there was almost no support and training to help them develop their skills. Without adequate knowledge and training non-statutory organisations risk perpetuating the mis-information we found to be rife within newcomer communities.

Most organisations had to refer some clients to other organisations because they could not offer the full range of support required. Referral destinations included both statutory and non-statutory organisations but most were in the non-governmental sector. Non-statutory providers showed some mistrust about the quality of service provision in the statutory sector. They were asked to rate the effectiveness of key organisations in the sector on a scale of 1-5, where 5 was highly effective, and 1 not at all effective (see Table 6.2). Organisations rated Connexions as the most effective of the statutory services in meeting the needs of asylum seekers and refugees.

Services provided by the Education Authority and Primary Care Trusts were ranked closely behind Connexions, while services provided by JCP, other employment agencies and Leisure Services were perceived to be below average. The vast majority of organisations in our research struggled to identify any

Statutory organisations	Average score out of 5
Connexions	3.1
Education Authority	3.0
Primary Care Trusts	3.0
Leisure Services	2.9
Jobcentre Plus/ Employment Agencies	2.7
Housing	2.6
Social Services	2.6

Table 6.2: Perceived effectiveness of statutory services in meeting the needs of asylum seekers and refugees

other organisations they believed to represent good practice in providing services for newcomers.

Improving IAG services for newcomers

There are clearly a number of serious gaps in service provision. Education and training opportunities were seen as essential to assist newcomers' settlement in the UK, as were accurate and reliable IAG and ongoing support to help access learning and employment. IAG providers recognised that newcomers needed more individually tailored advice, offered over time, so they could link the qualifications and experience they had gained in other countries to learning and employment in the UK. Providers argued that newcomers needed one-to-one support to develop personal pathways to learning and employment so they could utilise their skills more effectively. ETE programmes tailored to different sections of the community needed to be developed. This might entail combining additional elements of support, such as vocational ESOL and mentoring, with mainstream provision to make existing learning opportunities newcomer friendly.

Whilst access to ETE related IAG was seen as vital, providers also argued for the need to enhance their knowledge of crucial areas such as benefits, housing, health and immigration. A number of organisations were concerned about the lack of help for refugees during the 28 day transition period, the lack of assistance to enable dis-benefited asylum seekers to subsist until the point of deportation and the lack of provision for newcomers with mental health issues. Many dis-benefited asylum-seekers who feared returning to their home countries were both destitute and statusless. Not being able to do anything for them distressed the IAG providers as well as the newcomers affected. Providers recommended that advisers receive specialist training to improve the delivery of such services, even to offer the most general or basic advice. Such training would equip advisers to accurately direct newcomers to all the appropriate services available, ideally in a system of mutual referral.

Partnership working

The advisers in our studies wanted to see coherent partnership working, so that organisations could play to their strengths and deliver services across the spectrum of needs they had identified. Fifty six per cent of non-statutory organisations already worked with other providers but there was scope for far greater co-operation. Strengthening the relationships between and across statutory and non-statutory sectors would allow the organisations to develop a coordinated multi-agency approach to support the wider delivery of services, and to increase awareness in all sectors about the services on offer and how to access them. A well co-ordinated system would enable providers to direct clients to the most suitable information and support services.

The providers argued that, strategically, they wanted approaches that were systematic, so that all organisations could access relevant and up-to-date information about newcomers' needs and ever-changing entitlements. However, developing a more co-ordinated approach to service delivery is challenging given the vulnerability of the non-governmental sector and the uncertainty surrounding policy and funding regimes.

Organisations experienced rapid changes in fortune. In the relatively short time since this research was conducted, a number of those which participated have ceased to operate, and some have had their activities severely constrained because of lack of funding. The statutory sector also has difficulties in providing services for newcomer client groups and they too have had to cope with funding changes recently, particularly for ESOL.

IAG providers emphasised their need for flexibility and creativity so they could respond to changes in a client's circumstances. The need to respect and promote diversity, whilst investing time in developing relationships and trust with clients was seen as important. RCOs in particular prided themselves on the trust they developed with the new communities they served but seldom had the capacity and expertise to deliver the level of services required.

Building the capacity of organisations working with new migrants

Nearly all the voluntary and community sector organisations in our research emphasised the need for more resources. Thirty five per cent of them wanted training to improve their knowledge about potential sources of funding, how to tap into available funding streams and, specifically, how to write successful funding applications. Whilst some organisations could see how they would use additional funds to tailor and improve their IAG services, others needed additional funding to survive.

Many of the non-statutory providers were, or had been, heavily dependent on volunteers because resources in the sector were so scarce. Some of the most experienced and specialised services had evolved from entirely voluntary organisations, though many were now employing staff as well. Twenty seven per cent of organisations required additional funds for salaries. Providers stressed the need for IAG staff, tutors with relevant language specialism, employment link officers, outreach workers, interpreters, ESOL trainers and for resources to pay for volunteer expenses. A number of organisations wanted to employ or train dedicated workers to serve the needs of newcomer groups, and 12 per cent indicated that they would channel further resources into capacity building activities for existing managers and management committees.

Over 25 per cent of IAG providers felt they needed to develop the knowledge and expertise of existing staff. Smaller and less established organisations required general IAG training, whereas mature providers specified the need to build expertise in areas such as legal advice, financial management, public relations, asylum legislation and web design. Training in cultural awareness and diversity and about how to deal with clients with mental health problems were considered a worthwhile investment for generalist organisations that were beginning to serve newcomer clients:

> We need to be aware of cultural differences before we begin working with new-comers and be aware that their cultural needs may be misinterpreted. We need training and to do research on the background of newcomers we are working with ...we should begin from where they are starting e.g. don't put city-dwellers in isolated rural areas. Take time and be patient when explaining how our basic services work – education, employment and health service etc. (IAG provider)

Further resources for equipment such as computers, printers, photocopiers, books, directories, Internet access and software to translate materials into relevant languages were required by 25 per cent of organisations. Acquiring a permanent base or expanding premises and services was impossible without adequate funding. Organisations either used the premises of other organisations, which they believed limited their effectiveness, or worked in inadequate and overcrowded conditions. Thirty per cent wanted to acquire or expand premises to add new facilities such as childcare provision, counselling, translation and interpretation.

Our research findings pointed to the need for organisations to develop better monitoring and tracking so they could build a comprehensive picture of their clients, their referral destinations, including learning providers and employers. Some organisations wanted evaluation and feedback systems so they could assess the value of their services and predict future needs. IAG providers across the board were keen to see mechanisms developed that would enable best practice to be shared and reports and publications on newcomer issues to be disseminated.

Conclusion

This chapter explored the range of IAG services offered to newcomers by statutory and non-statutory providers and examined some of the challenges they face when trying to support them. Many of the pressures upon IAG organisations stemmed from the arrival over such a short time of a diverse range of clients with intense personal needs. The lack of core funds to enhance or develop new services to meet the needs of new migrants have strained statutory and non-statutory organisations alike.

Other than the Home Office's SUNRISE pilot areas, there is at present no support for refugees entering the testing 28 day transition period. So the responsibility for helping new refugees find homes, benefits and all the other help they need has defaulted to non-statutory and to some extent, statutory IAG providers. All newcomers need help to locate learning and employment opportunities or IAG services as soon as leave to remain has been granted if they are to be successfully integrated into society.

IAG organisations have a role in this. Access to accurate and relevant information and advice about learning or employment remains vital. But sadly, the reality we found was that most newcomers experience misinformation and language difficulties. Together with cultural differences and the constraints of the asylum system, newcomers struggled to identify and access mainstream services.

It was clear that newcomers were not well served by either the statutory or non-statutory sectors. There was evidence in both sectors of gaps in knowledge, reach, and resources, and the services IAG organisations are funded or commissioned to provide were seldom comprehensive or satisfactory.

Changes have been made since our research. The ability of JCPs to work specifically with newcomers has been enhanced through provision of dedicated 'refugee champions', and the SUNRISE programme to support the integration of newly recognised refugees is about to be rolled out. However, the experience of various national programmes funded through EQUAL, a European Social Fund initiative, suggests that these innovations will not meet the needs of all refugee groups (Gray *et al*, 2007; Waddington, 2007). Despite the developments in statutory support in the months after this research was undertaken, shortcomings in the statutory sector are still evident. As long as these persist, the voluntary and community sector will take the brunt of helping newcomers deal with their problems and gain access to ETE related IAG.

Significantly more funding is needed by non-statutory providers so they can develop their capacity and build new skills, knowledge and expertise in working with newcomers. Although a major source of funding for RCOs, the Home Office Challenge Fund has now been withdrawn. The trend is away from supporting voluntary sector organisations and towards funding centralised support for new refugees under the proposed National Refugee Integration Service. This service will only be available to refugees who gain status after the new service commences operation. Questions arise about how other refugees are to get advice about how they can access learning and employment.

An overarching problem affecting organisations we researched was the difficulty of providing them with accurate and helpful information about ETE so they could match the needs of newcomers to the appropriate provision. IAG providers argued for a more holistic approach which could provide a broader spectrum of support in an integrated manner. In the concluding chapter we argue that under current policy and funding regimes such an approach would require that existing services be co-ordinated through multi-agency partnership working.

A collaborative approach that seeks to offer a portfolio of services would be a major step forward. The services might emanate from several different organisations, but be delivered as a coherent integrated package of support. Our final research-based chapter considers newcomers' access to employment and the main challenges faced by newcomers and potential employers in linking refugees to jobs.

7

Employing new migrants

Give us the opportunity to get a job, whatever the colour of our skin, culture or religion. (Cameroonian woman, 31)

Despite the skills, experience and qualifications newcomers bring with them from their countries of origin, gaining employment is blocked by one obstacle after another. They struggle to locate work commensurate with their skills, due largely to the attitudes of employers. Many of the problems the newcomers encountered are discussed in Chapter Two. Here we bring together the accounts of new migrants and the employers in the hope that such detail will aid the understanding of how and why newcomers experience so much greater under-employment and unemployment than the wider population or other ethnic minority groups (Aldridge and Waddington, 2001; Bloch, 1999, 2000; Feeney, 2000; Phillimore and Goodson, 2001; Walters and Egan, 1996). What does employment mean to newcomers? What do they have to offer the economy and society? And what are the difficulties they face in securing work? And, finally, what can be done to reduce the high levels of unemployment in newcomer communities?

Estimates suggest that between 60 per cent and 90 per cent of newcomers are unemployed and that finding secure employment continues to be a problem (Bloch, 2002). Disappointingly few newcomers return to their former careers and many remain long-term unemployed (Phillimore and Goodson, 2001). A report published by the Industrial Society suggests that newcomers are being actively hampered from working because of a combination of 'muddled' Government policy, employer ignorance and media backed public prejudice. Clearly the Government's declared intent of creating full employment and opportunity for all will come to nothing if newcomers continue to be excluded in such large numbers from the labour market (Sargeant and Forna, 2001).

The newcomer data in this chapter is based on responses from 44 focus group participants, 66 one-to-one interviews and 1597 quantitative interviews that were undertaken as part of a household survey. Employer data is based on interviews with 44 employers.

The importance of employment to new migrants, and specifically refugees, is an ongoing theme in this book. Refugees want to work as soon as they can. As we saw in Chapter Four, they see employment as a priority because of the social and economic benefits of being in paid work and because of their own self-esteem. Newcomers find it distressing when they are prevented from using the skills and experience they brought with them, and a gap opens between their status in their home country and in the UK:

> We are seen as educated back home, but here we are nothing (Kurdish Iraqi man, 23)

> ...they think that you came ... for good jobs, in fact I was having a much better job than I have now. I had a much better life style than I have now (Zimbabwean woman, 40)

New migrants who had not worked since arriving in the UK were unhappy about their economic inactivity. Some worried about the burden they placed upon the state by having to rely on benefits while some were conscious of the negative impact on their own well-being. The absence of a daily routine and the social interaction of the work place made them feel isolated and in some cases depressed:

> [When I first came] I couldn't see my family and I became depressed ... newcomers can't see their family, can't study and can't work. So they become depressed and suicidal. (Kurdish Iraqi woman, 26)

> It was terrible when I first came ... like I was in prison. I had no friends and I could not work. First of all when you come to a different country, you don't speak English. When you cannot express yourself the door is closed, the window is closed so there is a huge barrier between you and the world. (Afghani man, 31)

Looking first at refugees' employment experiences in their home country we can see that many have brought valuable skills and experience to the UK. It is clear that newcomers could make a significant contribution to the economy and society if given the appropriate guidance, learning and employment.

What can newcomers offer?
Employment in county of origin

The work histories of newcomers involved in our studies show that their experiences varied hugely, due to factors including age, gender, family circumstance and the political situation in their home country. Exogenous factors clearly played a large part in influencing the nature of newcomers' past work experience. Take Iraq as an example: it is not difficult to understand why in the current and past political situation, people may not always have worked in employment of their choice, or worked at all.

There were specific cases, where people's political activism had directly jeopardised their jobs and in some extreme cases endangered their families. Other people's mental health had been affected by compulsory military service. As one Congolese man explained:

> I can no longer sleep well, I have insomnia, I dream that I am in war, I see what was happening and I have headaches. I am no longer able to concentrate on things as I used to be.

It was clear that continued upheaval and the experience and effects of war had prevented some newcomers from developing career paths in their country of origin. They worked in family businesses, maybe selling goods in the market, for instance, rather than seeking independent employment, since working for family was often the safest or only available option in a chaotic society. Newcomers from Somalia spoke of being unable to work during the past fifteen years because of civil war. Many had eked out a living by selling goods at the market.

Despite these conditions and their impact on the employment history of some newcomers, survey results showed that the majority, 59 per cent, of those dispersed to the West Midlands had been economically active in their home country and had held a variety of jobs. At one end of the spectrum were the highly qualified professionals, and at the other, people with no formal education and with no experience of structured paid employment. Of those who had been employed, 31 per cent had worked in skilled trades and occupations; 16 per cent had been employed as managers and senior officials; 10 per cent were process plant and machine operatives; 8 per cent were professionals; 9 per cent were associate professionals and technicians; 8 per cent worked in elementary trades; 5 per cent were in administration and secretarial work and 2 per cent in personal services.

Economic activity rates varied. Men were more likely to have been employed than women, and older adults more likely than young adults. Most of those employed before arriving in the UK were over the age of 25. Such employment patterns come as no surprise, as we saw in Chapter Four, many young adults had been engaged in education when they had had to flee. In fact one in ten newcomers had left their country of origin before completing their education. This helps explain why a proportion of the newcomers involved in our research prioritised re-entering education.

Regardless of the political conditions in their past lives many newcomers were clear about the type of career path they wished to pursue in their country of origin and many retained their original aspirations. Their high aspirations were evident from the type of job they were either working in or working towards before they left. These included journalism, academia, teaching, professional engineering and consultancy, medicine, nursing and midwifery. Professionals, skilled and semi-skilled workers in particular had been striving for promotion. But we also found low aspirations. These appeared to be linked to the political and economic situation and culturally determined gender roles in their countries of origin. Women were constrained from gaining employment or seeking progression in some countries.

It was clear from this snapshot of newcomers' employment experiences that they possessed a wide range of skills, interests and aspirations. While many retained those aspirations once they had moved to the UK, they found them far harder to achieve than in their country of origin. For people who had fled war or persecution, arrival in the UK marked the end of a long and sometimes hazardous journey. Those who managed to negotiate the system, prove themselves to be legitimate refugees and gain leave to remain, were then faced with the reality that their opportunities and employment trajectories were not as they had been in their home countries.

Employment in the UK

Our examination of the employment rates and kinds of jobs refugees had secured in the UK indicates how they fared since their arrival. Our findings revealed that most (60%) wanted to 'work as soon as possible' – generally as soon as they had been granted permission to work, or as soon as they could speak English. A further 29 per cent wanted to 'return to work soon' but were unsure when this would be. Only 6 per cent stated that they 'do not wish to return to work' and this figure included older adults, disabled newcomers and women with childcare responsibilities. Our research however supports the findings of previous studies on the employability of new migrants and presents a bleak picture.

Of respondents permitted to work, 27 per cent (23% full time) were employed whilst some 23 per cent were economically inactive and a further 50 per cent unemployed, a far higher proportion than the 4 per cent regional average and the average rate of unemployment (13%) among ethnic minority groups generally (see Bloch, 2004; Twomey, 2001). Table 7.1 details refugees' economic activity rates compared to the regional average population.

Economic Status	Refugee average% *	Regional average%
Employed	27	71
Unemployed	50	4
Economically inactive	23	24

Base: *respondents who currently have permission to work in the UK*

Source: combined data from three LSC studies (cf. Phillimore *et al*, 2003, 2004; Goodson *et al*, 2005b)

Table 7.1 Economic status of refugees compared to the regional average

Except for those who found work in the refugee sector as newcomer support workers or interpreters, the type of employment that newcomers did secure was poorly paid, low skilled and in temporary, part-time or voluntary positions. Most worked in jobs well beneath their ability and skills. Our survey revealed that 79 per cent of the respondents working in the UK were employed as process, plant and machine operatives or in elementary occupations. Many newcomers obviously had to endure a reassessment of their economic positions. Some who had held professional and skilled positions had to seek jobs that were not commensurate with their capabilities. This evidence of down-skilling was reinforced by our qualitative research findings, which suggested that many new migrants were prepared to accept any job including elementary or unskilled positions so they could at least be financially self-sufficient in the short term. Such low aspirations were particularly evident amongst those from cultures without a strong ethos of career development.

Although some of the new migrants initially regarded low-skilled employment as a stop-gap until something better came along we found that the hope for transition to higher-level jobs was seldom realised. Some of these respondents had become trapped in low skilled work; others kept hoping to return to their former career and aspired to get work in the UK as health care professionals, teachers or journalists.

We saw in Chapter Four that for various reasons professionals rarely managed to secure places on courses that enabled them to re-train, or to get their qualifications recognised. Even the few who did manage to gain UK qualifications had difficulty in using them in the job market. Mohammed, a 31 year old refugee from the Sudan, is typical. Mohammed graduated with a degree in Electronic Engineering and worked as a computer engineer for six years before leaving the Sudan. His employers provided him with work-based training and sent him on short courses. In the UK he worked as a security guard to raise funds to cover his university fees. After completing a Masters' in Electronic Engineering at Sheffield Hallam University, he moved to the West Midlands and started a PhD programme. Since gaining leave to remain, Mohammed had tried to find a job that suits his qualifications and has applied for many without being offered a single interview. He felt that all migrants struggled to find decent employment regardless of their qualifications or personal qualities. Like most of his friends, Mohammed was anxious about finding sufficient funds to complete his doctorate. Nonetheless, when he looked back at his experience of education and how learning had transformed his life, he remained optimistic. He hoped eventually to work in academia.

Our survey results confirm the findings from our interviews that the largest proportion of respondents were seeking unskilled work: 17 per cent were looking to work as process plant and machine operatives and a further 24 per cent in elementary occupations. Sixteen per cent wished to work in skilled trades. Figure 7.1 illustrates the types of occupations newcomers would be seeking once they were able to work in the UK.

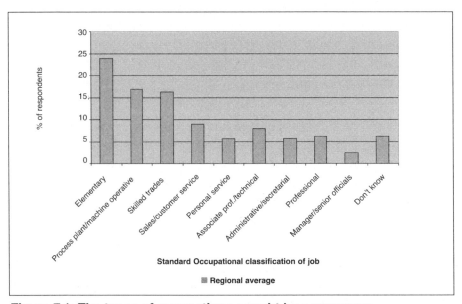

Figure 7.1: The types of occupations sought by newcomers

Except for a handful who had managed to gain secure contracts as advice workers, most of the working migrants in our sample spoke about having jobs that were beneath their capability and which afforded little job satisfaction. Poor pay, unsociable and unpredictable hours, being asked to carry out tasks without receiving any training or demonstration, the temporary nature of the work and the lack of job security were amongst the problems. Over half of all newcomers had gross annual earnings of less than half the regional average of £19,296 per annum and none of those in our sample earned more than £12,949. Interviews with the clients of a housing advice centre indicated that a quarter of all those who worked there had been paid less than the minimum wage and the rest at, or very close to, the minimum wage.

Few knew much about employment rights so they could not assess whether the way they were treated at work was fair or even legal. Some told us they were discontent with their workplace because of their treatment by their workmates. Some newcomers spoke of intimidation or being ignored by their peers. They assumed they were being harassed because they were refugees:

> People see you differently as a refugee and it makes me sad, because of the stigma attached to the name refugee. (Kosovan man, 32)

> People don't take refugees as being human beings, I am ashamed to say that I am a refugee. (Rwandan man, 22)

> Sometimes people are racist. When you go to work sometimes and if you are black, they can fire you. But the white people can't be touched, even if s/he is not doing well. (Rwandan woman, 27)

The way they were treated by their employers could be a problem too. Much has been written about employers' attitudes to appointing newcomers, but there is almost no empirical evidence about what employers actually think and are looking for when recruiting. In the next section we examine employers' attitudes to taking on newcomers by means of in depth interviews. What qualities did employers seek from their employees, and how did their expectations marry with their perceptions and the realities of employing newcomers?

Employers' attitudes to employing newcomers
What do employers want?

For newcomers to improve their chances of gaining employment they and their advisers have to understand what employers are seeking when they recruit staff. The vast majority of organisations interviewed were encountering some difficulties in recruiting and retaining staff and were keen to identify solutions. The employers we interviewed tended to look for a range of personal qualities and characteristics such as motivation, a desire to succeed, the ability to work as part of a team, being well presented and punctual. Evidence of past qualifications and work experience was usually an automatic requirement. In nearly all cases employers would, as standard practice, request UK work references or evidence of a traceable work history. Some employers were simply not prepared to make exceptions to this rule and others said they would feel 'uncomfortable' about an applicant who could not demonstrate their employment background. One employer had encountered a refugee who could prove his work history for only seven years out of the previous ten years and explained that:

> ...as security has been heightened post 9/11 we can't give people the benefit of the doubt anymore.

However Monti's (2005) study suggests that whilst employers may take into account work experience in the applicant's country of origin as background information, what they are really interested in is work experience in the UK. Overall our research revealed varying attitudes towards proof of work histories. Employers wishing to fill low skilled posts were generally more lenient. Although most employers requested UK work references, some were prepared to explore other means of testing an applicant's suitability for the job. For example, an excellent character reference might compensate for the lack of employer references, or a work trial could give the candidate the chance to demonstrate their commitment, motivation and competence. One employer said he would be willing to pursue overseas references if a candidate performed well at interview. Four employers did not require references but relied on the application and interview process to determine suitability for employment. One personnel officer went so far as to say that:

> [Employers] don't obtain references. There was too much paperwork and you didn't really get anything [of use] from the previous employer.

Some employers recognised that a vicious circle existed – newcomers could not gain UK work experience without UK references and could not get these without being given the chance to work. But they were nervous about taking the leap of faith required to give a refugee their first UK job.

As well as UK work experience and references, employers sought evidence of qualifications. Proof was particularly important for post-secondary school qualifications and for any vocational training completed. On top of the problem of not being able to provide evidence of past qualifications, newcomers also had to ensure they had the correct paperwork to prove their eligibility to work in the UK. National Insurance Numbers and P45s were routinely required, as were checks on the legal status and identity of new recruits, sometimes through the Criminal Records Bureau.

Rather more surprising was the number of employers who thought it necessary to ask for proof that a refugee was securely housed. Hursfield *et al* (2004) found that fears about retention made employers reluctant to invest resources in training for newcomer groups. Employers in our study had heard that refugees were a transient group so wanted an applicant to provide a tenancy agreement showing that they were established or intending to settle in the area. Finally, employers who required their employees to be mobile in order to carry out their duties wanted applicants to have a UK driving licence and access to a vehicle. Some employers were concerned lest employees working shifts might struggle to get home when no public transport was running.

Application, induction and training procedures

We also explored employers' application and recruitment procedures. Some examples of good practice were identified, including the positive recruitment campaigns operated by three companies, one of which was a healthcare provider which had recruited 80 professionals from the Indian sub-continent and dealt with all their immigration and work permit procedures. Although they were not asylum seekers or refugees, their programme would have been equally appropriate: it entailed an induction programme aimed to train staff to UK standards and to acquaint them with British healthcare procedures through an orientation package and ESOL classes. Employers aimed at offering strategies such as mentoring and job shadowing to assist newcomers into employment.

Larger organisations in particular had formalised and stringent recruitment systems that usually began with a written application form, followed by an interview and/or an aptitude test. Success was determined by a set of criteria matched to applicants' qualifications, skills and experience. Candidates who failed to meet requirements or to comply with the system were simply discounted. These employers thought that those with English as a second language would be unlikely to progress satisfactorily through the stages of their application procedures unless they could find someone to help them to complete their application form. And language proficiency would be a potential problem at interview stage.

We have seen how unfamiliar newcomers were with UK employment culture and with obtaining training which would help them to learn how to complete application forms correctly, even if they could write English well. Systems to provide feedback to unsuccessful applicants were not standard practice, so they could not learn from unsuccessful applications. Newcomers who were unfamiliar with recruitment systems – the large majority – would inevitably find themselves disadvantaged in the labour market, as reported in Aldridge *et al*'s (2005) study on the employability of newcomers in the East Midlands. All the companies in our study demanded written application forms that were completed 'clearly with a competent level of English' before they would process any application.

Six organisations (5%) however, operated more flexible recruitment procedures, offering candidates an opportunity to discuss at interview where they might be best suited within the organisation. These were mainly in the hotel, retail, machine and plant operative sectors. They intimated that language difficulties could be accommodated if a candidate was considered the 'right person for the job'. Not surprisingly, greater flexibility was apparent in the organisations that had employed newcomers in low skilled positions.

New migrants who reached interview stage in less flexible organisations had to communicate how their skills and experience fitted a particular job. Some had to pass aptitude tests, which ranged from basic numeracy and language tests to more demanding tests of written and communication skills. For example, very basic number and language aptitude tests were a requirement for warehouse work. Maths and English tests which entailed applicants writing 1,000 words about 'why you are suitable for the job' were expected for retail work. For data processing, new recruits were asked to complete a practical IT test to demonstrate their ability to use equipment and a general knowledge exercise to demonstrate spelling and written skills as well as memory recall. One organisation anticipated that certain aspects of the application procedure would be particularly challenging for applicants with poor language skills, especially as the content of their aptitude tests 'have a UK bias'. But they maintained that the nature of the test closely reflected the type of skills and tasks that any successful applicants would routinely have to carry out and that the system afforded little scope to assess skills in alternative ways.

Induction programmes aimed at familiarising new recruits with organisational procedures, such as health and safety, were standard practice. Depending on the type of work and the skills required for the job, training varied in length and intensity, and across sectors and within organisations. It was suggested that a data processor, for example, would be required to undertake specialist training for sixteen weeks followed by a further 36 week programme for successful trainees. A newsagent would follow at least a seven week programme, reviewed at the end to see if further training was needed and a twelve week training period was offered for warehouse work, mainly through mentoring on the job.

Employers were generally reluctant to take on personnel whom they felt would be unable to complete induction and initial training. Hurstfield *et al* (2004) found that employers were concerned about the additional costs associated with the extra time they thought would be needed to induct and train newcomers. Our findings demonstrate the weight employers placed upon written and spoken communication skills. Next, we examine their attitudes to newcomers.

Experiences of employing new migrants

Nineteen of our sample of 44 employers had some experience of employing new migrants. Three public sector employers could not say whether they employed refugees as they did not keep records. Our research suggested that once employers had some experience of employing newcomers their attitudes tended to become more positive. They described them as being 'good workers', with a strong work ethic and a 'genuine commitment to the job'. They considered newcomers to be enthusiastic and committed to learning English ways of working and of being more flexible over working hours than indigenous workers as they did not abide by the 'typical UK 9am to 5pm work pattern'. Some employers even asserted that newcomers brought a 'fresh perspective to the job' and skills that other employees could not offer. In the retail sector, for example, where employers had customers from multicultural backgrounds, they found the newcomers' language skills and cultural knowledge extremely valuable. They felt that reflecting the customer base and communities they served in their workforce made 'good business sense' and helped them to improve the quality of their service.

However, as the literature suggests and as our interviews with newcomers confirm, the type of work newcomers actually gained was generally low skilled. This was certainly true of the nineteen organisations employing newcomers and was in line with what newcomers had told us. The types of organisations in our study employing refugees were manufacturers, distributors, hoteliers and retailers. Distribution and hotel jobs typically amounted to doing laundry, housekeeping, portering, shelf-stacking and car park attending, none of which required fluent English and were thus perceived not to be too challenging for newcomers.

Thus new migrants had difficulty in accessing the labour market, or in finding jobs commensurate with their experience. We now draw on the accounts of new migrants and employers to look at the main barriers facing newcomers in the West Midlands, taking account of both perceived and actual experiences.

Barriers to employment

As we saw in Chapter Four, new migrants experienced barriers and constraints in accessing resources to enable them to learn. They then had to deal with similar issues when they tried to get a job.

Language

Their poor English hampered the job prospects of new migrants in numerous ways. It prevented their accessing and understanding the relevant information like job adverts and the skills and qualities called for certain posts. As we have seen, those who managed to access and understand information about a vacancy and considered themselves suitable for a position then had to complete an application form to a certain standard or sell themselves at interview.

Once in employment, newcomers had to deal with a new set of language related problems and this undermined their confidence to do the job and integrate in the workplace. They could find it hard to follow instructions, understand workplace culture and mix with colleagues formally, as part of a team, and informally in social situations. If their spoken English was poor they felt 'stressed' and 'worried', first about their ability to communicate with people at different levels in their organisation, and secondly about losing their job. Some newcomers did not have the confidence even to try to get work or, in some cases, engage in other activities. As Burim, a 33 year old Albanian, explained:

> I sit home and look in the window, it is boring to stay home but if you can't speak English here, you can't do nothing at all.

Employers were concerned about newcomers' English competence in case it jeopardised their performance or created more work for other staff and they worried about how it might affect their general well-being and ability to settle. In larger organisations, where it was harder to create alliances, employers expressed particular concerns about newcomers becoming marginalised. They were also concerned about compliance with health and safely regulations, specifically with completing health and safety inductions, and about whether the newcomers would be able to read safety notices, follow safety instructions, wear protective clothing or operate safety guards. This was especially so in warehouse work, cleaning and engineering where employees handle toxic substances or machinery. Being unable to comply with health and safety guidelines was considered to be a significant safety risk for the employee but also for those around them, and employers feared the legal consequences if they were found to be in breach of UK safety regulations.

Newcomers who had been recruited from agencies for temporary work felt that their employers did not explain or provide adequate induction about the workplace generally or about health and safety issues. They maintained that employers did not consider them worth spending time on and simply wanted to maximise the productivity of agency workers without caring about their well-being. They felt they were 'working in the dark' and were 'scared' to admit that they did not understand certain aspects of the job for fear of being laid off. The fact that many of these workers were dependent on agency work and did not want negative feedback from employers compounded the problem. Some of those on temporary contracts lived in hope of being offered permanent employment and felt that admitting to any shortcoming on the job could jeopardise their chances. They found constantly moving between benefits and short-term work stressful and desperately wanted to improve their situation.

Some new migrants, especially those with only basic English, believed that they would be restricted to low skilled and poorly paid work regardless of their skills and prior experience. Several employers acknowledged that although some may have been highly qualified in their countries of origin, they were offered work that had little prospects of progression. Lack of confidence stemming from poor competence in English, or a perception of poor competence, held some newcomers back from even applying for anything other than low skilled positions, whilst others decided to stay in ESOL classes until they were more fluent. Newcomers perceived their employment opportunities to be intrinsically linked to their proficiency in English and that their chances of securing better work improved alongside their English. Ironically, however, those already in low skilled work often found accessing ESOL support difficult, especially if they had to do shift work. Some were resigned to being unable to improve their English whilst they were working. And without a sufficient command of English they had little prospect of progression within their workplace.

The employers' tolerance of employees' communication skills varied across sectors and the type of work they did. Having a good standard of English was considered essential for jobs where employees came into contact with the public, especially in direct customer care roles. Some organisations in the hotel and distribution sectors could be flexible because they had a range of backstage positions and this enabled newcomers to be employed in out of sight jobs. In these sectors applicants with little English could be started in positions that required little communication, and when their English improved, they could move front stage. Laundry porters, chamber maids and shelf stackers all worked when stores were closed or rooms empty.

In larger organisations with an ethnically diverse workforce, employers seemed more sympathetic and accommodating to those who spoke little English. Some already routinely offered translation and interpretation as well as having staff who spoke numerous languages. As one employee remarked: '...whenever complex information needs to be relayed to the workforce, there is always another employee who could act as an interpreter'.

Smaller organisations with less diverse workforces were unable to help people learn enough English for the job or to offer bilingual trainers in house for on the job training. Only three employers in our sample offered language support to migrant employees either as part of an induction process or on a continual basis and these were in the distribution, hotel and public sectors.

Immigration status, employment legislation and entitlement to work

Asylum seekers were often excluded from the labour market because of their immigration status. Many of the asylum seekers in our sample were eager to work and felt frustrated that they were forced into unemployment by Government policy:

> I would be better if I had a chance to do what I am good at. (Congolese woman, 34)

Finding work clearly affected how newcomers felt about themselves and their status:

> ...getting a job would make me integrate more and make me think more positively about my life. (Kosovan woman, 34)

While some wanted to work so they would have something constructive to do, others were so overwhelmed with anxiety about their future that they struggled to do anything and were certainly not prepared to make plans for the future, such as attempting education and training which could make them more employable if they did gain leave to remain. Mental health issues, in particular post-traumatic stress disorder, triggered by experiences which led them to flee, the shock of leaving everything behind, and even the journey to the UK itself, rendered some unfit for work even if permission was granted.

Once they were given leave to remain and associated permission to work, another common problem the refugees faced was the employers' ignorance of employment legislation and entitlement to work. Only two thirds of those employing newcomers in our studies claimed to understand the legislation. Others, especially those who had never employed newcomers, had no grasp whatever of these issues. Our findings did however reveal some geographical disparities and differences according to the size of organisations. Larger organisations and employment agencies, except for one, appeared well briefed on current legislation.

Organisations which had no idea about the documentation newcomers needed to determine their work status were unlikely to recruit refugee workers as they assumed that employment law was too complicated and might require professional legal advice. One employer, for example, maintained that they always used a solicitor to check applicants' employment status, which at a flat fee of £1,000 per candidate made employing newcomers unattractive. Several organisations said they had never had to clarify someone's employment status but would consider checking out a good candidate although they did not know where to begin. They suggested Birmingham Chamber of Commerce and Industry or Jobcentres as sources of guidance. Some employers were deterred from appointing migrants lest they incur financial penalties because they were caught employing people who were not legally entitled to work.

Employers who were more in tune with employment law had researched the legislation themselves through official websites, for instance the Department for Work and Pensions (DWP) or the Home Office. The larger organisations received internal briefs with updates on employment law from their Personnel or Human Resource teams. Some companies in the hotel and catering sector had seen significant increases in the number of newcomers applying for seasonal work, and had decided to offer staff training specifically on employment legislation. Others sought advice from employment agencies about the legal working status of applicants and gave them the responsibility for screening candidates. Employers also expected applicants themselves to take responsibility for the declarations made on their application forms and for providing evidence of their right to work. Employees would normally be expected to produce documentation when they started work and those who failed to do so within a certain time faced dismissal.

The ambiguity surrounding newcomers' entitlement to work and the ignorance about employers' legislation are clearly significant barriers to employment. Findings from other studies have identified yet more difficulties for employers in determining an applicant's entitlement to work. Unclear immigration documents, identity forgeries and the bureaucracy and time required to check documents have all been cited. And many employers were unaware of the agencies which could support the process, (cf Bloch, 2004; Dunn and Somerville, 2004; Hurstfield *et al*, 2004; Sargeant and Forna, 2001).

Prejudice and negative stereotyping: a pool of unskilled labour

It was clear that some employers were cautious about engaging individuals whose entitlement to work was not straightforward, fearing that establishing an applicant's legality could be complex and burdensome. The reluctance to engage with relevant employment legislation could be described as discriminatory. New migrants themselves spoke of the prejudice they encountered from employers and the community. One Zimbabwean woman who had lived in South Africa said she preferred living under apartheid to living in the UK. Apartheid had clear rules dictating what black people could do whereas the rules in the UK were unclear and refugees were unsure about what they were allowed to do because racism was hidden 'but it is still here killing people inside'. Whilst prejudice was not always overt newcomers believed that some employers discriminated against them.

Our interviews with employers revealed stereotypical assumptions that cultural differences would cause problems with customer service etiquette and over 'understanding what we do here'. Some employers argued that cultural differences would influence newcomers' working practices and that if they were to succeed in the UK labour market they had to understand and accept UK working culture. Whilst we might view cultural concerns as a challenge to be overcome through orientation training and support on the job, the negative stereotyping was harder to deal with.

In organisations based outside the city where the workforce was less diverse, employers were reluctant to engage newcomers. They argued that the media had exacerbated, if not generated, the 'poor image' and 'bad reputation' of asylum seekers and refugees but that such portrayals affected workforce relations. They feared upsetting their workforce or their customers by employing people who had been labelled as 'bogus' or 'scroungers' and were unwilling to risk employing new migrants, whose image had been 'coloured by stories they have heard or read in the media'. Such employers expressed concern lest, as new members of staff tended to be used as scapegoats, newcomers would be 'likely targets', so might not work well as part of a team. Smaller employers recruited and managed their staff personally and claimed to know whether or not a potential recruit would 'fit in'. Larger organisations were concerned that workplace discrimination would go unnoticed and that unless cases of harassment were formally reported, they would not be addressed. Rather than having to deal with discrimination and workplace bullying they thought it safer not to employ newcomers.

Public sector employers maintained that having equal opportunities policies and grievance procedures acted as a safeguard against discriminatory be-haviour. These organisations were often so large that they did not know whether they had employed newcomers. They thought that refugees were un-likely to disclose their status voluntarily, keeping a low profile to avoid intimi-dation in the workplace. The issue of potential tensions within the workforce was raised by fifteen employers. Respondents from other organisations spoke of the 'inherent prejudice' held by some UK employers. They cited the media and its influence on the attitudes of staff and also their managers' opinions about taking on newcomers. Was this protectionist rationale for not employ-ing them simply thinly veiled racism? Where employers were prepared to con-sider employing newcomers it was as a pool of unskilled cheap labour:

> They [refugees] would do for unskilled labour, I am sure they would be good at warehouse work and cleaning. (Manufacturing sector)

> ...we have not had any refugees but we have clients in manufacturing who do. They seem honest and hardworking and they do the jobs British Asians wouldn't do. [There is a] need to make [employers] more aware of their availability and that they are cheaper to employ. (Finance sector)

Whilst in theory refugees do have full employment rights, our research found that in practice employer and workplace discrimination obstructed their em-ployment and advancement. Although negative attitudes appeared more marked – or were more frequently voiced – in small and medium sized busi-nesses, we wonder how prevalent they were in the larger national and public sector companies too. These companies were obviously mindful of their equal opportunities policies, but they too failed to facilitate career progres-sion amongst refugees and merely used them to fill low skilled posts.

Some of the employers who realised that refugees included educated and professional people thought that refugees should be content with low-paid jobs and be prepared to 'work their way up the ladder gradually'. Some British Asian employers, for example, argued that refugees should do the menial jobs previously allocated to immigrants, perhaps remembering their own experiences of being immigrants who had to struggle to gain workplace recognition or the discrimination against immigrants from the New Commonwealth and Ireland. However, four other British Asian employers were clearly sensitive to the difficulties faced by refugees and made special provisions, such as the use of interpreters, to facilitate communication with their immigrant staff.

Recognition of skills, experience and past qualifications

Some employers were aware that the new migrant workforce offered a valuable range of skills and qualifications levels but showed little interest in any skills or experience gained outside the UK. As we saw in Chapter Four, only a few newcomers tried to get their qualifications translated and only a handful had succeeded. The absence of Accreditation of Prior or Experiential Learning (APEL) procedures to aid re-qualification made matters worse:

> They don't accept our qualifications here. If they want to help, they should provide training, work experience and job replacement. Send them to work. The governments should create more jobs for them. Not to give them welfare benefit, it is better to send them to work. (Afghani man, 31)

Newcomers' rarely succeeded in getting recognition of their skills and qualifications when they tried to get a job. Little attention was paid to their past experience and qualifications, as a newcomer from Burkina Faso observed:

> Some countries accept the qualifications but I think I would have problems with it here ... nobody at all has asked me about my qualifications before and I have been here for more than six months.

Practical obstacles to work

Practical barriers stood in the way of taking a job even when one was offered. Before 2005 it was hard to obtain a national insurance number. Some refugees waited several months for a NINO and employers would only engage them if they had a P45. Banks were reluctant to allow newcomers to open bank accounts without documentation proving they had lived in the UK for three years. Most employers and employment agencies insisted upon payment going directly into employees' accounts.

We saw that women were denied learning and employment because they could not access affordable childcare. Much of the work offered to refugee women was shift work, in cleaning and hotels and catering, and childcare was usually only provided during the daytime. Some refugees had no suitable clothing for interviews or for work. One recruitment agency described how it often happened that migrants they could not send for interviews or to do certain work 'as the agency is always given guidelines and we have to send appropriately dressed people'. It did not tell their client why they were rejected lest this upset them, explaining 'we won't tell them why as it isn't their fault'.

Employment advice and guidance

Both newcomers and providers expressed to us their concern about the lack of specialist advice on access to appropriate learning. Our studies found the same to be true of advice to help newcomers access work. Newcomers wanted assistance to understand how their skills and abilities related to the UK labour market, and information about the work opportunities available and how to access them. People who had specialised or specific areas of interest found no way of accessing these. Although ESOL providers and voluntary organisations offered generic support to their newcomer students and clients, they were seldom able to give them advice on specific areas of employment.

Few, if any, new migrants had obtained effective specialist advice from statutory bodies such as Jobcentre Plus. Although information about job vacancies was available within the agency, advisers were under pressure to get claimants off benefits as soon as possible and as a result matched newcomers to low quality, short-term work regardless of their ability or experience. As we have noted, there was a reluctance to allow individuals to access training or employment that would be more sustainable in the medium or long term. Government employment targets, which apparently influenced the way in which advisers worked, were believed to underpin their approach.

Very few professional newcomers obtained interviews for jobs commensurate with their skills. One refugee felt 'people should be given better advice on where they want to be'. Newcomers saw word of mouth as the best way to get a job, but this grapevine discouraged others from applying for skilled or professional posts. Refugees who had been unable to get their skills recognised or to re-qualify, became disillusioned and told other skilled refugees not to bother. This negativity, reflecting as it did the reality, goes a long way to explain why employment aspirations were low and why many newcomers said they would accept any type of work just in order to be earning a wage.

Several newcomers had found work through the recommendation of a fellow refugee who worked for a company known to employ refugees. There was evidence that such work sometimes paid rates below the minimum wage and was located within the grey economy. It was often offering work on a day-by-day basis, and afforded no job security whatsoever.

Improving the employability of the new migrant workforce

Some of the problems that prevented newcomers from gaining employment or that pigeonholed them into unskilled jobs were due to the employers' ignorance about the capabilities of the new migrants and their rights and entitlements. Until employers become confident about recruiting new migrants skilled newcomers will not be able to fill skills shortages. So what can be done to assist newcomers and help maximise their contribution in dispersal areas? We draw on suggestions by the employers about making newcomers more attractive to UK employers.

Recruitment was blocked by the inadequate understanding and access of employers to information about employing new migrants. Organisations need clear and comprehensive information about the legislation concerning the employment of newcomers: the entitlement to work, national insurance numbers and tax codes. While employers were aware of equal opportunities legislation and took care not to breach it, the decisions they made about who to interview were based on mistaken assumptions and negative stereotyping. When we promised the employers confidentiality some spoke openly about how these impressions had influenced their decisions and suggested that the government do more to help employers filter out misinformation by means of an 'easy to understand and accessible' internet site, and through awareness raising campaigns. They also suggested that a legal helpline or access to appropriate local agencies specialising in employment law, translation and interpretation be set up and that active intervention from employment agencies or JCP should actively clarify employment entitlement.

The negative attitudes of employers and workers prevented newcomers' being employed, so measures should be taken to help break down preconceptions and tackle negative stereotypes. The 'automatic mistrust' bred by the media could be challenged by getting to know newcomers, listening to their stories and understanding their experiences. The employers in our studies who had never worked with newcomers recognised that their introduction into the workplace, albeit in 'restricted numbers to deal with the sensitivity', could in fact help educate existing staff, whilst offering the newcomers a chance to prove themselves.

Because of labour shortages employers might need to look to non-traditional workers in the future, even in areas with no history of diversity. This is already the case with Eastern European migrants from the A8 countries, who are working in traditionally white middle class areas. We found that employers were beginning to appreciate that their employees needed to understand that

174

filling vacant posts could be a problem and newcomers could help their organisation thrive. The tensions they anticipated might thus diminish, and circulating information about the sort of skills newcomers possessed might also help to capitalise on the skills available locally. Providing training opportunities for newcomers to get their skills recognised and accredited to UK standards was considered essential.

Ultimately, employers wanted better recruitment and retention and not to be short of staff with the relevant skills. They were open to ideas about what they might do to improve matters.

Facilitating new migrants' access to work

Employers welcomed the notion of an orientation course to assist newcomers' transition into the labour market: it would enable them to demonstrate some knowledge of UK work culture and would enhance their employability. Voluntary and work experience placements would also allow newcomers to familiarise themselves with UK work culture and enable them to get a UK reference.

Many newcomers were keen on work placements because they hoped to be able to prove themselves and enhance their employment prospects. Yet although the employers we interviewed said they were willing to offer such placements, few newcomers had found places. Perhaps the employers they approached did not understand what voluntary placements entail, or their obligations as employers. They might be more willing to offer placements if financial assistance was offered to subsidise the training undertaken and if they were set up by an advocate, such as an IAG worker, who could negotiate the exact terms and expectations of the placement.

Employers generally used job shadowing and mentoring in their standard induction and training programmes and this could help newcomers on placements to fit into the workplace. But the employers said that resource constraints did not allow for giving enough one-to-one support.

Only two organisations in our sample extended mentoring type systems beyond initial induction to longer term 'buddying' arrangements. Employers believed that new recruits who were still learning English would need intensive periods of shadowing and mentoring, particularly if the job was their first time in a UK workplace. Employers were concerned that this level of support might diminish the productivity of core staff. Organisations were thus more likely to offer work placements to newcomers if their loss of productivity could be reimbursed, perhaps by subsidised training and induction grants.

175

On the whole employers were positive about attending events such as job fairs for migrants. They believed gaining access to a new source of labour might benefit their organisation, in both the immediate and long term, and enable them to learn about issues such as how to tackle negative attitudes, and give them the opportunity to meet organisations which had employed newcomers. Job fairs were particularly attractive for those experiencing difficulties filling vacancies, and gave a chance to network and develop local and regional partnerships. Both employers and newcomers suggested that such events needed to be easily accessible and promoted in ways that would avoid negative press coverage.

Thus various initiatives could be implemented with the help of development and funding. There is scope to make such initiatives widely available through partnership working between employers, funders and training providers. In the first instance some assistance is required to help build the confidence of employers and to encourage them to provide practical work placement opportunities and job trials. A priority would be to provide information on employment legislation, ESOL support, mentoring and opportunities for top up training. Partnership working between funders, trainers and employers could all raise employers' confidence about recruiting refugees.

Conclusion

A number of general conclusions can be drawn from the research findings discussed in this chapter. Downward professional mobility is the norm for skilled newcomers living in the dispersal areas of the West Midlands, as it is for refugees residing just about anywhere in the UK or Europe (Phillimore and Goodson, 2006; Sargeant and Forna, 2001). In principle refugees, once they are granted status, have the same employment entitlements as British citizens – but in reality they do not enjoy equality of opportunity in the work place. With many barriers to overcome and so little support to help them into the labour market it is no surprise that refugee unemployment rates are so high. Such high unemployment and the predominance of low paid, unstable jobs will inevitably have major economic implications for deprived urban areas. On an individual level it is not difficult to see how the pattern of unemployment, de-skilling and demotivation we have described leads to the increasing exclusion of refugees in society.

Our research demonstrates the lack of opportunities for newcomers to gain work experience through structured work placements or voluntary work and of work-based learning opportunities for newcomers to earn an income whilst developing their skills and work competences. Vocational courses such as National Vocational Qualifications (NVQs) should be promoted to both employers and newcomers. The lack of opportunity for newcomers to develop their employability could well lead to the long-term exclusion of refugees from jobs with progression opportunities and will exacerbate problems of social exclusion in deprived areas where they have settled.

A multi-faceted approach is required. The employers need help to recruit, support and encourage career progression, whilst the newcomers need prompt and accessible advice, guidance and training opportunities. There is immense scope for improving newcomers' position in the labour market and compelling reasons for doing so. As the concluding chapter shows, exclusion from economic and social opportunities undermines integration, inclusion and cohesion in dispersal areas. It goes onto suggest what can be done to help new migrants into employment that is commensurate with their skills, qualifications and employment experience.

8

From exclusion to integration
via employability

Research undertaken over the past decade has demonstrated that asylum seekers and refugees are amongst the most economically disadvantaged groups in the UK, with women the worst affected (Bloch, 2004; Dumper, 2002). We have seen that the situation in the West Midlands is particularly acute. The region currently houses over 50,000 newcomers, nearly 1 per cent of the overall population, with most in the most deprived urban centres. The newcomer population in the West Midlands comes from over 100 countries and speaks over 100 languages. Unemployment levels recorded amongst newcomers who have the right to work are strikingly high, exceeding those of the most deprived ethnic and social groups in the region and of refugees living in London.

New migrants are struggling to access the language provision they need to work and to study. The provision they are able to access is often poor and has little relevance to their vocational needs. Now that free ESOL for asylum seekers who have waited less than six months for a decision has been withdrawn, access to ESOL is set to decline. Speaking little English impedes access to education and training but even when they become more proficient they cannot access education and training opportunities. JCP regulations actually prevent newcomers from getting the training they need to enhance their employability.

There is little in the way of specialist advice for refugee jobseekers and a tendency for refugees to be pointed to unskilled, unsustainable employment regardless of their education, qualifications or experience. Many have no proof of their qualifications and those that do possess a certificate find it is often downgraded by the National Academic Recognition Information Centre (NARIC). Those who do attend college find no mechanisms such as APEL exist to help recognise their skills and experience. The main route to re-qualification is to begin their studies again. Many refugees cannot afford such a lengthy process and end up seeking paid employment in the short term rather than investing the time to improve their long term prospects.

The detailed picture we have painted of the challenges faced by newcomers trying to access ETE shows them to be multiple, overlapping and interwoven. English is a problem for many newcomers and problems accessing ESOL classes, or the poor quality or unsuitability of these classes, can mean it takes years for them to acquire workplace appropriate language skills.

New migrants face the uncertainty of awaiting a decision and the disruption of the 28-day transition period. They have their identity as refugees constantly thrown into doubt by immigration officials and the media. The impact on their self-esteem is severe and they may also have psychological problems caused by their experience of war.

All new arrivals also have to deal with having no references from a UK employer or any work experience in this country. These are compounded by not understanding how the system works or how to locate jobs, contact employers, complete application forms or prepare CVs in a thorough manner. Fewer still have any concept of selling oneself at interview. And employers are, as we have seen, not keen to engage newcomers thanks to media portrayals of refugees as 'lazy' or 'criminal' and fear their customers or employees will be offended if they are appointed. The confusing documentation surrounding immigration makes employers nervous lest they unwittingly break the law.

Misinformation appears to be endemic amongst employers, educators and refugees alike. Education and training providers struggle to find out about the rights and entitlements of newcomers. Non-statutory agencies, while seeking to work with newcomers, lack the knowledge or resources to provide support. Many of the organisations providing support to newcomers are trapped in a short-term funding cycle and forced to spend time competing for funding instead of delivering their services. Few newcomers have access to childcare and travel so women in particular struggle to access and sustain their learning. Newcomers striving to find out about education and training often have to rely on their peers for information, which, as we have shown, is often inaccurate.

On the whole and despite the barriers they faced, most newcomers were highly motivated to work and learn. Their general educational achievement levels were slightly lower than the regional average but they varied from complete illiteracy to post-graduate qualifications. Many young people had experienced a break in their education because they had to flee their homeland. Women from some backgrounds had been forbidden access to learning.

Some newcomers had never worked in a formal environment, having eked a living in an agrarian economy, whilst others had been government ministers, academics, factory managers, doctors and teachers. That they could not bring their skills and experience, some of which were in chronic shortage in the UK, deprives their local economies and communities. The lack of opportunity undermines the employment aspirations of refugees, who come to believe that employers would not consider them for skilled or professional jobs. The presence of large numbers of new migrants, who have a wide range of skills and qualifications, should be seen as an opportunity to revitalise deprived areas where the indigenous population is low skilled and ageing.

For a dispersal area to be sustainable its population needs to become self-sufficient and to have prospects for the future. How engaged a person is in their local community and in society and their willingness to participate in civic activities depends largely on their employment status. There is no evidence that skilled refugees are obtaining work commensurate with their skills. Large-scale longitudinal surveys are needed to examine social mobility. Qualitative research will help us understand the processes that underpin mobility and opportunity among newcomer populations.

Chapter Two began with notions of newcomer integration and the relationship between ETE and integration. The research findings from across the West Midlands indicate that while ETE are key functional aspects of newcomer integration the ability to access them is too often problematic. The few who did gain access to ETE found that being engaged in learning, and particularly in employment, facilitated their access to other aspects of integration such as social networks and secure housing. A chicken and egg situation exists. Having stable housing, or at least being housed, generally made it possible to study and obtain work but those with jobs were better able to get housing because private landlords saw people who were employed as more attractive tenants.

Access to ETE increased the likelihood of newcomers being able to build some social capital through informal and formal social networks. Speaking English at work or college helped newcomers to improve their language skills and thus become more self-sufficient. Having a network of social contacts opened up access to advice, emotional support and increased self-confidence. For newcomers, integration was first of all about getting work and becoming financially self-sufficient. In many cultures, being unable to support oneself is seen as a sign of failure. Newcomers wished to contribute to society so they could feel they were equal members of it. Being employed and having an income also meant they had some control over their lives and could make decisions and become active consumers. For people with a professional background working in their own field was part of their identity. They could feel they had regained some of their status.

At present most new migrants in the region are unemployed. The increase in the level of unemployment in already deprived dispersal areas has implications for the future of both the individuals and the areas in which they reside. Greater unemployment increases the difficulty of sustaining basic local institutions; or achieving adequate social organisation; structural resources are removed; and cultural resources, such as positive role models, are lost. Wilson (1998) demonstrates how in Chicago, high joblessness was associated with isolation from mainstream society and feelings of having little control over the local environment. As joblessness increases so does the clustering of poverty, so that social exclusion spreads across wider areas and becomes ever more concentrated in the most deprived areas. All the disadvantages associated with poverty become accentuated and breaking the cycle becomes ever more difficult. As more poor people are added to poverty clusters it becomes harder to turn the area around. In such circumstances, unemployment is likely to be long-term, the skills that newcomers offer are wasted. And regeneration initiatives in dispersal areas will not be helped by high concentrations of disaffected unemployed refugees living below the poverty line, as our research shows.

How a large influx of unemployed migrants affects the attitudes and behaviour of indigenous communities is an issue that has attracted much attention (Audit Commission, 2007). Many of those who took part in our studies expressed concern about the attitudes and behaviours exhibited by local people towards newcomers and many of the newcomers felt vilified by the media and some local people.

On first arriving in the UK newcomers spent several months coping with culture shock, the climate and the trauma of losing family members and material goods in their homeland. The gradual realisation of how 'despised' they were made them feel unable to mix with local people because they would be 'looked down upon' or people would be 'scared' of them. Women in all our studies experienced greatest isolation. The effect of dispersal on social inclusion and integration, both integral components in creating social cohesion, has been the subject of increasing debate. Findings presented in the Cantle report (2001) indicated that even third generation ethnic minority groups were not integrated and society appeared to be divided along racial lines in which the various communities led 'parallel lives'. In his investigation of the 2001 riots Cantle (2001) identifies ghettoisation as a key contributor to social unrest. In his recent book Cantle (2005) argues that the segregation of communities in the UK is one of the greatest threats facing British society and demands prompt action to facilitate social contact and reduce structural inequalities.

The dispersal programme has undoubtedly added to the complexity of issues facing deprived neighbourhoods. The socio-demographic composition of areas is changing with the arrival of large numbers of young, predominantly male migrants, from a range of ethnic backgrounds new to these areas (Phillimore *et al*, 2003, 2005). Many arrive already marginalised by the state, because they have been dispersed away from any family or friends already resident in the UK, and excluded from work and from mainstream education. Many argue that restrictionalist policies that explicitly aim to exclude asylum seekers are simply storing up problems for the future (Brochmann, 1999). In addition, the state has politicised asylum and the media have created images of asylum seekers as 'scroungers' who take advantage of tax payers' money and resources. The implicit and explicit discourse of the legislation since the introduction of the National Asylum Support Service (NASS) (Robinson *et al*, 2003) reflects these attitudes and is echoed in the popular press.

A few measures have been put in place to help integrate refugees into their new 'communities'. Recognising a gap in policy, the Government has recently proposed the rolling out of the SUNRISE programme so that all new refugees will be provided with advice about how to locate housing and how to use Jobcentre Plus. We have shown that JCP is part of the problem rather than the solution, and has exacerbated refugees' feelings of exclusion and worthlessness. Certainly their approach to working with new migrants needs to be reviewed.

There is little data to suggest that newcomers are moving out of dispersal areas. There is little accommodation that they could afford anywhere else and they do not know the full range of housing options which are available to them (Goodson *et al*, 2005; Phillimore, 2005; Phillimore *et al*, 2004). Without jobs there are few opportunities for newcomers to mix with local people. Unable to become self-supporting, they have little choice but to remain in their dispersal area. So prospects for the future are bleak.

Whether looking at the debate in academic or policy terms it is clear that asylum seekers and refugees are being socially excluded. In policy terms the UK Government argues that the problems experienced by the socially excluded are linked and mutually reinforcing: low income, being from an ethnic minority, living in a deprived neighbourhood, living in poor housing and family instability. The nature of the asylum system and the situation that led people to claim asylum are the very factors likely to precipitate exclusion. Most newcomers are unemployed, the dispersal areas are located in deprived neighbourhoods, newcomers are almost all from ethnic minority backgrounds and they have been separated from their friends, family and material belongings and their accommodation is sub-standard (Zetter and Pearl, 2000). Decent employment is critical for breaking this downward spiral and for the economic stability and social cohesion of the areas in which they have been placed.

The social exclusion of refugees has also been considered from an academic perspective. Looking for some common ground in discussions of social exclusion Atkinson (1998) found three recurring elements: relativity, agency and dynamics. People are excluded from society only if they are excluded from the mainstream. Thus, unemployment will exclude refugees because poverty and isolation from local people will also exclude them from other aspects of society such as consumption and social interaction. Social exclusion also results from actions, whether by the individual electing to drop-out of the market economy or by others, for example, the action or inaction of employers or the government on behalf of refugees. Finally, people are excluded not just because of their present position but because they have few prospects for improvement in the future; in the case of refugees this book has demonstrated that few have any prospect of gaining work of any kind, let alone skilled jobs.

Supporting the integration of newcomers through education, training and employment

There is a serious discrepancy between the policy objectives of improving the living and working conditions of EU citizens, and the deliberate social exclusion of migrants from these societies (Sales and Gregory, 1996). Unlike reception countries such as the Netherlands, where a right to work is granted for up to three months a year, and Sweden, where asylum seekers are entitled to work if their claim is anticipated to take more than four months to process, asylum seekers in the UK are excluded from the labour market and wider society until leave to remain has been granted. Upon being granted refugee status UK refugees are expected to integrate but are given no access to mechanisms or resources to help them do so.

We have shown that unless refugees living in dispersal areas are helped to be economically active they will be excluded. Dispersal areas have all the ingredients: frustration, disaffection and racial segregation, which Cantle (2001) pointed to as key causes of the social unrest in northern British cities. Following Berry's (1997) integration model, successful integration requires state institutions to take account of newcomers' needs and to respect diversity. It is important to ensure that the costs of integration are covered centrally before the far greater social and economic costs of marginalisation are felt locally, regionally and nationally.

While the new move towards cohesion may bring some measures for building bridging capital between old migrant communities and new, it is vital to tackle the striking structural inequalities experienced by newcomers. Employment, education and training have the potential for integration precisely because many refugees have skills that are in short supply. Creating initiatives and revising policies to improve the employability of refugees would be a major advance towards inclusion and cohesion.

If the ban on asylum seekers working were revoked, those who gain leave to remain would already have made some progress towards economic inclusion and not be pushed into the grey economy while they await the legal right to work. Undertaking a skills audit on their entry to the country would build a comprehensive picture of the skills and experience offered by newcomers. This information about newcomer skills, combined with training providers and employers working collaboratively, and funding from the Department for Innovation, Universities and Skills (DIUS), would help to facilitate programmes to help refugees adapt their skills to UK requirements. And advisers working within mainstream agencies who have been trained to understand the complex problems that refugees face when seeking work should provide specialist advice to each individual.

In Norway a new profession of integration advisers has been developed. They link refugees to language, learning, and employment opportunities and this has markedly enhanced refugee employment (FAFO, 2004). And the Dutch experience shows that work experience and apprenticeship programmes will enable refugees to gain access to the labour market in the first instance (Scheldler and Glastra, 2000).

The stereotyped attitudes of employers to the UK will need to be changed dramatically. Coussey (2000) suggests that employers be the focus of integration strategies because they can provide training and development for ethnic minority workers. Such moves might run alongside education to help refugees meet employers' normative demands with respect to customs and manners, flexibility and ability to learn (Gowricharn, 2002). The programme would also speed up their move towards fluency in English and support their development in English literacy.

Moving skilled refugees into skilled work is a major challenge for agencies working in deprived areas. The experience of organisations in the UK seeking to place minority groups into work has demonstrated that general measures for tackling exclusion from the labour market are not effective for all groups (Coussey, 2000). There is a need for personalised support based within mainstream services that can provide comprehensive information and a wide range of initiatives (Feeney, 2000). The Refugee Council (1997) argue the need to remove legal, cultural and language obstacles so that new arrivals can benefit fully from existing opportunities. This would require public institutions to adapt to changes in the population profile, to accept refugees as part of the community and critically, to take specific steps to facilitate their access to resources (Schibel *et al*, 2002).

The current expectation is that refugees will access employment through the state employment agency, the job centres of JCP. Until very recently JCP received no extra funding to help support the additional costs of working with refugees, such as interpretation, no staff training or even guidance (Phillimore and Goodson, 2001; Phillimore *et al*, 2003). It has been reported that JCP often steer refugees towards low skilled work because it is quicker than trying to explore sustainable options (Phillimore and Goodson, 2001; Phillimore *et al*, 2003a, 2003b). We have found that JCP policies actively prevent many refugees from engaging in activities which would help them to gain access to skilled employment.

A policy of directing certain groups of clients to employment that has no prospects can be described as institutionally racist (Ogbonna, 1998). It restricts particular ethnic groups to particular kinds of work and is ultimately counterproductive because it condemns those groups to the poverty trap (Preece and Walters, 1999). Resources are now being targeted at JCP to help them cope with the influx of refugees, and some sub-regions with access to European funding are seeking to develop specific programmes. The focus will remain, however, on outputs and thus emphasis will be placed on locating employment in the short term rather than helping refugees to obtain work commensurate with their skills. If social exclusion is not to be intensified in deprived dispersal areas then measures that enable refugees to meet their potential are urgently needed, and must include the development of programmes acknowledging and accrediting newcomers' prior knowledge and experience.

When we looked for good practice in enhancing the employability of newcomers we found well-established mechanisms in other European countries that had a proven impact on economic activity levels. Holland, France and Germany have long-established APEL systems, which are open to the general population. In Scandinavia systems are newer but have been extensively evaluated to determine the most effective approaches and the target groups for each. In the UK we have no national APEL system. There are OSAT tests for individuals working for registered construction employers and NVQs for those who have managed to find a job in an area where they have skills, but no systems exist for unemployed people who wish to have their skills and abilities proven. Furthermore, resources are centrally provided for APEL in Northern European countries as part of the funds earmarked for integration. Organisations in the UK, however, must compete for local or national funds and thus have been able to develop only small-scale APEL programmes, which work with small numbers of people in small geographical areas, for a short time.

To make the most of refugees' skills and experience, however, we need a national APEL system. And creating an effective and meaningful system requires substantial funding. Holland, France and Germany have used software or interpreters to adapt long-established APEL systems for use with migrants in a wide range of languages. Work-based skills testing enables newcomers to demonstrate their skills in a real work situation and minimises the need for demonstrable written language skills. The system is used to accredit migrants' skills but also as a diagnostic system to enable assessors to identify the person's gaps and weaknesses and to recommend courses to address them. The portfolio approach developed in the Netherlands and Scandinavia enables newcomers to prepare a detailed account of their skills and how they might be applied.

All these methods have some possibilities for the UK. The most practical approach is work-based skills assessment. This would give refugees with largely practical skills a rapid solution to re-qualification and would not require the UK to set up specialist test centres, such as those used to accredit skills in France and Germany. Practical skills recognition might be developed in association with work experience initiatives so that refugees can accredit their skills whilst gaining UK work experience, a reference and all the other benefits associated with work placements. NVQ assessors might be involved in this accreditation. Refugees who have construction skills might take OSAT tests whilst working in unpaid placements. But the cost of these tests is likely to be beyond the reach of most refugees so a source of funding has to be identified.

The skills portfolio approach may also be of use to refugees but only if this can be standardised and employers educated about how to use it. The Dutch system provides a suitable model for the UK. Ideally the system would be developed by employer-focused organisations such as the National Employer Panel or the Sector Skills Councils in conjunction with an organisation such as the Refugee Council, to ensure its suitability for both employers and refugees.

In addition, trained advisers are needed to support refugees completing portfolios. With Learning and Skills Council (LSC) funding these could be provided as part of the ESOL process. Perhaps one role of the new SUNRISE workers could be to assist refugees in the development of their portfolio. There might also be a role for mentors working with refugees under the Timebank project to advise them about their portfolios. It is unlikely that a national APEL system will be developed unless an organisation is charged with the responsibility for this and allocated sufficient funds for setting up the training and systems. We suggest that overall responsibility be placed with the LSC.

Our survey of employability initiatives (Phillimore *et al*, 2005) indicated that the provision of work experience places is critical to increasing refugees' employability, their knowledge of the labour market, their English proficiency and their self-worth. Work experience is also an important means of expanding existing skills and orientating to the labour market. Many organisations in the UK offer work experience places but most are on an *ad hoc* basis and on a small scale and so have little impact on refugee unemployment and underemployment overall. The situation is somewhat different in Northern Europe and particularly in Scandinavia where refugees are provided with placements as part of Government initiatives.

The development of a successful work experience programme depends on engaging employers and this could be done through existing employer networks. Programmes must be well structured and everyone must know what is expected of them. A job specification and, ideally a subsequent contract between organisation and newcomer are important for re-enforcing what is expected from all concerned. Support for newcomers and employees has to be offered on a regular basis but must also be available for problem solving or even damage limitation should problems emerge.

Finding the right newcomer for the right job is crucial. Approaches in Scandinavia and the Netherlands indicate that it is necessary to provide the wide range of support they might need including a caseworker, an 'in-work' mentor and ideally an 'out-of-work' mentor. The 'in-work' mentor helps newcomers fit into their new organisation and encourages them to gradually take on more tasks so their contribution to their employer develops iteratively. Ideally this mentor has received training to provide support to newcomers and, in the longer term, other staff.

Evaluation of the success of such initiatives is essential so that learning and problems can be identified and influence the ongoing evolvement of the integration programme. Organisations need to keep track of their clients and how their work experience initiative contributed to the refugee's success. The success achieved in Scandinavia and the Netherlands where refugee unemployment rates are far lower than the UK, – although the Netherlands' general unemployment rate is 7 per cent higher – is testimony to the emphasis placed on work experience and core funding for these initiatives. UK initiatives, in contrast, are small-scale, based in localities rather than across regions or nationally, and struggle to attract funding for expansion or even sustainability. This situation in the UK needs to change.

A model for the UK

We brought together the main ideas and initiatives around APEL and work experience to construct a model that we have piloted in the West Midlands with a wide range of partners. The model is illustrated in Figure 8.1. It aims to help skilled newcomers enhance their employability by recognising and accrediting their skills simultaneously and facilitating their access to work experience opportunities. The model, or Employability Pathway, recognises the skills of newcomers in particular vocational areas – to date construction, healthcare, business administration, general maintenance and social research (Phillimore *et al*, 2007). The Pathways generally operate with no more than 20 refugees at a time.

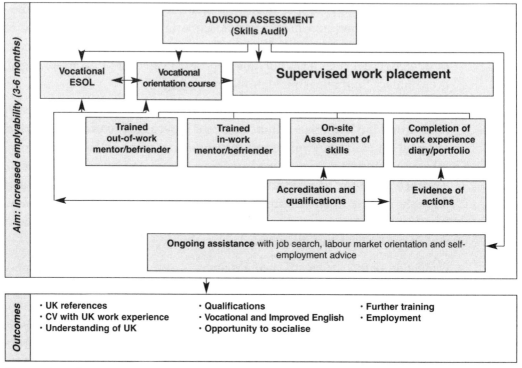

Figure 8.1: Route to work based accreditation of prior and experiential learning

The model is intended to work in stages. First is the recruitment and assessment phase, where skilled refugees seeking work enter a refugee community organisation or JCP or are registered with organisations as seeking employment. The support staff at the organisations have been briefed about the establishment of the pathways and are actively recruiting refugees to take part. The recruits are briefly assessed, either individually or at an open day. Once their skills and experience are identified, they are referred to an appropriate project. Assessments are undertaken by a project worker who has responsibility for running the programme day to day and is based at the premises of the training provider.

At the initial assessment the refugees meet the project worker and hear about the programme. Their suitability for it is gauged through a short skills audit and a formal or informal evaluation of their proficiency in English as required in the vocational area. Those whose English language skills are inadequate are referred to a suitable ESOL course. Those whose wider skills could not be brought quickly up to standard are referred to training courses in conjunction with local colleges. Those on the programme who cannot reach a standard where they are job ready are referred to a short workplace orientation course and then return for referral. Once they are job ready, they are encouraged to return to their project worker for re-assessment.

The second stage entails training and vocational orientation. The refugees undertake a range of activities offered by various training providers. But ideally, to aid continuity, as many of the programme components as possible are located at one site for a maximum of sixteen hours per week for up to fourteen weeks. Pathway components vary according to vocational area. A construction pathway, for example, needs to incorporate health and safety training and provide the opportunity to take the Construction Skills Certification Scheme (CSCS) test, as refugees need a CSCS card to work on a UK construction site. Healthcare workers need support to apply for a Criminal Records Bureau (CRB) check, without which they cannot work in the health sector.

Some elements are common to all pathways. Each pathway incorporates some training provider based work where the refugees demonstrate their skills through role-play or practical activities and can get training and advice about how to locate their skills within the labour market. All are given vocational ESOL so they can learn the technical language they will need in the workplace. The project worker explores with the refugees the ways in which their skills can be accredited at different stages in the pathway. The options available may vary according to the refugee's ability to undertake written assignments or practical demonstrations. A key role of the project worker is to identify a work experience place for each refugee on the programme.

All the refugees attend an interview with their prospective employer, having been offered interview training and support to prepare a CV. Refugees who are unsuccessful are given feedback from their interview by their project worker and then introduced to another potential employer. Employers are encouraged to offer their trainee an in-work mentor and supervisor, to make line management straightforward. The project worker negotiates on the trainees' behalf to secure agreement from the different parties as to hours, tasks and responsibilities and amends the job description accordingly.

The in-work mentor smooths the refugee's transition into the workforce. They will have received training to develop their mentoring skills and to understand refugee issues. Mentors are expected to continue with their routine work whilst, in the first instance, describing their actions to their mentee. They explain how the workplace routinely operates. They also introduce their mentees to colleagues and ensure that they do not feel isolated. Where possible, mentors are matched to refugees by age and gender. Over time refugees can take on more and more by themselves until they can work more or less independently. By this stage they are treated the same as their colleagues and their tasks are allocated by the supervisor.

Through the Timebank Programme refugees on the pathways will also be offered an out of work mentor. This mentor provides support mainly on a personal level and guides them through any personal difficulties that threaten to affect their work. Ideally they will support the refugee's ongoing job search, help seek jobs and advise on interview techniques.

Their project worker will have introduced the refugee to a college assessor. The assessor advises refugees, their mentors and supervisors, of the evidence that needs to be collected and regularly checks to assess progress and identify any difficulties. The assessment methods should be agreed by both the refugees and employers. They might entail diaries, discussions, and testimonials from their in work mentor and photographs of practical work, which must be verified by their supervisor. Trainees will be encouraged to keep a diary of their activities. This may contribute towards their assessment and will act as a record of achievement helping their supervisor to write references or testimonials. Diary records could possibly be used to create a portfolio contributing to an NVQ. The supervisor is the refugee's line manager and will deal with any work related problems. The supervisor must ensure that the refugee is able to undertake all the tasks needed to provide evidence of skills and will work with the mentor to identify any skills gaps and discuss them with the refugee and their project worker so that appropriate training can be given in house or elsewhere. When the work experience ends the supervisor will be responsible for writing the refugee's references, using their records of achievement to inform a detailed account of their ability and achievements.

Five vocational employability pathways have been piloted in the West Midlands, based on this model. Each pathway brought together a range of organisations to collaboratively develop vocationally focused integrated packages of employability products. Some of the organisations had no experience of working with refugees. Although few of the services offered were new, pulling them all together in one package was an innovative way of engaging refugees and getting their skills recognised. Funding from the EU EQUAL programme paid for expertise required to identify and bring partners together. Evaluators tracked the progress of each of the 143 refugees who followed the pathways. Early findings suggest that only 9 per cent of refugees were unemployed at the end of the programmes compared with 73 per cent at the beginning, and many had gained access to skilled work, skilled self-employment or higher level education (see Phillimore *et al*, 2007).

We have demonstrated through this book that newcomers in the UK are struggling to access education, training and employment and that it is virtually impossible for refugees to get skilled employment. Early indications are that migrant workers from the A8 EU accession countries also struggle to access work commensurate with their skills, although not to the same extent as refugees (McKay and Winkelmann-Gleed, 2005). The structural inequalities embedded in the treatment of new arrivals to the UK have long been of concern to commentators. Rex and Moore (1967) highlighted concerns around segregation and inequality in their work based in Birmingham forty years ago. And recently reports have emphasised the social costs of segregation (Cantle, 2005; Icoco, 2007).

We have shown how agency, a key dimension of exclusion, underpins newcomers' exclusion from education, training and employment. The restrictionalist asylum policy and lacklustre, under-resourced integration policy combine to separate newcomers from society. These policies have marginalised newcomers, and only positive policy action to include them can bring about change. We need to learn from countries which focus on the hardest to serve (Evans, 2001). The UK's present Welfare to Work policy concentrates on a single transition to employment as soon as possible: the emphasis is on any employment, not on sustainable employment. Astonishingly, JCP define sustainable employment as a job that is retained for thirteen weeks.

Yet there is great reluctance to change the system for refugees. One Department for Work and Pensions minister, quoted by the Employability Forum (2006) said:

> We cannot afford to drive a coach and horses through our whole welfare to work programme for the sake of this group. We cannot make exceptions – and if we did we would put refugees at even greater risk from sections of the media that already try to suggest that refugees receive more favourable treatment than the host community.

But without concerted action the situation cannot improve. The system needs to be made more dynamic and focus on career progression for those who are unemployed. Workers on short-term or part-time contracts are shown to receive far less work-related skills training than someone with a permanent job (Arulampalam and Booth, 1998). Yet they are the ones for whom training will enhance Britain's economic activity.

Nothing less than a total shift in policy and practice will do. Instead of paying passive benefits to encourage engagement in low paid employment with no prospects, a comprehensive and concerted programme of training, re-skilling, re-qualifying, work experience and up-skilling needs to be put in place. Initiatives such as the Employability Pathway would provide a shortcut to skilled employment or a fast-track to re-qualification. The innovative pathways, offered to a small number of refugees, proved their worth. Similar Pathways need to be rolled out across the whole country. But the key statutory agencies would have to change their approach. The quality of jobs is all-important in ensuring that newcomers become included and can maximise their contribution to their neighbourhood. The Government's Welfare to Work policies must be directed at enabling new migrants – and the unemployed generally – to access stable jobs that offer prospects. Such a policy shift would also benefit the refugees who move in and out of work whilst remaining excluded. Instead of being a drain on dispersal areas, refugees would contribute to their own stability and to the social cohesion and economic prosperity of the UK.

References

ABNI (2006) *Progress towards Integration*: 2005/6 Annual Report. London: Home Office

Advantage West Midlands (2004) *Delivering Advantage. The West Midlands Economic Strategy and Action Plan 2004-2010*. Advantage West Midlands: Birmingham

Aferiat, Y (1999) *Good Practice Guide on the Integration of Refugees in the European Union: Vocational Training for Refugees*. ECRE Task Force on Integration. Brussels: OCIV

Ager, A and Strang, A (2004) Indicators of Integration: Final Report. *Home Office Development and Practice Report 28*. London: HMSO

Alba, R and Nee, V (1997) Rethinking Assimilation Theory for a New Era of Immigration. *International Migration Review* 31 (4), pp 826-874

Alba, RD (1998) Assimilation, Exclusion or Neither? Models of the Incorporation of Immigrant Groups in the United States. In Schuck, P and Munz, R *Paths to Inclusion: The integration of immigrants in the US and Germany*. Oxford: Becghahn

Alcoff, L and Potter, E (1993) *Feminist Epistemologies*. London: Routledge

Aldridge, F, Dutton, Y, Gray, R, McLoughlin, A, Sterland, L and Waddington, S (2005) *Working to Rebuild Careers: An assessment of the provision to assist refugees seeking employment in the East Midlands*. Leicester: National Institute for Adult Continuing Education

Aldridge, F, Gray, R *et al* (2005) *Skills Audit for Asylum Seekers and Refugees: A Practitioners' Manual*. Leicester: National Institute for Adult Continuing Education

Aldridge, F and Waddington, S (2001) *Asylum Seekers' Skills and Qualifications Audit Pilot Project*. Leicester: National Institute for Adult Continuing Education

Anderson, B (1983) *Imagined Communities: Reflections on the origin and spread of nationalism*. London: Verso

Arulampalam, W and Booth, A (1998) Labour market flexibility and skills acquisition: is there a trade off? In Atkinson, A and Hills, J (eds) *Exclusion, Employment and Opportunity*. CASE paper 4. London: LSE pp 65-85

Ashe, P, Brown, K, Huremovic, D, Olimide, G, and Walters N (1997) *On the HORIZON, Final Report of the European Employment HORIZON project, European refugees and migrants: advice and guidance into employment*. University of Surrey: School of Educational Studies

Atfield, G, Brahmbhatt, K and O'Toole, T (2007) *Refugees' Experiences of Integration,* University of Birmingham and Refugee Council

Atkinson, A (1998) Social exclusion, poverty and unemployment. In Atkinson, A and Hills, J (eds) *Exclusion, Employment and Opportunity*. CASE paper 4. London: LSE pp 1-24

Baker, R (1990) The Refugee Experience: Communication and Stress, Recollections of a refugee survivor. Oxford: *Journal of Refugee Studies* 3 (1)

Banton, M (2001) National integration in France and Britain, *Journal of Ethnic and Migration Studies* 27 (1, Jan) pp 151-68

Baubock, R (1994) *The Integration of Immigrants*, CMDG Report. Strasbourg: Council of Europe

BBC News Online (2001) *UK Attacked over Refugee Racism*. BBC News Online, 3rd April 2001

Beauvais, C and Jenson, J (2002) Social Cohesion: Updating the state of research, *Canadian Policy Research Networks*. Ottawa: Canadian Heritage

Beresford, P (1996) *Challenging the 'Them' and 'Us' of Social Policy Research, Ethics and Social Policy Research*. Luton: University of Luton Press

Berry, J W (1997) Immigration, Acculturation and Adaptation. *Applied Psychology: An International Review* 46, (1) pp 5-68

Berry, J W (1994) Acculturation and Psychological Adaptation: An overview. In Bouvy, A, van de Vijver, F, Boski, P and Scmitz, P (eds) *Journeys into cross-cultural psychology*. 11th International Conference Liege.

Berthoud, R (2000) Ethnic employment penalties in Britain. *Journal of Ethnic and Migration Studies* 26 (3) pp 389-416

Bhui, K, Abdi, A *et al* (2003) Traumatic events, migration characteristics and psychiatric symptoms among Somali refugees. *Social Psychiatry and Psychiatric Epidemiology* 38(1) pp 35-43

Birmingham Chamber of Commerce (2005) *Demographic Change in Birmingham and Solihull* Birmingham: Chamber of Commerce

Black, R (2001) Fifty years of refugee studies: from theory to policy. *International Migration Review* 35 (1) pp 57-78

Bloch, A (2004) Labour market participation and conditions of employment: a comparison of minority ethnic groups and refugees in Britain. *Sociological Research Online*, 9, no2, http://www.socresonline.org.uk/9/2/bloch.html

Bloch, A (2002) *Refugees' Opportunities and Barriers in Employment and Training*. DWP Research Report series (179) pp 83

Bloch, A (2000) Refugee settlement in Britain: the impact of policy on participation. *Journal of Ethnic and Migration Studies* 26 (1) pp 75-88

Bloch, A (1999) Carrying out a survey of refugees: some methodological considerations and guide-lines, *Journal of Refugee Studies*, 12/4, Oxford

Bloch, A (1999) Refugees in the job market: a case of unused skills in the British economy. In Bloch, A and Levy, C, *Refugees, Citizenship and Policy in Europe*, Basingstoke: Palgrave, pp 187-210

Bloch, A and Atfield, G (2002) The Professional Capacity of Nationals from the Somali Regions in Britain, London: Refugee Action and the International Organisation for Migration, unpublished report

Bloch, A and Schuster, L (2005) At the extremes of exclusion: deportation, detention and dispersal. *Ethnic and Racial Studies*, pp 491-512

Bloch, A and Schuster, L (2002) Asylum and welfare: contemporary debates. *Critical Social Policy*, 22 (3) pp 393-414

Bourdieu, Pierre (1965) *Travail et Travailleurs en Algerie*. Paris: Editions

Bourn, J (2004) *Improving the Speed and Quality of Asylum Decisions*. London: The National Audit Office.

Bouvy, A, von de Vijver, F, Boski P and Schmitz, P (eds) *Journeys into cross-cultural psychology*. Amsterdam: Swets and Zeitlinger

Brochmann, G (1999) Controlling immigration in Europe. In Brochmann, G and Hammar, T (eds) *Mechanisms of immigration control: a comparative analysis of European Regulation Policies*. Oxford: Berg

Burgess, S and Propper, C (2002) The dynamics of poverty. In Hills, Le Grand and Piachaud (eds) (2002) *Understanding social exclusion*. Oxford: OUP

Burnett, A and Peel, M (2001) Asylum Seekers and Refugees in Britain: Health needs of asylum seekers and refugees. *British Medical Journal*. 322 pp 544-547

Cantle (2005) *Community cohesion: a new framework for race and diversity*. London: Palgrave Macmillan

Cantle, T (2004) *The end of parallel lives? Report of the community cohesion panel*. Home Office. London: HMSO

Cantle, T (2001) *Community Cohesion: a report of the independent review team*. Home Office. London: HMSO

Carey-Wood, J (1997) *Meeting Refugees' Needs in Britain: the role of refugee-specific initiatives*. London: Home Office

Carey-Wood, J, Duke, K, Karn, V and Marshall, T (1995) The settlement of refugees in Britain, *Home Office Research Study* 141 London: HMSO

Carlson, E B and Rosser-Hogan, R (1991) Trauma Experiences, Posttraumatic Stress, Dissociation, and Depression in Cambodian refugees. *American Journal of Psychiatry*. 148 pp 1548-1551

Castles, S (2003) Towards a sociology of forced migration and social transformation. *Sociology* 77 (1) pp 13-34

Castles, S and Davidson, A (2000) *Citizenship and migration: globalisation and the politics of belonging*. Basingstoke: Palgrave

Castles, S, Korac, M Vasta, M, and Vertovec, S (2002) I*ntegration: Mapping the Field* (Report of a project carried out by the University of Oxford Centre for Migration and Policy Research and Refugee Studies Centre for the Home Office Immigration Research and Statistics Service (IRSS). London: HMSO

Cliff, D (2000) Helping Refugees, Asylum Seekers and Migrants to Use Their Wealth of Talents and Experience, in *Local Economy* 15 (4) pp 339-342

Code, L (2003) Taking subjectivity into account. In Alcoff, L and Potter, E (eds) *Feminist Epistemologies*. London: Routledge

Cohen, R (1994) *Frontiers of Identity: the British and Others*. London: Longman

Colardyn, D and Bjornavold, J (2004) Validation of formal, non-formal and informal learning: policy and practices in the EU Member States. *European Journal of Education* 39 (1) pp 69-89

Commission for Integration and Cohesion (CIC) (2007) *Our shared future*. Commission on Integration and Cohesion or www.integrationandcohesion.org.uk

Confederation of Indian Organisations (1996) *Cry for Change – An Asian Perspective on Developing Quality Mental Health Care*. London: CIO.

Council of Europe (2000a) *Diversity and Cohesion: New Challenges for the Integration of Immigrants and Minorities*. Available on www.social.coe.int/en/cohesion/actionpubli/ migrants/ diversit.htm

Council of Europe (2000b) *Strategy for Social Cohesion and Quality of Life*. Available on www. social.coe.int/en/cohesion/strategy/CDCS/docstrat.htm

Coussey, M (2000) *Framework of integration policies*, Directorate General III-Social Cohesion. Strasbourg: Council of Europe Publishing

Craig, G *et al* (2004) *The Local Impact of International Migration*, Working Paper available from Social Policy, Hull: University of Hull

Crick, B (2003) *The New and the Old: interim report for consultation of the 'Life in the United Kingdom'* Advisory Group. London: Home Office

Crisp, J (2004) *New Issues in Refugee Research: The local integration and local settlement of refugees: a conceptual and historical analysis.* Geneva, Global Commission on International Migration

Crowley, P (2003) *An Exploration of the Mental Health needs of Asylum Seekers in Newcastle.* The Tyne, Wear and Northumberland Asylum Seeker Health Group

Cutler, S and Ceneda, S (2004) *They took me away: Women's experiences of immigration detention in the UK London:* Bail for Immigration Detainees and Refugee Women's Resource Project. Asylum Aid. Available at: http://www.biduk.org/pdf/women/women_in_detention_in_word_02Sep04.doc

Denzin, N and Lincoln, Y (eds) (1998) *Handbook of qualitative research.* Thousand Oaks: Sage

DeWind, J and Kasinitz, P (1997) Everything Old is New Again? Process and theories of immigrant incorporation. In *International Migration Review* 31 (4) pp 1096-1111

DfES (2000) *Labour Force Survey.* London: DfES

DfES (2003) *Skills in England,* Vol.1, Coventry: Learning and Skills Council. London: DfES

Dick, M (2004) *Birmingham and the refugee experience.* Birmingham: University of Birmingham

Directorate-General Justice, Freedom and Security (2004) *Handbook on Integration for policy makers and practitioners.* Brussels: European Commission

Dörr, S and Faist, T (1997) Institutional Conditions for the Integration of Immigrants in Welfare States: A comparison of the literature on Germany, France, Great Britain, and the Netherlands. *European Journal of Political Research,* 31 (4) pp 401-426

Dumper, H (2002) *Missed opportunities: a skills audit of refugee women in London from teaching, nursing and medical professions.* London: GLA

Dumper, H (2006) *Is it Safe Here? Refugee women's experiences in the UK.* Refugee Action

Dunn, L and Somerville, W (2004) *Barriers to Employment.* London: Centre for Economic and Social Inclusion

Dustmann, C *et al* (2003a) *Labour market performance of immigrants in the UK labour market.* Home Office Online Report 05/03

Dustmann, C *et al* (2003b) *The local labour market effects of immigration in the UK.* Home Office Online Report 06/03

Düvell, F and Jordan, B (2002) Immigration, asylum and welfare: the European context. *Critical Social Policy,* Vol. 22, No. 3, pp 498-517

DWP (2004) *Building on New Deal: Local solutions meeting individual needs.* London: DWP

DWP (2005) *Working to rebuild lives: a refugee employment strategy.* London: DWP

Employability Forum (2006) *Rebuilding Lives – Groundwork: Progress report on refugee employment.* London: NRIF Employment and Training Subgroup

European Commission (2001) *Report of the third European Conference on the integration of refugees.* Brussels: European Commission

European Commission (2000a) *The Social Policy Agenda.* Available on http://europa.eu.int/comm/employment_social/general/com00-379/com379_en.pdf

European Commission (2000b) *COM 757 on a Common Immigration Policy.* Available on http://europa.eu.int/eur-lex/en/com/cnc/2000/com2000_0757en01.pdf

Evans, M (2001) *Welfare to work and the organisation of opportunity: Lessons from abroad.* Case paper 15. London: LSE

Evans, N (1989) Assessing prior experiential learning. *Industrial and Commercial Training* 21 3-5

Expósito, S and Favela, A (2003) Reflective Voices: Valuing immigrant students and teaching with ideological clarity. *The Urban Review,* Vol. 35, No. 1, pp 73-91

REFERENCES

Favell, A (1998) *Philosophies Of Integration: Immigration and The Ideal Of Citizenship In France and Britain.* Basingstoke: Macmillan

Feeney, A (2000) Refugee Employment. *Local Economy,* Vol. 15, No. 4, pp 343-349

Field, S (1985) HO Research Study No. 87. *Resettling Refugees: the lessons of research.* London: HMSO

Fieldhouse, E A and Gould, M I (1998) Ethnic minority unemployment and local labour market conditions in Great Britain. *Environment and Planning,* Vol. 30, pp 833-853

File, N and Power, C (1981) *Black Settlers in Britain 1555-1958.* London: Heinemann Educational

Finnan, C R (1981) Occupational Assimilation of Refugees. *International Migration Review,* Vol.15, No.1

Fitzgerald, R, Finch, S and Nove, A (2001) Black Caribbean young men's experiences of education and employment, in *Labour Market Trends,* 109 (2) pp 123-124

Flanagan, J, Baldwin, S and Clarke, D (2000) Work-based learning as a means of developing and assessing nursing competence. *Journal of Clinical Nursing,* 9 pp 360-368

Fletcher, S (2001) Accreditation of prior learning: a contribution to national economic objectives. *Journal of European Industrial Training* 14 9 pp 8-11

Forrest, R and Kearns, A (2001) *Social Cohesion, Social Capital and the Neighbourhood.* Urban Studies, 38 (12)

Franz, B (2003) Bosnian refugee and socio-economic realities: changes in refugee and settlement policies in Austria and the United States. *Journal of Ethnic and Migration Studies* 29 (1) pp 5-25

Fry, P (1984) *Staying Power: Black People in Britain.* London: Pluto Press

Fryer, P (1984) *Staying Power: Black People in Britain.* London: Pluto Press.

Fyvie, A, Ager, A, Curley, G and Korac, M (2003) *Integration Mapping the Field, Volume II: distilling policy lessons from the 'mapping the field' exercise.* Home Office Online Report 29/03

Gameledin-Adhami, M, Cooper, L and Knight, J (2002) *Refugee settlement: can communities cope?* London: Evelyn Oldfield Unit

Gans, H (1997) Toward a Reconciliation of 'Assimilation' and 'Pluralism': The interplay of accultura-tion and ethnic retention. *International Migration Review,* 31 (4) pp 875-892

Gans, H (1992) Ethnic invention and acculturation: a bumpy line approach. *Journal of American Ethnic History.* 12 (1) pp 45-52

Garnett, J, Portwood, D, and Costley, C (2004) *Bridging rhetoric with reality: accreditation of prior experiential learning (APEL) in the UK.* Report for UVAC

Garvie, D (2001) *Far From Home.* London: Shelter

Geddes, A (2003) Migration and the Welfare State in Europe. In Spencer, S (ed) *The Politics of Migration: Managing opportunity, conflict and change.* Oxford: Blackwell.

Geddes, A (2000) *Immigration and European Integration: Towards Fortress Europe?* Manchester: Manchester University Press.

Goodson, L and Phillimore, J (2008) Social capital and integration: the importance of social relationships and social space for refugee women. *The International Journal of Diversity in Organisations, Communities and Nations,* 7 (1)

Goodson, L, Beider, H, Joseph, R, and Phillimore, J (2005a) *Black and Minority Ethnic Communi-ties in the Eastern Corridor: Aspirations, Neighbourhood 'Choice' and Tenure.* Birmingham: Birmingham City Council

Goodson, L, Phillimore, J, Black, J, Jones, P, Lutz, J, Tice, A, and Williams, A (2005b) *New migrants communities: education, training, employment and integration matters.* Sandwell: Learning and Skills Council, Black Country

Gorst-Unsworth, C, and Goldenberg E (1998) Psychological Sequelae of Torture and Organised Violence Suffered by Refugees from Iraq: trauma-related factors compared with social factors in exile. *British Journal of Psychiatry* 172 pp 90-94

Gott, C and Johnston, K (2002) *The Migrant Population in the UK: Fiscal Effects*. London: Home Office Research, Development and Statistics Directorate

Government Office West Midlands (2005) *Regional profile* www.gos.gov.uk/gowm /OurReg/?a= 42496.

Gowricharn, R (2002) Integration and social cohesion: the case of the Netherlands. *Journal of Ethnic and Migration Studies*, Vol. 28, No. 2, pp 259-273

Gradstein, M and Justman, M (2002) Education, Social Cohesion and Economic Growth. *American Economic Review* 92 (2) pp 1192-1204

Gras, M and Bovenkerk, F (1999) Migrants and Ethnic Minorities in the Netherlands: Discrimination in Access to Employment. In Wrench, J, Rea, A and N Ouali, N (eds) (1999) *Migrants, Ethnic Minorities and the Labour Market: Integration and Exclusion in Europe*. Hampshire: MacMillan pp 93-107

Gray, R, Sterjland, L and Aldridge, F (2007) *Advising for adaptation*. Leicester: NIACE

Greater London Authority (GLA) (2004) Home Office Consultation on *Integration Matters: a National Strategy for Refugee Integration*. Response by the Mayor of London, October 2004

Green, A, Preston, J and Ricardo, S (2003) Education, Equality and Social Cohesion: a distributional approach. *Compare* 33 (4) pp 253-470

Griffiths, D (2003) *English language training for refugees in London and the regions*. Home Office Online Report 14/03

Griffiths, P (1998) Khat use in London: A study of Khat use among a sample of Somalis living in London. *Drug Prevention Initiative Paper* No. 26. London: Home Office

Griffiths, D, Sigonda, N, and Zetter, R (2006) Integrative paradigms, marginal reality: refugee community organisations and dispersal in Britain. *Journal of Ethnic and Migration Studies* 32 (5) pp 881-898

Grover, D (2006) *More Than a Language: NIACE Committee of Inquiry on English for Speakers of Other Languages*. NIACE

Hannah, J (1999) Refugee students at college and university: improving access and support. *International Review of Education* 45 (2) pp 153-166

Haque, R (2003) *Migrants in the UK: a descriptive analysis of their characteristics and labour market performance, based upon the Labour Force Survey*. London: DWP.

Harrell-Bond (1988) The Sociology of Involuntary Migration: An Introduction. *Current Sociology* 36 (1)

Hasluck, C (2000) *Early Lessons from the Evaluation of New Deal Programmes. A report prepared for the Employment Service*. Institute for Employment Research: University of Warwick

Haynes, M (1999) Setting the Limits to Europe as an 'Imagined Community'. In Dale, G and Cole, M (eds) *The European Union and Migrant Labour*. Oxford: Berg, pp 17-42

Heath, T and Hill, R (2002) *Asylum Statistics United Kingdom 2001*. National Statistics for the Home Office

Heath, T, Jeffries, R and Lloyd, A (2003) *Asylum Statistics United Kingdom 2002*. National Statistics for the Home Office

Heyworth, F and Peach, E (2004) *A rough guide to navigating secondary sources of data and information on refugees and asylum seekers in the UK*. Second Annual Postgraduate Conference on Forced Migration, Coventry March 2004

Hills, J, Le Grand, J, and Piachaud, D (eds) (2002) *Understanding social exclusion.* Oxford: Open University Press

Home Office (2006) *Second Quarter 2006 asylum figures.* Home Office RDS website

Home Office (2005a) *Integration Matters: National Strategy for Integration.* London: HMSO.

Home Office (2005b) *Controlling our borders: Making migration work. Five year strategy for asylum and immigration.* London: HMSO.

Home Office (2003) *Asylum statistics: United Kingdom.* London: HMSO

Home Office (2002) *Secure Borders Safe Haven: Integration with diversity in modern Britain.* London: HMSO.

Home Office (2001) *Asylum statistics: June 2001 United Kingdom.* London: HMSO

Home Office (2000) *Full and Equal Citizens: a strategy for the integration of refugees into the United Kingdom.* London: HMSO.

Home Office (1998) *Firmer, faster, fairer: a modern approach to immigration and asylum.* London: HMSO.

Home Office (undated) *The New and the Old.* The Interim Report for Consultation of the 'Life in the United Kingdom' Advisory Group.

Hondius, A, van Willigen, L, Kleijn W and van der Ploeg, H (2000) Health Problems among Latin-American and Middle-Eastern Refugees in the Netherlands: Relations with Violence Exposure and Ongoing Sociopsychological Strain. *Journal of Traumatic Stress.* 13 pp 619-634

House of Commons Home Affairs Committee (2003) *Asylum removals.* Fourth Report of Session 2002-2003. London: HMSO

Houston, L, Hoover, J and Beer, E (1997) Accreditation of prior learning: is it worth it? An evaluation of a pilot scheme. *Nurse Education Today* 17 pp 184-191

Hubbard, P (2005) Accommodating Otherness: anti-asylum centre protest and the maintenance of white privilege. *Transactions of the Institute of British Geographers*, 30 (1) pp 52-65

Hudson, D and Mårtenson, H (1999) *Good Practice Guide on the Integration of Refugees in the European Union: Employment*, ECRE Task Force on Integration. Brussels: OCIV

Hurstfield, J, Pearson, R, Hooker, H, Ritchie, H and Sinclair, A (2004) *Employing Refugees. Some Organisations' Experiences.* Institute for Employment Studies Paper for the Employability Forum

Huysmans, J (1995) Migrants as a security problem: dangers of 'securitizing' societal Issues. In Miles, R and Thränhardt, D (eds), *Migration and European Integration: The Dynamics of Inclusion and Exclusion.* London: Pinter, pp 53-72

Hynes, T (2003) *The issue of 'trust' or 'mistrust' in research with refugees: choices, caveats and considerations for researchers.* Geneva: UNHCR

Icoco (2007) *Estimating the Scale and Impacts of Migration at the Local Level.* Coventry: University of Coventry

Immigration and Nationality Directorate (IND) (2004) *Asylum statistics: United Kingdom.* London: HMSO

Indra, DM (1989) Ethnic Human Rights and Feminist Theory: Gender Implications for Refugee Studies and Practice. *Journal of Refugee Studies*, 2/2, Oxford

INTEGRA (undated) *Combating Social Exclusion: A comparative study of Bosnian, Kurdish, Somali and Senegalese Communities in the UK, Germany, Denmark and Italy.* Brussels

Institute of Public Policy Research (2003) *States of conflict: causes and patterns of forced migration to the EU and policy responses.* London: IPPR.

Jacobsen, K and Landau, L (2003) *Researching refugees: some methodological and ethical considerations in social science and forced migration.* Geneva: UNHCR

Jenson, J (2001) *Social Cohesion and Inclusion: What is the Research Agenda?* Canadian Policy Research Network

Jobbins, G (2004) Translators, trust and truth: cross-cultural issues in sustainable tourism research. In Phillimore, J and Goodson, L (eds) *Qualitative research in tourism: ontologies, epistemologies and methodologies.* London: Routledge pp 311-323

John, A *et al* (2002) *Experiences of Integration: Accessing resources in a new society – the case of unaccompanied minor asylum seekers in Milton Keynes.* Oxford: Refugee Studies Centre

Joly, D (1996) *Haven or hell: asylum policy in Europe.* London: Macmillan

Kearns, A and Forrest, R (2000) Social cohesion and multi-level urban governance. *Urban Studies,* vol 37, nos 5-6, pp 995-1017

Kelley, N and Stevenson, J (2006) *First Do No Harm: Denying health care to people whose asylum claims are failed.* Refugee Council and Oxfam UK

Kempton, J (2002) *Migrants in the UK: Their Characteristics and Labour Market Outcomes and Impacts.* RDS Occasional Paper 82. London: HMSO

Kershen, A (ed) (2000) *Language, Labour and Migration.* Aldershot: Ashgate

Kincheloe, J and McLaren, P (1998) Rethinking critical theory and qualitative research. In Denzin, N and Lincoln, Y (eds) *Handbook of qualitative research.* Thousand Oaks: Sage

Kinzie, J, Boehlein, J, Leung, P, Moore, L, Riley, C, and Smith D (1990) The Prevalence of Post-traumatic Stress Disorder and its Clinical Significance among Southeast Asian Refugees. *American Journal of Psychiatry* 147 pp 913-917

Kirk, R (2004) *Skills Audit of Refugees.* London: HMSO

Klusmeyer, D (2001) A 'guiding culture' for immigrants? Integration and diversity in Germany. *Journal of Ethnic and Migration Studies,* 27 (3) pp 519-532

Knox, K (1997) *A credit to the nation: a study of refugees in the United Kingdom.* London: Refugee Council

Korac, M (2003) Integration and How We Facilitate It: A comparative study of the settlement experiences of refugees in Italy and the Netherlands. *Sociology* 37 (1) pp 51-68

Kuepper, W G *et al* (1975) *Ugandan Asians in Great Britain. Forced Migration and Social Absorption.* London: Croom Helm

Learning and Skills Council (2005) *Priorities for Success: Funding for Learning and Skills, 2006-2008.* Coventry: Learning and Skills Council.

Learning and Skills Council (2006a) *Funding Guidance for Further Education in 2006/2007.* Learning and Skill Council. http://www.lsc.gov.uk/ (accessed 24.10.2006)

Learning and Skills Council (2006b) News Release, 18 October 2006. Learning and Skill Council http://www.lsc.gov.uk/ (accessed 24.10.2006)

Learning and Skills Council (2006c) *Learner Support Fund: Funding Guidance for 2006/2007.* Learning and Skill Council, http://www.lsc.gov.uk/ (accessed 24.10.2006)

Learning and Skills Council (2005) *Level 2 Entitlement: Guide for Providers, Stakeholders and Intermediaries.* Learning and Skill Council. http://www.lsc.gov.uk/ (accessed 24.10.2006)

Learning and Skills Council (2004) *The approach: recognising and recording process and achievement in non-accredited learning.* LSC consultation paper

Learning and Skills Council (2003) *National Employers Skills Survey 2003: Key findings.* Coventry: Learning and Skills Council

Learning and Skills Council (2002) *Skills in England 2002. Volume 1,* London: DfES

Leitch Review of Skills (2006) *Prosperity for all in the global economy world class skills.* London: HM Treasury

Lemos, G (2005) *Challenging and changing racist attitudes and behaviour in young people.* Joseph Rowntree Foundation Findings

Ley, D, and Smith, H (2000) Relations between Deprivation and Immigrant Groups in Large Canadian Cities. *Urban Studies* 37(1) pp 37-62

Lloyd, C 2000 Anti-Racist Responses to European Integration. In Koopmans, R and Statham, P (eds) *Challenging Immigration and Ethnic Relations Politics: Comparative European perspectives,* 389-406. New York: Oxford University Press.

London Asylum Seekers Consortium (2002) *Asylum Seeker and Refugee Integration in London.* London: Association of London Government

Marfleet, P (2006) *Refugees in a global era.* London: Palgrave

mbA (1999) *Creating the conditions for refugees to find work.* Report for the Refugee Council, London

McKay, S, and Winkelmann-Gleed, A (2005) *Migrant Workers in the East of England* (PDF). East of England Development Agency, 2005

McLoughlan, G and Salt, J (2002) *Migration Policies Towards Highly Skilled Workers, Report to the Home Office.* University College London: Migration Research Unit

McQuaid, R, Lindsay, C and Grieg, M (2005) Job guaranteed, employability training and partnerships in the retail sector. *Local Economy* 20 (1) pp 67-78

Menz, G (2002) Patterns in EU labour immigration policy: national initiatives and European responses. *Journal of Ethnic and Migration Studies* 28 no 4: 723-742

Mestheneos, E and Charapi, A (1999) *Good Practice Guide on the Integration of Refugees in the European Union: Community and culture.* ECRE Task Force on Integration. Brussels: OCIV

Mestheneos, E and Ioannidi, E (2002) Obstacles to Refugee Integration in the European Union Member States. *Journal of Refugee Studies* 15 (3) pp 304-320

Midlands Refugee Council (2001) *Asylum Seekers: Developing Information, Advice and Guidance on Employment, Training and Education in the West Midlands.* EQUAL bid July 2001

Miller, K (1999) Rethinking a familiar model: psychotherapy and the mental health of refugees. *Journal of Contemporary Psychotherapy* 29 283-306

Miles, R and Cleary, P (1993) Migration to Britain: racism, state regulation and employment. In Robinson, V (ed) *The International Refugee Crisis: British and Canadian responses.* London: Macmillan

Mollica R, Sarajlic, N, Chernoff, M, Lavelle, J, Vukovic, I., Massagli, M (2001) Longitudinal Study of Psychiatric Symptoms, Disability, Mortality, and Emigration Among Bosnian Refugees. *The Journal of the American Medical Association* 286 pp 546-554

Monti, F (2005) *Pathways to employment.* London: RETAS. 87

Morris, L (2002) Britain's asylum and immigration regime: the shifting contours of rights. *Journal of Ethnic and Migration Studies* 28 (3) pp 409-425

Moya, J (2005) Immigrants and associations: a global and historical perspective. *Journal of Ethnic and Migration Studies* 31 (5) pp 833-864

Murphy, A, Lynch M, Bury, G (1994) An Assessment of the Screening of 178 Bosnian refugees to Ireland. *Irish Medical Journal* 87 pp 174-175

Murphy, D, Ndegwa, D, Kanani, A, Rojas-Jaimes C and Webster A (2002) Mental Health of Refugees in Inner-London. *Psychiatric Bulletin* 26 pp 222-224

National Statistics Online (2003) *Unemployment rates: by ethnic group and age 2001-02* www. statistics.gov.uk/cci/nugget http://www.statistics.gov.uk/downloads/

Nevin, B, Lee, P, Goodson, L, Murie, A and Phillimore, J (2000) *Changing housing markets and urban regeneration in the M62 Corridor.* Birmingham: University of Birmingham Centre for Urban and Regional Studies

Nikolou-Walker, E and Garnett, J (2004) Work-based learning. A new imperative: developing reflective practice in professional life. *Reflective Practice* 5 (3) pp 297-312

Noon, M and Ogbonna, E (1998) Unequal Provision? Ethnic minorities and employment training policy. *Journal of Education and Work,* 11 (1) pp 23-39

Oatley, N (2000) Initiatives to Support Refugees and Asylum Seekers. *Local Economy,* 15 (4) pp 338-339

ODPM (2004) *Indices of Deprivation 2004.* http://www.neighbourhood.gov.uk

ODPM (2000) *Preventing social exclusion. Social Exclusion Unit.* London: ODPM http://www.neighbourhood.gov.uk/page.asp?id=1057

ODPM (1998) *Index of Local Deprivation* (Regeneration Research Summary No.15)

Ogbonna, E (1998) British ethnic minorities and employment training: redressing or extending disadvantage? *International Journal of Training and Development,* 2 (1) pp 28-41.

OHCHR (1951) *Convention Relating to the Status of Refugees.* Geneva

ONS/Home Office (2007) *Control of Immigration Statistics:* United Kingdom 2006 Command Paper 7197. Cabinet Office/HMSO

Oppenheim, A (1992) *Questionnaire design, interviewing and attitude measurement.* London: Pinter

Ouali, N and Rea, A (1999) Young Migrants in the Belgian Labour Market: Integration, Discrimination and Exclusion In Wrench, J, Rea, A and Ouali, N (eds) *Migrants, Ethnic Minorities and the Labour Market: Integration and Exclusion in Europe.* Hampshire: MacMillan Press, pp 21-34

Overbeek, H (1995) Towards a new international migration regime: globalisation, migration and the internationalization of the state. In Miles, R and Trändhart, D, (eds) (1995) *Migration and European Integration.* London: Pinter

Pahl, R E (1991) The search for social cohesion: From Durkheim to the European Commission. *Archives of European Sociology* 32 pp 345-360

Parson, T (1937) *The Structure of Social Action.* New York and London: McGraw- Hill

Patle, S, and Wright, L (2005) *Khat use among Somalis in Four English Cities.* London, Home Office Online Report 47/05

Peabody Trust (1999) *Refugee SkillsNet: the employment and training of skilled and qualified refugees,* London: Peabody Trust

Peach, E and Henson, R (2005) *Key statistics about asylum seeker arrivals in the UK.* ICAR Statistics Paper 1

Peacock (2006) *Designing a programme for Refugee health Professionals.* 4th Annual Conference of Teaching and Learning in Higher Education, 'The Challenge of Diversity' 8-9 June 2006, Galway, Ireland

Phillimore, J (2005) *Evaluating the outcomes of refugee support.* Report for Birmingham City Council

Phillimore, J (2004) *The housing needs and aspirations of asylum seekers and refugees living in the Birmingham Sandwell Pathfinder Area.* Urban Living, HMRA

Phillimore, J, Craig, L and Goodson, L (2006) *Employability initiatives for refugees in Europe: looking at, and learning from, good practice.* Report for EQUAL and the Home Office

Phillimore, J, Ergün, E, Goodson, L, Hennessy D and BNCN Community Researchers (2007b) *'Now I do it by myself': Refugees and ESOL.* University of Birmingham for Joseph Rowntree Foundation

Phillimore, J, Ergün, E, Goodson, L, Hennessy, D and BNCN Community Researchers (2007c) *'They do not understand the problem I have': Refugee well being and mental health.* University of Birmingham for Joseph Rowntree Foundation

Phillimore, J and Fathi, J (2003) *The housing needs and aspirations of asylum seekers and refugees living in the Birmingham Sandwell Pathfinder Area.* Birmingham: University of Birmingham Centre for Urban and Regional Studies

Phillimore, J and Goodson, L (2006) Problem or opportunity? Asylum seekers, refugees, employment and social exclusion in deprived urban areas. *Urban Studies* 43 (10) 1715-1736

Phillimore, J and Goodson, L (2005) *West Midlands Regional Housing Strategy West Midlands Regional Spatial Strategy shared evidence-base Asylum seekers and refugees.* Report for the Regional Housing Board

Phillimore, J and Goodson, L (2002) *Asylum seeker and refugee employability initiatives: models for implementing a super pathway in the West Midlands.* Discussion paper prepared for West Midlands Executive Consortia.

Phillimore, J and Goodson, L (2001) *Exploring the integration of asylum seekers and refugees in Wolverhampton into UK labour market.* Birmingham: University of Birmingham, Centre for Urban and Regional Studies

Phillimore, J and Goodson, L, Beebeejaun, Y and Ferrari, E (2004) *The access, learning and employment needs of newcomers from abroad and the capacity of existing provision to meet those needs.* Birmingham: Learning and Skills Council, Birmingham and Solihull

Phillimore, J, Goodson, L, Hennessy, D, Ergün, E and Joseph, R (2007) *Employability pathways: an integrated approach to recognising the skills and experiences of new migrants.* Birmingham: University of Birmingham

Phillimore, J, Goodson, L, Oosthuizen, R, Ferrari, E, Fathi, J, Penjwini, S and Joseph, R (2003) *Asylum Seekers and Refugees: Education, Training Employment, Skills and Services in Coventry and Warwickshire.* Coventry: Learning and Skills Council, Coventry and Warwickshire

Pickersgill, D (2007) Educating Refugee Doctors and Nurses. The Sheffield College unpublished report from Progress GB Development Partnership Equal project

Pile, H (1997) *The Asylum Trap: The Labour Market Experiences of Refugees With Professional Qualifications.* London: Low Pay Unit

Pithers, R and Lim, R (1997) A Non-English Speaking Background in Adult Vocational Education: Breaking Through the Barriers. *Vocational Education and Training* 49 (4) pp 531-544

Porter, M and Haslam, N (2001) Forced Displacement in Yugoslavia: a Meta-analysis of Psychological Consequences and their Moderators. *Journal of Traumatic Stress* 14 pp 817-834.

Portes, A (1998) Divergent Destinies: Immigration, the Second Generation and the rise of Transnational Communities. In Schuck, P and Munz, R (eds) *Paths to inclusion: the integration of migrants in the United States and Germany,* 33-57. Migration and refugees series, v.5. New York and Oxford: Berghahn Books and American Academy of Arts and Sciences

Portes, A (1997) Immigration Theory for a New Century: Some Problems and Opportunities. *International Migration Review,* 31 (4) pp 88, 799-825

Power, A and Wilson, W (2000) *Social exclusion and the future of cities* CASE paper 35. London: LSE

Preece, J and Walters, N (1999) Accommodating refugee identity transitions: how adult education hinders or helps refugee lifelong learning needs. In *The Final Frontier – Exploring Spaces in the Education of Adults,* University of Warwick: SCUTREA

Putnam, R (2002) Bowling together: the American prospect. 11th February 2002. (www.prospect.org/print/V13/3/putnam-r.html)

RAGU (2006) *Refugees and Asylum Seekers: an education, training and employment guide for advisers.* London Advice Resources (www.advice-resources.co.uk)

Rawley, A (1981) *The Transatlantic Slave Trade.* New York: Norton

Rea, A, Wrench, J and Ouali, N (1999) Introduction: Discrimination and Diversity. In Wrench, J, Rea, A and Ouali, N (eds) *Migrants, Ethnic Minorities and the Labour Market: Integration and Exclusion in Europe.* Hampshire: MacMillan p 1-18

Refugee Action (2006) *I could use these skills to do something: refugee women and the voluntary sector on Merseyside.* London: Refugee Action.

Refugee Council (2005) *The Government's Five Year Asylum and Immigration Strategy.* Refugee Council Briefing February 2005

Refugee Council (2003) *Response to Home Office Consultation on Juxtaposed Controls Implementation,* Dover-Calais November 2002. London: Refugee Council

Refugee Council (2002) *Refugees in today's world.* London: Refugee Council

Refugee Council (1999) *ECRE Task Force on Integration, Refugees and Employment: the European Context.* London: Refugee Council

Refugee Council (1997) *Just existence: The lives of asylum seekers who have lost entitlement to benefits in the UK.* London: Refugee Council

Rex, J and Moore, R S (1967) *Race, Community and Conflict.* London: Oxford University Press

Richmond, A (2000) Refugees and Asylum Seekers in Britain: UK Immigration and Asylum Act, 1999. *Refuge* 19 (1) 35-41

Robinson, V (1998a) The Importance of Information in the Resettlement of Refugees in the UK. *Journal of Refugee Studies*, 11 (2) pp 146-160

Robinson, V (1998b) Cultures of Ignorance, Disbelief and Denial: Refugees in Wales. *Journal of Refugee Studies* 12 (1) pp 78-87

Robinson, V (1993) Marching into the middle classes? The long-term resettlement of East Asians in the UK. *Journal of Refugee Studies.* 6 (3)

Robinson, V (1986) *Transients, Settlers, and Refugees: Asians in Britain.* Oxford: OUP

Robinson, V, Andersson, R and Musterd, S (2003) *Spreading the burden? A review of policies to disperse asylum seekers and refugees.* Bristol: Policy Press

Robinson, V and Segrott, J (2002) *Understanding the decision making of asylum seekers.* Home Office Research Study 243. London: HMSO

Rumbaut, R G (1997) Assimilation and Its Discontents: Between Rhetoric and Reality. *International Migration Review* 31 (4) pp 923-960

Sales, R (2002) The deserving and the undeserving? Refugees, asylum seekers and welfare in Britain. *Critical Social Policy* 22, (3) pp 456-478

Sales, R and Gregory, J (1996) Employment, Citizenship and European Integration: The implications for Migrant and Refugee Women. *Social Politics* 3 pp 331-351

Salinas, M, Pritchard, D and Kibedi, A (1987) Refugee-based organisations: their function and importance for the refugee in Britain. (Cited in Griffiths, D, Sigonda, N and Zetter, R (2006) Integrative paradigms, marginal reality: refugee community organisations and dispersal in Britain.) *Journal of Ethnic and Migration Studies* 32 (5) pp 881- 898

Sargeant, G and Forna, A (2001) *A Poor Reception – Refugees and Asylum Seekers: Welfare or Work?* London: The Industrial Society.

Schaffer, H (2001) Domestic Violence and Asylum in the United States: In Re R- A-, 95 Nw. U.L. Rev. 779 (Winter 2001)

Schedler, P and Glastra, F (2000) Adult Education between Cultural Assimilation and Structural Integration. Settlement programmes for 'newcomers' in The Netherlands. *Compare* 30 (1) pp 53-66

Schellekens, P (2001) *English Language as a Barrier to Employment, Education and Training.* RBX3/01. Sheffield: DfES

Schibel, Y *et al* (2002) *Refugee Integration: Can research synthesis inform policy?* Feasibility study report, RDS ON-line Report 13/02

Scholten, A (2001) International; Credential Evaluation (ICE) and Prior Learning Assessment and Recognition (PLAR). Nuffic recommendations to the Kenniscentrum-EVC (APL Knowledge Centre)

Schuster, L (2003) *The Use and Abuse of Political Asylum in Britain and Germany.* London: Frank Cass

Schuster, L and Solomos, J (1999) The politics of refugee and asylum policies in Britain: historical patterns and contemporary realities. In Bloch A and Levy C (eds) (1999) *Refugees, Citizenship and Social Policy in Europe.* Basingstoke: Macmillan Press

Scottish Refugee Council (2001) *Responding to the needs of asylum seekers.* Glasgow: Scottish Refugee Council

Seedat, M (ed) (2001) *Community psychology theory, method and practice: South African and other perspectives.* Cape Town: Oxford University Press

Shields, M A and S Wheatley Price (2003) *The labour market outcomes and psychological well-being of ethnic minority migrants in Britain.* Home Office Online Report 07/03

Shiferaw, D and Hagos, H (2002) *Refugees and progression routes to employment.* Refugee Council in association with the Pan-London Refugee Training and Employment Network, London

Shmyr, Z (2003) *Recognition of prior learning (RPL) within the newcomer community: a needs assessment.* Prepared on behalf of the Saskatchewan Association of Immigrant Settlement and Integration Agencies (SAISIA)

Silove, D, Sinnerbrink, I, Field, A, Manicavasagar, V and Steel, Z (1997) Anxiety, Depression and PTSD in Asylum-Seekers: Associations with Pre- Migration Trauma and Post-Migration Stressors. *The British Journal of Psychiatry* 170 pp 351-357

Singh Ghuman, P A (1997) Assimilation or integration? A Study of Asian adolescents. *Educational Research* 39 (1) pp 23-36

Social Trends (2002) Unemployment rates: by region, 2002: *Social Trends* 33

Social Exclusion Unit (2001) *Preventing Social Exclusion.* March 2001, Cabinet Office, Social Exclusion Unit

Somerville, W (2006) *The newcomers handbook.* London Centre for Economic and Social Inclusion

Somerville, W (2007) *Immigration under New Labour.* Bristol: Policy Press

Soysal, Y (1994) *Limits of Citizenship: Migrants and Postnational Membership in Europe.* London: The University of Chicago Press

Srinivasan, S (1994) An overview of research into refugee groups in Britain during the 1990s. Paper presented at 4th International Research and Advisory Panel Conference, Oxford. Cited in Bloch, A (1999) Refugees in the job market: a case of unused skills in the British Economy. In Bloch, A and Levy, C (1999) *Refugees, citizenship and policy in Europe.* Basingstoke: Palgrave pp 187-210

Sriskandarajah D, Cooley, L and Reed, L (2005) *Paying their way; the fiscal contribution of immigrants to the UK.* London: IPPR

Stanley, L and Wise, S (1993) *Breaking out again: feminist ontology and epistemology.* London: Routledge

Steels, J and England, J (2004) *Emerging findings for the Refugee Employment Strategy: A Synthesis Report to the Department for Work and Pensions.* ECOTEC Research and Consulting Limited, Birmingham

Stewart, E (2004) Deficiencies in UK Asylum Data: Practical and Theoretical Challenges. *Journal of Refugee Studies* 17 (1) pp 29-49

Summerfield, D (2001) Asylum-seekers, Refugees and Mental Health Services in the UK. *Psychiatric Bulletin* 25 pp 161-162

Tait, K (2003) *Refugee Employment in the UK.* London: ICAR

Temple, B and Moran, R (2005) *Learning to live Together,* Joseph Rowntree Foundation, University of Salford

The White Paper Fairer, Faster and Firmer – A modern approach to Immigration and Asylum (http://www.archive.official-documents.co.uk/document/cm40/4018/4018. htm)

Thomas, H (1997) *The Slave Trade: The History of the Atlantic Slave Trade: 1440-1870.* New York: Simon and Schuster

Thomas, F and Abewaw, M (2002) *Refugees and Asylum Seekers in the Learning and Skills Council London North Area.* London: LSC London North

Thompsell, A (2001) Mental Health Problems of Asylum Seekers. *Psychiatric Bulletin,* 25 p360

Thranhardt D, Miles R (1995) Introduction: European integration, migration and processes of inclusion and exclusion. In Miles R, Thranhardt, D (eds) (1995) *Migration and European Integration: The Dynamics of Inclusion and Exclusion.* London: Pinter Publishers

Tomlinson and Egan (2002) From marginalisation to (dis)empowerment: organising training and employment services fro refugees. *Human Relations,* 55(8)

Treaty of Amsterdam (2007) amending the Treaty of the European Union, the Treaties establishing the European Communities and certain related acts

Twomey, B (2001) Labour market participation of ethnic groups. *Labour Market Trends,* January, pp 29-42

UDI (2004) *Annual Report: The Norwegian Directorate of Immigration.* Oslo: Norwegian Directorate of Immigration

UNHCR (2005) *2005 Global Trends: Refugees, Asylum Seekers, Returnees, Internally Displaces and Stateless Persons.* Annual Report, UNHCR

Valtonen, K (1998) Resettlement Of Middle Eastern Refugees In Finland: The Elusiveness Of Integration. *Journal Of Refugee Studies* 11 (1) pp 38-60

Visram, R (1989) The First World War and the Indian Soldiers, Indo-British Review. *A Journal of History* 16 (2)

Vourc'h, F, De Rudder, V and Tripier, M (1999) Foreigners and Immigrants in the French Labour Market: Structural Inequality and Discrimination. In Wrench, J, Rea, A and Ouali, N (eds) (1999) *Migrants, Ethnic Minorities and the Labour Market: Integration and Exclusion in Europe.* Hampshire: MacMillan pp 72-92

Waddington, S (2007) *Routes to Integration and Inclusion: a report from the progress* GB. Equal Development Partnership. Leicester: NIACE

Waddington, S (2005) *Asset UK Valuing skills and supporting integration:* A policy report on the lessons learned by auditing and developing the skills of asylum seekers as the basis for social and vocational integration. Leicester: NIACE

Walters, N and Egan, E (1996) *Refugee Skills Analysis Report for North West London.* Training and Enterprise Council. Guildford: University of Surrey

Watters, C (2001) Emerging paradigms in the mental healthy care of refugees. *Social Science and Medicine* 52 1709-1718

Weaver, H and Burns, B (2001) 'I Shout with Fear at Night': Understanding the Traumatic Experiences of Refugees and Asylum Seekers. *Journal of Social Work* 1 pp 147-164

Webster, A and Robertson, M (2007) Can community psychology meet the needs of refugees? *The Psychologist* 20 (3) pp 156-158

Weine S, Vojvoda, D, Becker, D, McGlashan, T, Hodzic, E, Laub, D, Hyman, L, Sawyer, M and Lazrove, S (1998) PTSD Symptoms in Bosnian Refugees 1 Year After Resettlement in the United States. *American Journal of Psychiatry* 155 pp 562-564

Weiner, M (1996) Determinants of Immigrant Integration: An International Comparative analysis. In Carmon, N (ed) *Immigration and Integration in Post-Industrial Societies: Theoretical Analysis and Policy Related Research.* London: Macmillan pp 47-62

Weiner, M (1995) *The Global Migration Crisis.* New York: Harper Collins

Wheatley Price, S (2001a) The employment adjustment of male immigrants in England. *Journal of Population Economics* 14 pp 192-220

Wheatley Price, S (2001b) The unemployment experience of male immigrants in England. *Applied Economics* 33 pp 201-215

White, P (1998) The Settlement Patterns of Developed World Migrants in London. *Urban Studies* 35 (10) pp 1725-1744

Wilson, W (1998) *When work disappears: new implications for race and urban poverty in the Global Economy.* CASE paper 17. London: LSE

Woolley, F (1998) *Social cohesion and voluntary activity: making connections*, paper presented at CSLS conference on 'The state of living standards and the quality of life in Canada, Ontario'

Zetter, R and Pearl, M (2000) The minority within the minority: refugee community-based organisations in the UK and the impact of restrictionism on asylum seekers. *Journal of Ethnic and Migration Studies* 26 no 4:675-697

Zetter, R, Griffiths, D, Sigona, N, Flynn, D, Pasha, T and Beynon, R (2006) *Immigration, social cohesion and social capital: what are the links?* York: Joseph Rowntree Foundation

Zetter, R, Griffiths, D, Ferretti, S and Pearl, M (2003) *An assessment of the impact of asylum policies in Europe 1990-2000.* Home Office Research, Development and Statistics Directorate. http://www.homeoffice.gov.uk/rds/pdfs2/hors259.pdf

Zetter, R, Griffiths, D and Sigona, N (2002) *A Survey of Policy and Practice Related to Refugee Integration.* Brussels: European Union

Index

accession countries 43
achievement 92, 98, 121, 181
advocacy 58-60, 141
agency 50, 184, 193
Amsterdam Treaty 12
APEL 39-42, 108-109, 187, need for 175
applications process 48, 163, 164, 174
apprenticeships 92
aspirations 36, 48, 91, 105, 119, 158, 159, 173, 181
assessment 98, 125, 126
assimilation 26, 35
asylum process 49, 104, 114, 123, 148, 184

barriers 47, 96-98, 100-102, 121-126, 131, 166-173
benefits 36, 48, 100, 110, 126, 137, 143, 156, 167, 173
Birmingham 22

childcare 106-106, 123, 124, 127-128, 158
citizenship 36, 40, 43, 144
Citizenship Test 41
cluster areas 78, 182
Commission for Racial Equality 7
community cohesion 34, 143, 146,
community researchers 84-85
Connexions 135, 137, 149
Council of Europe 16, 35

CRB check 163
culture issues 49, 92, 111, 113, 115, 118, 146, 152, 153, 164, 166, 170, 182
cultural orientation 128

data availability 67-69, 70, 71
Department for Work and Pensions 48, 68, 141, 169, 193
dependency 46
deprivation 7, 22, 34, 176, 183
de-skilling 44, 159, 176
definitions 61
detention 19
deterrent 18
disabled refugees 146, 158
discrimination 49, 170, 171-172
dispersal 1, 3, 14, 19, 23, 32, 34, 36, 47, 61, 144, 181-182, 183, 185
diversity 32, 151, 152, 165, 168, 174
drop-out rates 107, 122-126
Dublin Convention 11, 12, 16, 18
dyslexia 128

economic migrants 10, 43
education providers 43, 88-89
educational backgrounds 92
Educational Maintenance Allowance 38
employability 43, 45, 48, 89, 119, 141, 185

Employability Forum 68
employers 40, 44, 48, 51, 87, 139, 161-177, 186
employment see also unemployment 93, 102, 105, 155-161, 173-174
employment rights 161
English see language
Enoch Powell 6
enrolment 122
EQUAL 60, 88, 153, 192
equal opportunities 171, 174
equivalence 40
ESOL 37, 40, 60, 79, 96-100, 109, 112, 117-118, 123, 126, 129, 137, 144, 167
ethics 66-67
ethnic monitoring system 67
European Commission 35
European Social Fund 38
EU policy 44
exclusion 5, 176

faith groups 142, 143
family reunion 7, 8, 50, 62, 68
FENTO 124
flexibility in provision 113, 114, 147, 151, 164
Fortress Europe 11
Full and Equal Citizens 2, 36
functional integration 27, 31, 32, 49
funding 21, 130, 141, 143, 148, 151, 176, 180
further education 93, 102, 111, 119

Gateway protection
    programme 9
gender 27
Geneva Convention 11-12, 17
grey economy 185

harassment 29, 31, 107,
    145, 148, 161, 171
health 104, 120, 128, 143
health sector 108, 113, 159
health and safety 139, 164,
    166
higher education 39, 92, 93,
    97, 110, 113
history of immigration 4-8
Home Office 31, 50, 169
    Home Office Challenge
    Fund 154
housing 22, 102, 106, 127,
    143, 148, 163, 183

IAG 40-41, 102, 112, 119-
    120, 125-129, 131, 135-
    154 for
identity 32, 35, 61, 111, 180
IELTS 113
immigration controls 10, 14,
    147, 148
indicators 2, 25, 28, 29-31,
    46, 75
induction 164-165, 167, 168,
    175
information technology 93,
    101, 118, 128
Integration Matters 8, 29, 43
integration 1, 2, 20-21, 23-33,
    44, 46, 93, 114, 116, 125,
    131, 146, 153, 182, 185-
    186
Islam 107, 146
isolation 96, 104, 107, 120,
    156, 184

Jobcentre Plus 21, 38, 43,
    44, 68, 102, 110, 135,
    137, 141, 149, 153, 173,
    174, 183, 193
jobseekers' allowance 38, 40,
    100, 110, 137
job fairs 176

labour shortages 5
language 21, 29, 30, 31, 36,
    37, 40, 43, 45, 66, 76, 92,
    93, 104, 105, 120, 129,
    138, 153, 163, 166-168
Learner support fund see also
    Hardship Funds 38, 106,
    114, 130, 132
Learning and Skills Council
    38, 86, 121, 123, 136
learning provision 117-118
legislation 3, 4,6, 14, 18, 19,
    20, 23, 169
Leitch Review 136
Life in the UK test 36
low paid employment see
    also marginal employment
    33, 40

marginalisation 26, 27, 34,
    166, 185, 193
matrix standard 136
media 15, 18, 31, 46, 155,
    170, 174, 180
mental health 44, 104, 105,
    107, 120, 128, 146-147,
    150, 157, 168
mentoring 21, 131, 132, 139,
    141, 163, 175, 188, 192
methodology 57, 75, 79
monitoring and evaluation
    126, 145, 152, 189
motivations 54, 113, 119, 162

NARIC 40, 92, 110, 180
NASS 1, 19, 22, 36, 37, 61,
    68-69, 148
National Insurance number
    137, 163, 172
National Refugee Integration
    Forum 2, 20, 25
National Refugee Integration
    Service 25
New Commonwealth 5,6
New Deal 44, 138
New Nationality Act 7
NGOs 59
NIACE 136
NVQ 40, 92, 111, 187, 192

occupations 40, 156-158
on the spot fines/financial
    penalties 20, 44, 49, 169
Our shared future 35
overstayers 7, 69

partnerships 21, 133, 144,
    150-151, 154, 176
pathways to learning 150
pathways to employment
    model 190-193
persecution 10, 12, 62, 108,
    111, 157
policy 1, 28, 35, 37, 44, 58,
    91, 121, 155, 185
politics 15, 46, 132, 183
positivism 58
potential 21
professionals 21, 38, 39, 40,
    44, 108-111, 131, 157,
    159, 181

qualifications 37, 38, 39, 40,
    45, 51, 108, 119, 140,
    162, 172
qualitative and quantitative
    research 63-65, 85

race relations 6, 35
    Race Relations Act 7
race riots 5, 6
racism and xenophobia 5,6,8,
    16, 26, 125, 170, 186
references for work 40, 48,
    109, 162
refugee community
    organisations 21, 42, 63,
    97, 130, 141, 142, 143,
    145, 148
Refugee Council 19, 86, 188
refugee numbers 10, 13, 14,
    15, 17, 72-75
removal see also deportation
    7, 8, 17
research 57, 58, 59
restrictionalism 17, 18, 21,
    35-37, 183
retention 121, 122-126, 130
right to work 20, 44-45

sampling 63-66, 69, 83
Schengen 10-11, 16
school 112
self-esteem 32, 36, 40, 49,
    105, 115, 156, 180
self-employment 139
self-confidence 48, 112, 127,
    144, 148
segregation 26, 33, 193
sixteen hour rule 100, 110,
    113, 126
skills shortage 43, 47, 51,
    54, 88
slave trade 4
social capital 28, 30, 181-182
social cohesion *see also*
    community cohesion 32,
    34-35, 36-37, 114, 177,
    183, 184, 185, 194
social exclusion 32-33, 35,
    177, 182, 183-184, 187
social interaction 32, 107,
    156, 183
social space 96, 131
staff training 130
stereotyping 49, 140, 170-
    172, 174, 186
strategy 2, 16, 21, 30
subjectivity 27, 28, 57, 58,
    59, 60
SUNRISE 21, 25, 45, 153,
    183, 188
support 2, 19, 96, 99, 126-
    129, 130, 189

terrorism 16
translation and interpretation
    38, 66, 130, 139, 141,
    172, 174
transparency in research 58-
    59
transience 50, 67, 163
transport 105, 127, 163
trust 64-65, 142, 148, 151
tutors 96, 97, 101, 118, 127,
    130, 133, 151

under-employment 50, 155
unemployment *see also*
    employment 33, 47, 50,
    159-161,179
UNHCR 13

vocational provision 93, 99,
    113, 117, 118, 119, 141
voluntary sector 21, 143, 151
voluntary work 29, 109, 139,
    147, 149, 159

waiting lists 97, 107
West Midlands 22, 23, 53, 61,
    179
women 45, 47, 106-108, 114,
    116, 132, 145, 158, 172,
    179, 181
work-based learning 114,
    132, 176
work-based skills assessment
    187
workers registration scheme
    43
work experience 48, 109, 111,
    127, 140, 141, 175, 176
    initiatives 188, 191
workplace orientation 137,
    163, 170 need for 175,
    188
work trial 162
Working to Rebuild Lives 20,
    43

xenophobia 15, 26, 50

young people 111-112, 138,
    146, 148, 157